ELECTROPHILIC SUBSTITUTION
OF ORGANOMERCURIALS

MCGRAW-HILL SERIES IN ADVANCED CHEMISTRY

AMDUR AND HAMMES *Chemical Kinetics: Principles and Selected Topics*
BAIR *Introduction to Chemical Instrumentation*
BALLHAUSEN *Introduction to Ligand Field Theory*
BENSON *The Foundations of Chemical Kinetics*
BIEMANN *Mass Spectrometry (Organic Chemical Applications)*
DAVIDSON *Statistical Mechanics*
DAVYDOV (Trans. Kasha and Oppenheimer) *Theory of Molecular Excitons*
DEAN *Flame Photometry*
DJERASSI *Optical Rotatory Dispersion*
ELIEL *Stereochemistry of Carbon Compounds*
FITTS *Nonequilibrium Thermodynamics*
FRISTROM AND WESTENBERG *Flame Structure*
HELFFERICH *Ion Exchange*
HILL *Statistical Mechanics*
HINE *Physical Organic Chemistry*
JENSEN AND RICKBORN *Electrophilic Substitution of Organomercurials*
KAN *Organic Photochemistry*
KIRKWOOD AND OPPENHEIM *Chemical Thermodynamics*
KOSOWER *Molecular Biochemistry*
LAITINEN *Chemical Analysis*
McDOWELL *Mass Spectrometry*
MANDELKERN *Crystallization of Polymers*
MARCH *Advanced Organic Chemistry*
MEMORY *Quantum Theory of Magnetic Resonance Parameters*
PITZER AND BREWER (Revision of Lewis and Randall) *Thermodynamics*
POPLE, SCHNEIDER, AND BERNSTEIN *High-resolution Nuclear Magnetic Resonance*
PRYOR *Free Radicals*
PRYOR *Mechanisms of Sulfur Reactions*
RAAEN, ROPP, AND RAAEN *Carbon-14*
ROBERTS *Nuclear Magnetic Resonance*
ROSSOTTI AND ROSSOTTI *The Determination of Stability Constants*
SIGGIA *Survey of Applied Analytical Chemistry*
SOMMER *Stereochemistry, Mechanisms and Silicon*
STREITWIESER *Solvolytic Displacement Reactions*
SUNDHEIM *Fused Salts*
WIBERG *Laboratory Technique in Organic Chemistry*

ELECTROPHILIC SUBSTITUTION
OF ORGANOMERCURIALS

Frederick R. Jensen

Department of Chemistry
University of California
Berkeley

Bruce Rickborn

Department of Chemistry
University of California
Santa Barbara

McGraw-Hill Book Company

New York   San Francisco   St. Louis   Toronto   London   Sydney

ELECTROPHILIC SUBSTITUTION OF ORGANOMERCURIALS

Printed in the United States of America.

Library of Congress catalog card number: 68-11612

1234567890   MAMM   7543210698   **32466**

PREFACE

Physical-organic studies of aliphatic electrophilic substitution were, with few exceptions, nonexistent a decade ago. No doubt experimental difficulties and lack of stereoisomeric model systems contributed substantially to this neglect. Within the past ten years, however, the availability of new techniques and instrumentation has led to a rapidly increasing literature on this important subject.

Although here we treat only one aspect of this broad area, namely, electrophilic substitution reactions involving organomercurials, much of what has been determined and discussed is applicable to aliphatic electrophilic substitution reactions in general. The reactions of organomercurials for the most part may be classified as not involving carbanion intermediates, that is, they are S_E2 rather than S_E1 in nature. No effort has been made here to examine this closely related topic, for which the reader is referred to the recent excellent monograph by Professor Donald J. Cram.

It became apparent in reading reference materials that much of the physical-organic chemistry of organomercurials was incorrect, or that the conclusions reached by various authors would not withstand close scrutiny. A difficult decision was required as to how this work should be treated; it could be simply reported, ignored if clearly untenable, or subjected to critical evaluation. In fact all three courses were taken. In some instances the reader may feel that the treatment appears hypercritical, but a detailed analysis was deemed necessary where the original interpretation of results has been widely received as evidence for a specific mechanism.

A common difficulty in the study of electrophilic substitution of organomercurials is the occurrence of competing radical pathways. This problem was recognized and dealt with in some of the first careful work (Winstein and Traylor) in this area, but many other groups have not followed this lead and have largely ignored the possibility of competitive nonelectrophilic

v

reactions. Very recently, Hegarty, Kitching, and Wells [*J. Am. Chem. Soc.*, **89**:4876 (1967)] have commented on the too-frequent absence of critical work in many so-called electrophilic substitution studies of organometallics, where in fact the observations are associated with an oxygen-supported radical process.

Since an appreciable amount of the work cited in this text appears in Russian journals, many of which are now available in English translation with different pagination, it should be noted that the abbreviated journal names will indicate which course was used. In referring to an article in translation, the Americanized Consultants Bureau name is used, for examples *J. Gen. Chem., USSR* where the Russian paper appeared in *Zh. Obshch. Khim.* In cases where the present authors' interpretation of results differs from that presented in an article, both language versions were examined to ascertain whether misleading errors had occurred in translation.

The authors wish to express their indebtedness to their graduate students for many constructive suggestions and for reading the manuscript.

Frederick R. Jensen

Bruce Rickborn

TABLE OF CONTENTS

ELECTROPHILIC SUBSTITUTION
OF ORGANOMERCURIALS

1

ELECTROPHILIC ALIPHATIC SUBSTITUTION—GENERAL CONSIDERATIONS

1-1 Introduction

It is not possible to point to any particular historical development to mark the beginning of the broad, diverse field of the study of carbanionic reactions and concerted electrophilic aliphatic substitution. From a mechanistic viewpoint, however, it is clear that an understanding of reaction types has developed far more slowly than might be anticipated from the aspect of synthetic importance. One need only consider the Grignard reaction and a few of the numerous base-catalyzed condensations (e.g., aldol, malonic ester, Claisen) to visualize the vital place of carbanionic reactions in synthetic chemistry. In spite of the wealth of examples of aliphatic electrophilic substitution, no attempt was made to describe this area in a systematic manner until 1935, when Hughes and Ingold[1] undertook the task. This effort was directed toward developing a mechanistic nomenclature and descriptive system analogous to that proposed in their very successful treatment of nucleophilic substitution. This early work on electrophilic substitution was largely unsuccessful, partly due to the absence of meaningful stereochemical data, and partly due to an unfortunate choice of model reactions.

The terms S_E1 and S_E2 were introduced by these workers and formulated as follows:

$$R\!-\!H \rightleftharpoons R^- + H^+$$
$$R^- + X\!-\!Y \rightarrow RX + Y^- \qquad S_E1$$

$$\begin{array}{c} R\!-\!H \\ |\quad| \\ X\!-\!Y \end{array} \rightarrow R\!-\!X + HY \qquad S_E2$$

[1] E. D. Hughes and C. K. Ingold, *J. Chem. Soc.*, 244 (1935).

1

The Hughes-Ingold depiction of the S_E2 reaction, which as drawn will later be referred to as a four-center mechanism, was meant only to imply bimolecularity and not stereochemistry (reference 1). Such a depiction today would be taken as indicating a mechanism which requires retention of configuration. A comparable picture was drawn for the S_N2 mechanism (reference 1). In fact, inversion was tentatively suggested for the carbon seat of reaction for S_N2 and S_E2 reactions, and retention for S_N1 and S_E1 processes.

Hughes and Ingold further postulated the following relative rate order for an S_E2 process:

$$t\text{-Bu} > \text{isoPr} > \text{Et} > \text{Me}$$

This prediction was based on results of nitration and halogenation of alkanes, under conditions where it is now known that free-radical reactions can play important roles. The major contribution of this early work of Hughes and Ingold was thus to focus attention on a class of reactions different from the better understood nucleophilic substitutions, and to suggest a potential mechanistic nomenclature for these reactions.

The details and terminology of aliphatic electrophilic substitution mechanisms are discussed in later sections with appropriate examples.

1-2   Sources of Electrophilic Reagents

A nucleophile may be defined as any atom or molecular species capable of donating a pair of electrons to a nucleus. Common examples are anions (halides, alkoxides, carboxylates, etc.) and such materials as amines and alcohols. Conversely, an electrophile is defined as a nucleus capable of combining with an electron pair to form a bond. In theory both classifications are equally broad. In practice this should eventually prove to be true, but at present the number of different types of electrophiles that have been studied is relatively small.

By far the largest representative class of electrophiles consists of the proton donors (and their deuterium and tritium analogs). The reaction of an acid HY with a fully developed or potential carbanionic center can be sensitive to the group Y, that is, it is usually necessary to distinguish various protic

$$\overset{\diagdown}{\underset{\diagup}{-}}\text{C}-\text{M} + \text{HY} \rightarrow \overset{\diagdown}{\underset{\diagup}{-}}\text{C}-\text{H} + \text{MY}$$

acids in terms of their electrophilicity.

Other electrophile sources are cations, materials capable of accepting an electron pair (for example, $AlCl_3$), molecules such as the halogens which are potential cation donors ($\overset{\delta+}{Br}$—$\overset{\delta-}{Br}$), and unsaturated materials like ketones, aldehydes, and carbon dioxide. The application of a particular electrophile in any given reaction may be limited by unreactivity, formation of unstable products, or undesirable side reactions.

An exact relationship between the electronegativity or Lewis acid strength of the reagent and its electrophilicity does not necessarily exist. The electrophilicity of an atom or molecular species may be defined as the relative ease with which it forms a bond to a nucleus wherein the nucleus provides the electrons for the bond. In this text, the nucleus in question will always be carbon.

1-3 Leaving Groups

To the extent that generalizations can be made within a series of comparable reactions it is to be expected that a group bonded to carbon may be replaced in an electrophilic process by another group of greater electronegativity. Thus, the cationic form of any element is expected to replace a cation which has a lower electronegativity (Figure 1-1). Chemical experience is in accord with

F	Cl	Br	I	O	S	C	Hg
4.0	3.0	2.8	2.5	3.5	2.5	2.5	1.9

Tl	Pb	Sn	Zn	Al	Mg	Li	K
1.8	1.8	1.8	1.6	1.5	1.2	1.0	0.8

Figure 1-1 Electronegativities of some elements (L. Pauling, "The Nature of the Chemical Bond," 3d ed., p. 93, Cornell University Press, Ithaca, N.Y., 1960.)

these generalizations: Hg(II) and Tl(III) will replace Mg(II), and Br_2 will replace Sn(IV), but Br^-, which should have a very low "electronegativity" value, will not replace (by electrophilic substitution) Sn(IV).

The compound R—Y will in general be susceptible to nucleophilic substitution when the substituent is more electronegative than carbon, whereas electrophilic substitution will normally occur when Y is less electronegative than carbon. Since the atoms which fall in the former group are limited (halogens, oxygen, nitrogen, phosphorus, and a few others), the number of elements which can undergo electrophilic displacement predominate to a substantial extent. Thus, theoretically, electrophilic substitution reactions vastly outnumber their nucleophilic substitution counterparts. This becomes apparent when one considers that many of the elements susceptible to electrophilic displacement have multiple substitution. For example, the number of hypothetical electrophilic reactions of Sn(IV) compounds,

RSnXYZ (considering ten possible combinations such as $RSnX_2Y$, $RSnX_3$), is larger than the number of nucleophilic reactions of compounds RX, RY, and RZ by a factor greater than three.

A crude correlation exists between the ease of electrophilic cleavage and the electronegativity of the leaving group. When the electronegativity of the central atom in the leaving group is greater than 1.7, the C—M bond is not cleaved by water; but when the value is 1.7 or less, hydrolysis occurs readily.

For elements with valences higher than one, the relative tendency towards electrophilic scission is expected to vary with the electronegativities of the other attached groups. The carbon-mercury bond in the structure $\overset{\delta-}{C}$—$\overset{2\delta+}{Hg}$—$\overset{\delta-}{C}$ has about 8 % ionic character, whereas in the structure C—Hg—Cl the negative charge on carbon is decreased by the presence of the electronegative halogen atom. Since the $ClHg^+$ group is expected to be a poorer leaving group than RHg^+, it is reasonable to expect that electrophilic cleavage is slower with alkylmercuric salts than with dialkylmercury compounds.

The relative susceptibility of a group of atoms towards electrophilic reaction is expected to vary with small changes in structure. The polarization in the compounds should vary from positive carbon in CHgF to approximately

C—Hg—F			C—Hg—Cl			C—Hg—Br		
2.5	1.9	4.0	2.5	1.9	3.0	2.5	1.9	2.8

C—Hg—I			C—Hg—C		
2.5	1.9	2.5	2.5	1.9	2.5

Figure 1-2 Electronegativities of elements in a series of mercurials

neutral or negative carbon in CHgI and finally to negative carbon in CHgC. For the alkylmercuric halides, the compound with the least electronegative halogen would be expected to undergo electrophilic cleavage most readily. Thus, the alkylmercuric iodides are the only compounds in this series in which electrophilic cleavage by protic acid occurs below decomposition temperatures.[2] These compounds, however, do not cleave as readily as dialkylmercurials.

Caution is required in assuming that reactions take a particular course whenever the same elements are involved. For example, chemical experience leads to the expectation that cleavage of an organometallic halide by an electrophile takes the course

$$R—M—X + A^+ \rightarrow RA + MX^+$$

[2] H. Framherz and K. Lih, *Z. Physik. Chem.* (*Leipzig*), **A167**:103 (1933).

However, for cases where the carbon residue forms a very stable carbonium ion, an alternative course is plausible:

$$A^+ + R—M—X \xrightarrow{\text{(concerted)}} R^+ + A—M—X$$

This could occur in materials where the metal has become more electronegative than carbon. No well-authenticated examples are presently available, but this could become a fruitful area of research.

1-4   Effect of Substituents on Rate of Electrophilic Reaction

Electrophilic substitutions may be divided into two broad classifications: those involving formation of a fully charged carbanion (S_E1), and concerted reactions. It may be generalized with confidence that substituents on carbon which supply electrons destabilize the formation of carbanions and accelerate their reaction rates once formed.

A similar statement cannot be made for concerted substitution. Broad generalizations regarding the effect of structural changes in the leaving group on rate, which may not be quantitatively correct, were made in Sec. 1-3. However, there is no way of predicting a priori the relative change in charge density on carbon in going to the transition state. In fact, either response to variations in charge is reasonable; processes may exist which are accelerated or are retarded by substitution of either electron accepting or donating groups on carbon. It is therefore anticipated that steric considerations as well as inductive and resonance phenomena will affect reactivity orders in S_E2 and other concerned substitutions.

Reutov and coworkers[3] have taken a different view, namely that the electrical effects of substituents attached to the carbon seat are opposite to those observed in nucleophilic substitution. However, the presently available data for S_N2 reactions indicate that, depending on circumstances, rates may be accelerated by either electron withdrawing or donating groups.[4] Any analogy to be inferred by consideration of S_N2 processes leads to the conclusion that generalizations in the behavior of S_E2 reactions must await experimental investigation.

A consideration of the resonance forms of the transition state for concerted electrophilic substitution also leads to the conclusion that the change in

[3] O. A. Reutov and I. P. Beletskaya, *Proc. Acad. Sci. USSR, Chem. Sect.*, **131**:333 (1960). O. A. Reutov, I. P. Beletskaya, and G. A. Artamkina, *J. Gen. Chem. USSR*, (*Eng. Transl.*), **30**:3190 (1960). O. A. Reutov, *Record Chem. Progr.* (*Kresge-Hooker Sci. Lib.*), **22**:1 (1961).

[4] Cf. E. S. Gould, "Mechanism and Structure in Organic Chemistry," p. 282, Holt, Rinehart and Winston, Inc., New York, 1959.

charge density is not predictable. Figure 1-3 shows the possible resonance forms for the transition state for an S_E2 process. The effect of mesomerism

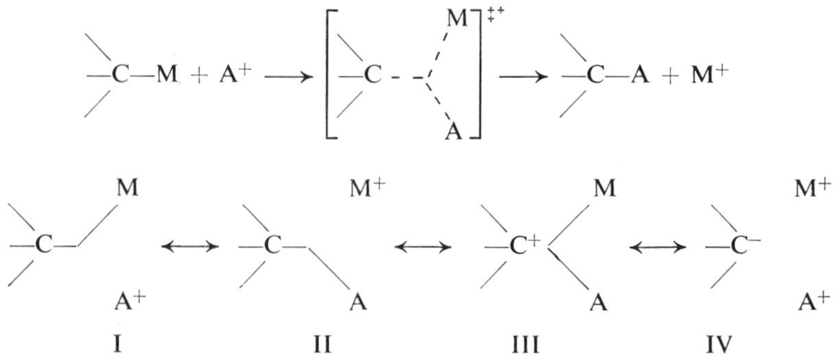

$$\ce{-C-M} + A^+ \longrightarrow \left[\ce{-C - -} \overset{M}{\underset{A}{\diagup}} \right]^{++} \longrightarrow \ce{-C-A} + M^+$$

Figure 1-3 An S_E2 reaction (top) and the resonance forms of the transition state (bottom)

on the charge density depends on the importance of the resonance forms III and IV.

1-5 Mechanisms for Concerted Substitution

Discussion in previous sections has been limited to the S_E1 and S_E2 types. Under the proper circumstances a gradual transition between these forms, as distinguished by the degree of negative charge generated on carbon in the transition state, can be expected. Other general types, analogous to nucleophilic counterparts, are also anticipated, for example, S_E2' and S_Ei.

Classification of limiting mechanisms involving carbanions should cause little difficulty. However, at the present stage of knowledge the same cannot be said of limiting concerted electrophilic reactions. Strictly speaking, an S_E2 reaction ("pure" S_E2) should involve reaction by an electrophile on carbon with no other interaction between the electrophile and the leaving

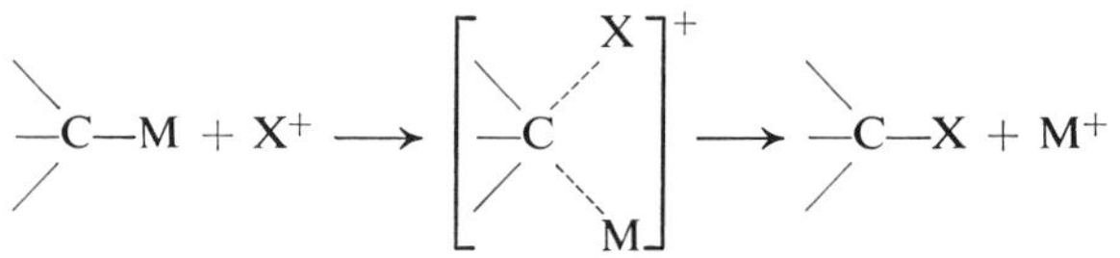

$$\ce{-C-M} + X^+ \longrightarrow \left[\ce{-C} \overset{X}{\underset{M}{\diagup}} \right]^+ \longrightarrow \ce{-C-X} + M^+$$

Figure 1-4 The pure S_E2 mechanism (inversion is also possible)

group. Most reactions studied thus far appear to be of another type wherein the incoming and leaving groups are joined by a "bridging" atom or group.

Reactions of this type are frequently referred to as four-center, closed transition state, or "no-mechanism" reactions, although extensive literature usage of the S_E2 designation dictates that the broader definition include these reactions.

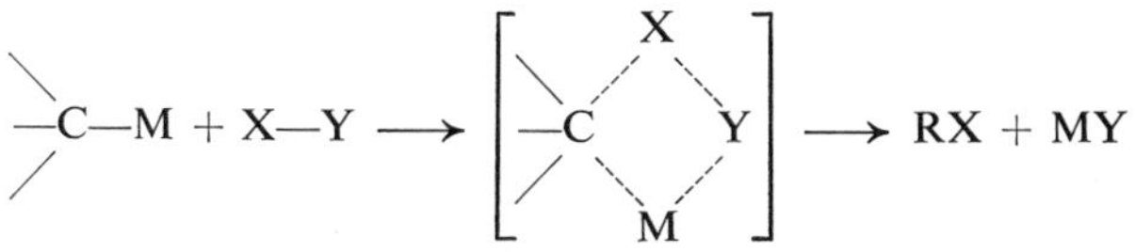

$$\overset{\diagdown}{\underset{\diagup}{\text{—C—M}}} + \text{X—Y} \longrightarrow \left[\underset{\diagup}{\overset{\diagdown}{\text{—C}}} \diagup\diagdown\overset{\text{X}}{\diagdown}\underset{\diagdown\text{M}\diagup}{\diagdown}\text{Y} \right] \longrightarrow \text{RX} + \text{MY}$$

Figure 1-5   A four-center electrophilic substitution process

Classification of reactions as electrophilic substitutions has often been arbitrarily made on the basis that the attacking reagent is electron deficient or potentially electron deficient. The development of either positive or negative charge (if any) on carbon will depend on the relative degree of bond making and bond breaking. Knowledge of the sign of this charge does not, in fact, suffice to allow definition of the reaction type. Assignment can properly be made only if the direction of electron flow is known, a seemingly impossible task (also of questionable meaning from a quantum mechanical standpoint). It is also conceivable that no net electron flow occurs in either direction, i.e., a four-center homolytic process.

Nevertheless, classification of reactions as examples of electrophilic substitution appears desirable whenever the gross features (effectively through considerations of electronegativities) suggest the reaction is electrophilic; difficulties then arise mainly because details of the mechanism are imperfectly known. A process which, due to the nature of the attacking reagent, may be termed electrophilic, and which involves a bridging group, is properly designated as S_Ei. Such a designation is actually broader than "four-center," allowing a description of mechanisms in which an ambident ligand, e.g., acetate ion, may serve as the bridging group in a six-centered cyclic transition state.

From a theoretical viewpoint the "pure" S_E2 reaction is of greater interest than the four-center process. Unfortunately, claims to the contrary notwithstanding, there is no authenticated example of a pure S_E2 reaction. The four-center mechanism explicitly requires retention of configuration at the carbon seat of reaction. Experimentally, stereospecificity in electrophilic substitution nearly always involves retention; the few documented examples where inversion occurs are associated with special structural features or other circumstances which will be discussed later. The most pressing current problem in the area of electrophilic aliphatic substitution is to find and conclusively demonstrate the mechanism and stereochemistry of a "pure" S_E2 process.

1-6   Transition States for Concerted Electrophilic Substitution

Considering the geometry and the atomic orbitals involved, inversion of configuration appears to be a resonable stereochemical outcome of S_E2 reactions. The central carbon atom in the transition state for this process

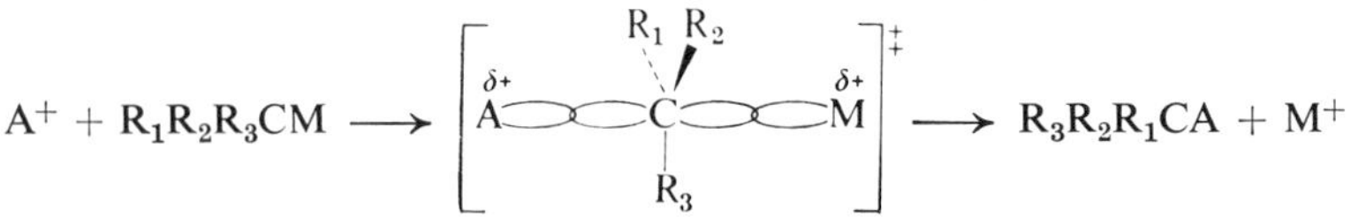

$$A^+ + R_1R_2R_3CM \longrightarrow \left[A \overset{\delta+}{\Longleftarrow} \overset{\overset{R_1\ R_2}{\diagdown\ /}}{\underset{R_3}{C}} \overset{\delta+}{\Longrightarrow} M \right]^{\ddagger} \longrightarrow R_3R_2R_1CA + M^+$$

Figure 1-6   A plausible S_E2 mechanism—inversion of configuration

undergoes a change of hybridization to sp^2 and p. The resonance forms of the transition state of this inversion mechanism are given in Figure 1-7.

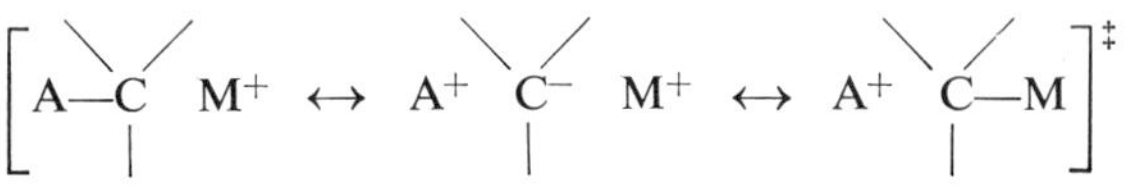

$$\left[A\overset{\diagdown\ /}{\underset{|}{C}}\ M^+ \ \leftrightarrow\ A^+\ \overset{\diagdown\ /}{\underset{|}{C^-}}\ M^+\ \leftrightarrow\ A^+\ \overset{\diagdown\ /}{\underset{|}{C}}{-}M \right]^{\ddagger}$$

Figure 1-7   Resonance model for an inversion S_E2 process

Reaction with retention of configuration may occur with no change in hybridization on carbon through attack on the bond rather than the carbon atom. Electron repulsion would make a similar mechanism for nucleophilic

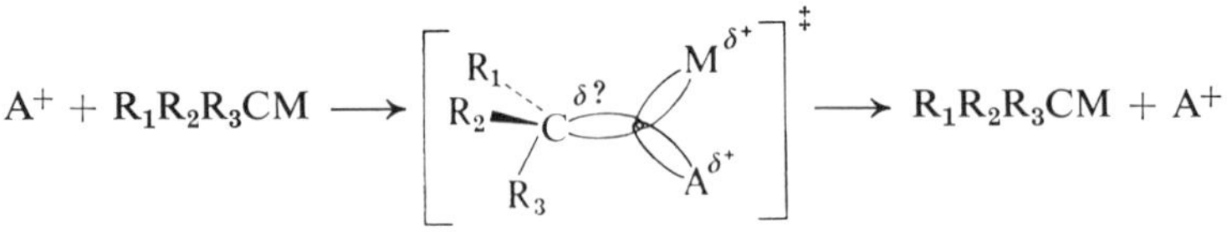

$$A^+ + R_1R_2R_3CM \longrightarrow \left[\overset{R_1}{\underset{R_3}{\overset{R_2}{\diagdown}}}C \overset{\delta?}{\diagdown}\overset{M^{\delta+}}{\underset{A^{\delta+}}{\diagup\diagdown}} \right]^{\ddagger} \longrightarrow R_1R_2R_3CM + A^+$$

Figure 1-8   The S_E2 retention mechanism

substitution unattractive. In the electrophilic reaction repulsion of charges (positive) will still occur, which may well account for the importance of bridging atoms between the electrophile and the leaving group in front-side attack reactions.

Metal ions are commonly encountered leaving groups in electrophilic aliphatic substitution. Invariably these atoms have vacant orbitals available for complex formation or readily expand their electron shells. The possibility of obtaining increased reactivities of the compound by complex formation of the metal and ligands has been recognized from the earliest investigations and the phenomenon has been verified many times experimentally. Interaction of the nucleophile and the metal causes an increase in the electron density on carbon, which increases the ease of scission to form a carbanion or enhances the reactivity with the electrophile.

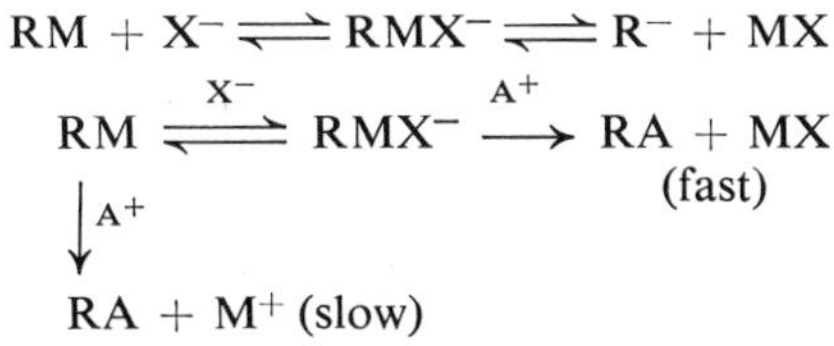

$$RM + X^- \rightleftharpoons RMX^- \rightleftharpoons R^- + MX$$

$$RM \underset{X^-}{\overset{}{\rightleftharpoons}} RMX^- \overset{A^+}{\longrightarrow} RA + MX$$
$$\quad\quad\quad\quad\quad\quad\quad\quad\quad\text{(fast)}$$

$$\Big\downarrow{\scriptstyle A^+}$$

$$RA + M^+ \text{ (slow)}$$

Figure 1-9   Consequences of
complex anion formation

Similarly, the possibility exists that the covalently bound electrophile and nucleophile react simultaneously with the leaving group and carbon. Interaction in this manner, depending on timing, may increase the charge density of carbon and increase the positive character of the electrophile. The net effect may be decreased charge separation during the course of the reaction as compared to the situation which exists when the electrophile and nucleophile act independently (Figure 1-10). The geometry of the transition

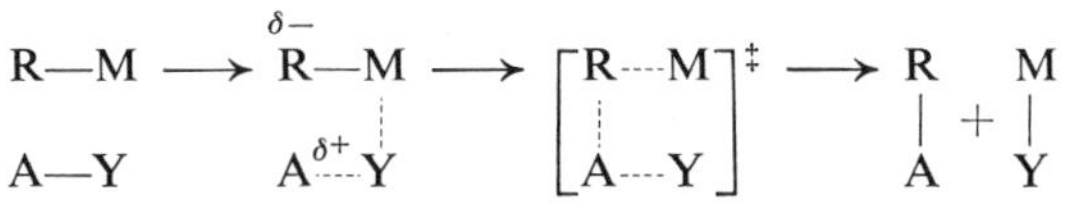

$$R{-}M \longrightarrow \overset{\delta-}{R}{-}M \longrightarrow \left[\begin{array}{cc} R \cdots M \\ \vdots \quad \vdots \\ A \cdots Y \end{array}\right]^{\ddagger} \longrightarrow \begin{array}{cc} R & M \\ | & + | \\ A & Y \end{array}$$
$$A{-}Y \quad\quad\quad A\overset{\delta+}{\cdots}Y$$

Figure 1-10   Predicted effect on charge distribution
by initial metal-nucleophile interaction

states of these four-center reactions does not appear to be particularly favorable (Figure 1-11).

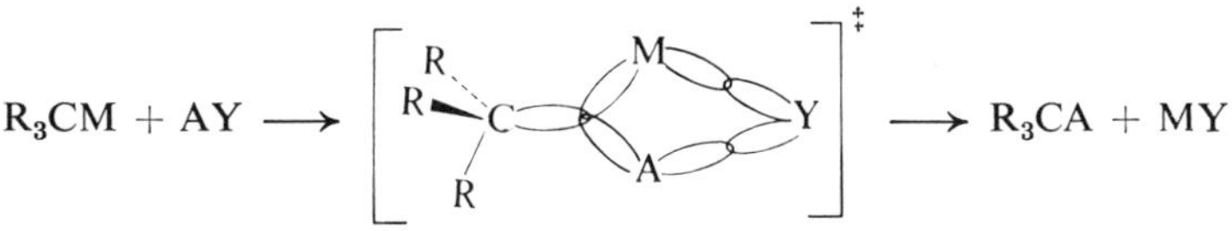

$$R_3CM + AY \longrightarrow \left[\begin{array}{c} R \\ R{-}C{=}\!\!\!\!=\!\!\!\!=M \\ | \quad\quad A{-}Y \\ R \end{array}\right]^{\ddagger} \longrightarrow R_3CA + MY$$

Figure 1-11   Orbital arrangement of a four-center
transition state showing unfavorable geometry

The four-center reaction may approach limiting forms depending on the relative degree of interaction of electrophiles and nucleophiles in the transition state. When the predominant feature of the reaction in the transition state is attack of the electrophile on carbon with little interaction of the nucleophile and the leaving group, the "pure" S_E2 mechanism is approached. With dominant bonding of the nucleophile to the leaving group and scission of the existing carbon bond to give a carbanion, the limiting S_Ei mechanism prevails. Between these extremes the transition state may either have similar degrees of bonding between all four atoms or dissimilar charge distributions.

The question of bridging in cyclic (closed) transition states is interesting, and numerous specific examples will be discussed in later sections. Insufficient information is available to predict the relative bridging efficiencies of various groups, but it may be safely generalized that bond lengths, bond angles, polarizabilities, availability of unshared pairs, and geometrical factors will be important. Thus, it is not possible to predict whether ions which are highly ionic but which may contribute several atoms to a bridge (for example, NO_3^-) with formation of a six-membered ring will be more favorable than groups which tend to form covalent bonds to metals (for example, Br^-) but require four-membered cyclic transition states.

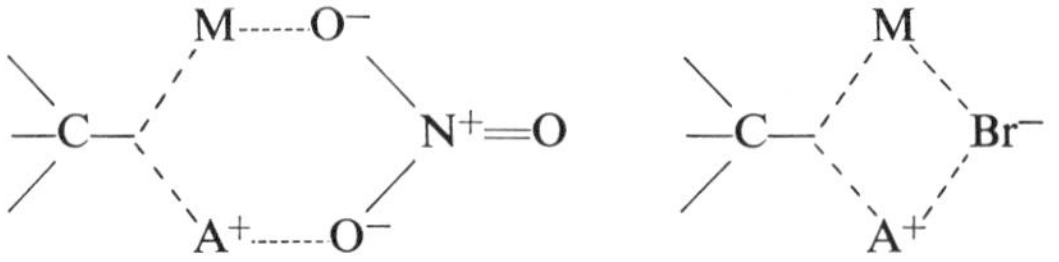

Figure 1-12 Six- and four-membered bridged species

Complications arise even in considering the simple case of bridging by bromide. Figure 1-13 shows orbital pictures for possible transition states for

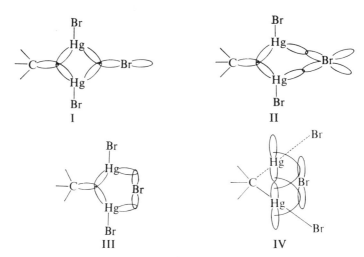

Figure 1-13 Various orbital involvements for bromine bridging (only bonding orbitals shown) in four-center transition states of the reaction

$$RHgBr + H\overset{*}{g}Br_2 \rightarrow RH\overset{*}{g}Br + HgBr_2$$

the four-center exchange reaction of mercuric bromide with an alkylmercuric bromide. Of these possibilities, structure II is assumed most probable because of the involvement of two electron pairs and reasonable geometry.

1-7 The Nature of Carbanions

The planar configuration as the preferred geometry of a carbonium ion is well accepted. The nature of a carbanion is, however, still a matter of conjecture. Arguments for an sp^2 planar configuration are based on the effective delocalization of negative charge that would be associated with such a structure. Proponents of the tetrahedral structure point out that a

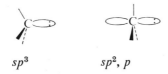

sp^3 sp^2, p

Figure 1-14 Tetrahedral and trigonal
configurations for a carbanion

carbanion is isoelectronic with an amine, for which a nonplanar configuration has been definitely established. The work of Bottini and Roberts[5] is especially relevant since it clearly shows that the nitrogen in N-alkylaziridines is both nonplanar and rapidly inverting. The rate of inversion of some N-alkylaziridines is however low enough to be measured by nuclear magnetic resonance techniques.[6]

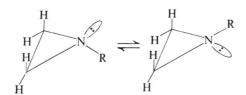

Figure 1-15 The inversion of N-alkylaziridines

Several interesting points may be made from the rate data given in Table 1-1. The ethyl- and benzyl-substituted materials invert at comparable rates, while the 2-phenylethyl is somewhat faster, and the t-butyl-derivative is too fast to measure,† indicating that steric interactions can greatly affect the rate of inversion. Similarly, the N-phenyl compound, where resonance interaction can occur, inverts too rapidly to measure (or has attained a planar configuration at $-77°$) (Fig. 1–16).

[5] A. T. Bottini and J. D. Roberts, *J. Am. Chem. Soc.*, **80**:5230 (1958).
[6] Below coalescence temperatures, the protons cis and trans to the N-alkyl group are distinguishable by nmr.
† Added in proof.

Table 1-1   Inversion rates of N-alkylaziridines

R	Temperature of coalescence	k, sec^{-1}
$CH_3—CH_2—$	108	60
 ⬡—$CH_2—$	105	60
 ⬡—$CH_2CH_2—$	96	69
t-Bu—	< -77	too fast
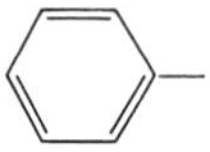 ⬡—	< -77	too fast

Bicyclic bridgehead organometallics are known and provide permissive evidence for the pyramidal carbanion structure. An example is found in

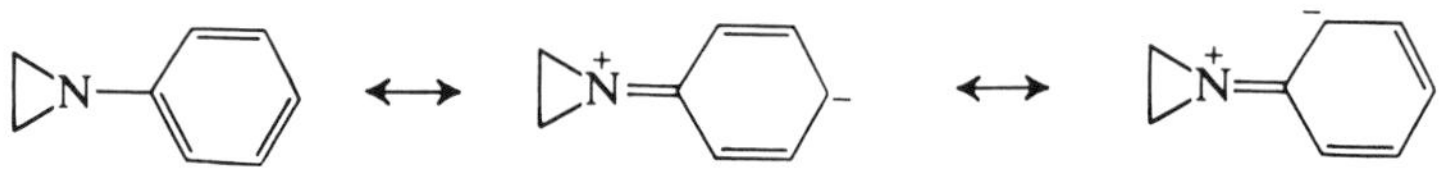

Figure 1-16   A possible resonance interaction leading to planar amine

the work of Wiberg and Lowry[7] on the bicyclo[2.1.1]hexane system. The reduction of 4-chlorocamphane with sodium in ethanol presumably

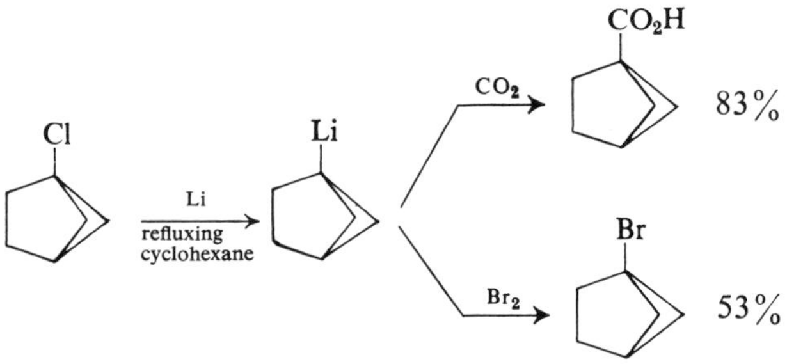

Figure 1-17   Formation and reactions of a bicyclic bridgehead organolithium reagent

occurs through bridgehead carbanion formation,[8] as does the reaction with

[7] K. B. Wiberg and B. R. Lowry, *J. Am. Chem. Soc.*, **85**:3188 (1963).
[8] W. von E. Doering and E. F. Schoenwalt, *J. Am. Chem. Soc.*, **73**:2333 (1951).

sodium-potassium alloy on the isomeric material, as shown in Figure 1-18. To the extent that these organometallics are representative of carbanions,

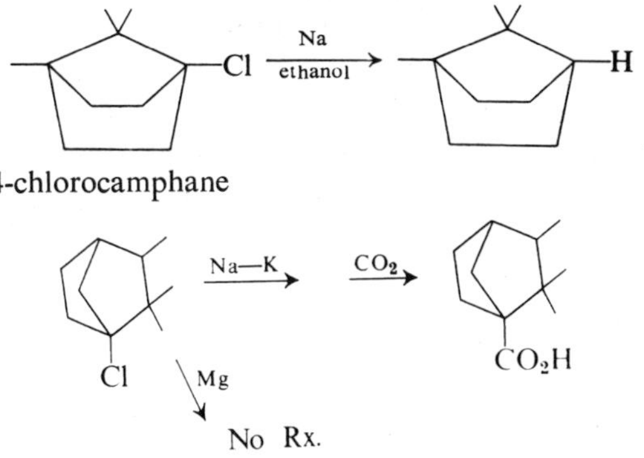

4-chlorocamphane

Figure 1-18   Reactions involving bridgehead organometallics

the tetrahedral configuration for carbanions is plausible. (In this context though it should be recalled that carbonium ion reactions also occur in comparable bridgehead systems, although at greatly diminished rates relative to open chain analogs;[9] see Figure 1-19.) Failure to form the Grignard reagent

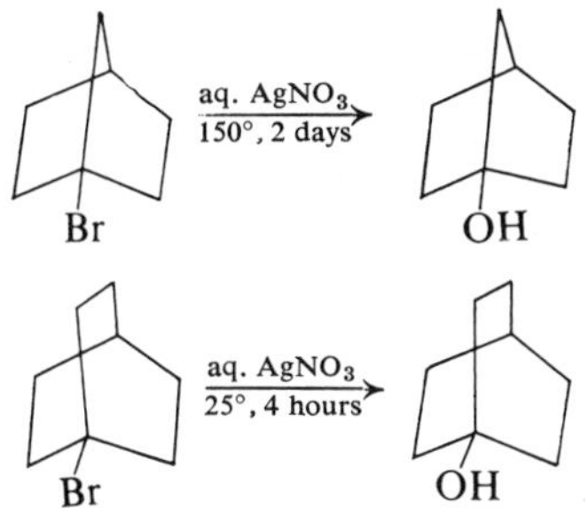

Figure 1-19   Bridgehead carbonium ion reactions

has been noted for some bridgehead halides (Figures 1-18, 1-20). While this

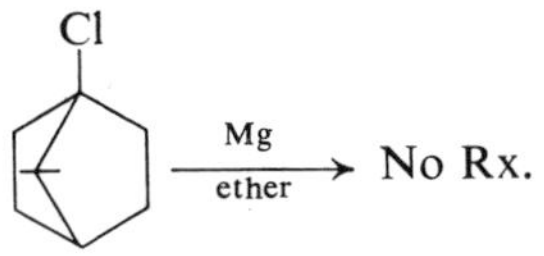

Figure 1-20   Failure of apocamphyl chloride to form a Grignard reagent.
[P. D. Bartlett and L. H. Knox, *J. Am. Chem. Soc.*, **61**:3184 (1939)]

[9] W. von E. Doering, M. Levitz, A. Sayigh, M. Sprecher, and W. P. Whelan, Jr., *J. Am. Chem. Soc.*, **75**:100 (1953).

behavior is not necessarily ascribable to the bridgehead structure (tertiary halides often react with difficulty), it is conceivable that such carbanions, like the analogous carbonium ions, are energetically unfavorable. Bartlett and Greene[10] have found that triptoic acid does not undergo base-catalyzed decarboxylation at 350°, a reaction which would presumably involve a carbanionic intermediate or transition state. The corresponding 1-tripticyl bromide also appears to be extremely inert to aqueous silver nitrate, i.e., apparently both anionic and cationic reactions are unfavorable in this system.

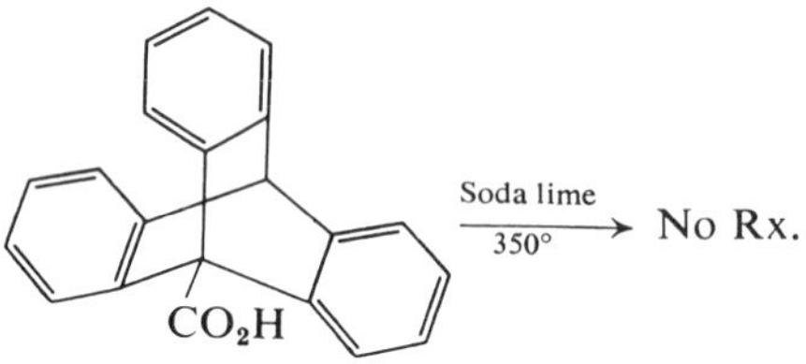

Triptoic Acid

Figure 1-21 An inert bridgehead system

While the preferred electronic configuration of a carbanion remains open to question, the foregoing indicates that the sp^3 state is a definite possibility and may be energetically favored or differ only slightly from the sp^2 state. It is possible that a fine balance exists between the two configurations, such that the structure of the molecule may determine the preference for one configuration or the other. Solvent effects and ion pairing must also be considered in individual systems. If the ion pair is very tight the cation can play an important part in the configurational stability of an organometallic compound.

1-8   Some Comparisons of the "Ionic" Organometallics

The Group IA (Li, Na, K, Rb, Cs) and Group IIA (Be, Mg, Ca, Sr, Ba) metals are the elements whose organic derivatives could be expected to exhibit ionic behavior. With the exception of lithium and magnesium compounds, these organometallics have received relatively little study. The chemical and physical properties of beryllium, calcium, strontium, and barium derivatives are the subject of a recent review.[11] No attempt will be made here to cover in detail this interesting area, although a few pertinent examples will be discussed.

Solid dimethylberyllium has a polymeric structure involving bridging methyl groups, with Be—C—Be bond angles of 66°.[12] Comparable structures

[10] P. D. Bartlett and F. D. Greene, *J. Am. Chem. Soc.*, **76**:1088 (1954).

[11] G. A. Balueva and S. T. Ioffe, *Usp. Khim.*, **31**:940 (1962).

[12] A. I. Snow and R. E. Rundle, *Acta Cryst.*, **4**:348 (1951).

have been suggested for dimeric and trimeric dimethylberyllium in the vapor state[13] (dimethylberyllium is a solid which sublimes at 217° at atmospheric pressure).

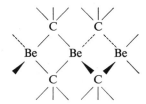

Figure 1-22   The structure of solid polymeric
dimethylberyllium

Dessy[14] has reported that diphenylberyllium does not undergo metal exchange with radioberyllium bromide in ether solution. This result precludes the formation of an RBeBr derivative in a Schlenk-type equilibrium under these conditions; the enhanced solubility of beryllium bromide in ether in the presence of diphenylberyllium suggests that a complex is formed (reference 14), which by analogy with dimethylberyllium might have the structure shown in Figure 1-23. This failure to undergo exchange suggests that "ionic" is

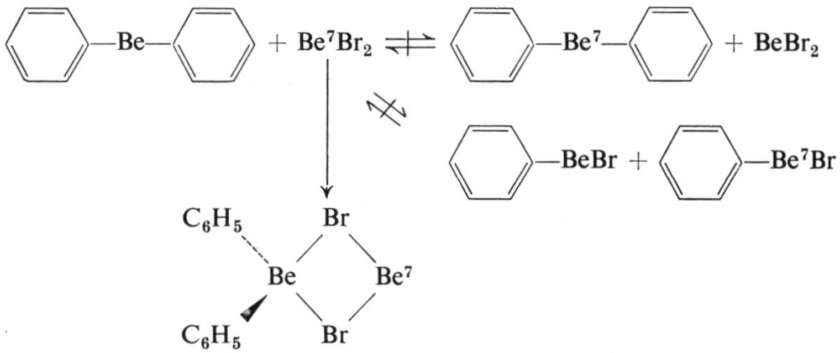

Figure 1-23   Lack of exchange between diphenyl
beryllium and radioberyllium bromide

a far from accurate description of these simplest of Group IIA organometallic derivatives.

Various data have been obtained recently which pertain to the properties of Group IA organometallics. Lampher[15] has examined the infrared spectra (in Nujol) of lithium, sodium, potassium, and magnesium allylic derivatives and has concluded that all, including the organomagnesium, are ionic.

[13] E. G. Coates, F. Glocking and N. D. Huck, *J. Chem. Soc.*, 4496 (1952).

[14] R. E. Dessy, *J. Am. Chem. Soc.*, **82**:1580 (1960).

[15] E. J. Lampher, *J. Am. Chem. Soc.*, **79**:5578 (1957).

Resonance stabilization of the allyl anion clearly plays an important role in determining the nature of the bonding in these systems. Calculations of the ionic character of various carbon-alkali metal bonds have been carried out by Ebel.[16] The anticipated increase in carbanionic contribution with increased s character in the carbon-metal bond is evident (Table 1-2).

Table 1-2 Dependence of ionic character on state of hybridization (reference 16)

Compound	% ionic character
CH_3Li	27
$CH_2{=}CHLi$	31
$HC{=}CLi$	39
CH_3Na	29
$CH_2{=}CHNa$	32
$HC{\equiv}CNa$	40
$(CH_3)_2Mg$	20

Differences caused by variations of the gegenion show up most strikingly in the reactivities of various organometallics. Lithium derivatives in general are stable in solution, as are organosodium compounds to a lesser degree. Potassium compounds, on the other hand, are extremely unstable and undergo reaction with solvent, rearrangement, and extensive degradation. The two general methods of producing these materials—by direct action of the metal on the alkyl halide and by metal cleavage of the dialkylmercury—give very poor yields of the desired product. That these low yields were caused by decomposition of the organopotassium compounds was not appreciated until the recent work of Finnegan,[17] and Benkeser, Trevillyan and Hooz.[18]

$$RX \xrightarrow{K} R^-K^+ + KX$$

$$R_2Hg \xrightarrow{K} 2R^-K^+ + Hg$$

Figure 1-24 Formation of organopotassium derivatives

In a study of the formation of n-amylpotassium from n-amyl chloride it was found (reference 17) that the major product was unsaturated, and that the simple unsaturates were converted to more stable dienyl anions on standing.

[16] H. F. Ebel, *Tetrahedron*, **21**:699 (1965).

[17] a. R. A. Finnegan, *Tetrahedron Letters*, 1303 (1962).
   b. *ibid.*, 429, 851 (1963).

[18] R. A. Benkeser, A. E. Trevillyan, and J. Hooz, *J. Am. Chem. Soc.*, **84**:4071 (1962).

The elimination of potassium hydride was postulated as a process leading to olefin. The results are summarized in Figure 1-25.

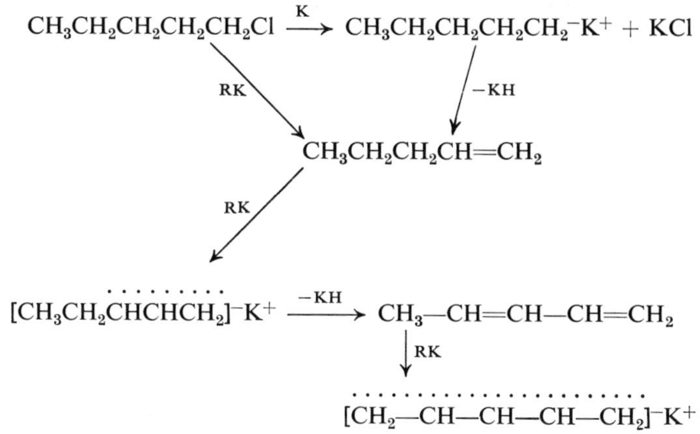

$$CH_3CH_2CH_2CH_2CH_2Cl \xrightarrow{\text{K}} CH_3CH_2CH_2CH_2CH_2^- K^+ + KCl$$

$$\text{RK} \qquad \qquad -KH$$

$$CH_3CH_2CH_2CH{=}CH_2$$

$$\text{RK}$$

$$[CH_3CH_2CHCHCH_2]^- K^+ \xrightarrow{-KH} CH_3{-}CH{=}CH{-}CH{=}CH_2$$

$$\downarrow \text{RK}$$

$$[CH_2{-}CH{-}CH{-}CH{-}CH_2]^- K^+$$

Figure 1-25 The formation of unsaturates in the preparation of an alkylpotassium

Generation of the dienyl anion, as established by protonation to give pentadiene, continued long after the initial reaction was completed; the yield of pentadiene increased from 2 to 12 to 20% after 0.2, 0.9 and 9 months, respectively.

Treatment of neopentyl chloride with potassium gave dimethylcyclopropane, 2-methyl-2-butene, and 2-methyl-1-butene along with minor amounts of hydrogen, methane, ethylene, acetylene, propene, and isobutylene (reference 17). The ratios of the major products were found to vary with reaction time (Table 1-3).

Table 1-3 Product ratios in the reaction of neopentyl chloride with potassium

$CH_3-\underset{\underset{CH_3}{|}}{\overset{\overset{CH_3}{|}}{C}}-CH_2Cl \xrightarrow{\text{K}}$	$\triangle$	$+ CH_3-\underset{}{\overset{\overset{CH_3}{|}}{C}}{=}CH{-}CH_3$	$+ CH_2{=}\underset{}{\overset{\overset{CH_3}{|}}{C}}{-}CH_2CH_3$
Initial	3.8	1.5	1
3 days	1.2	1.7	1
24 days	0.4	1.8	1

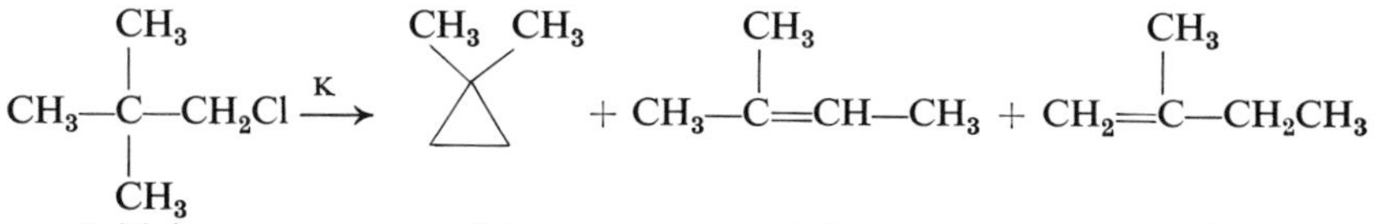

Dimethylcyclopropane is apparently formed by a carbene insertion reaction, which may also account for the 2-methyl-2-butene. The formation of

2-methyl-1-butene is less straightforward; the variations in ratio of the two major olefinic products with time suggests that they may not arise (entirely) from protonation of a common intermediate allylic anion.

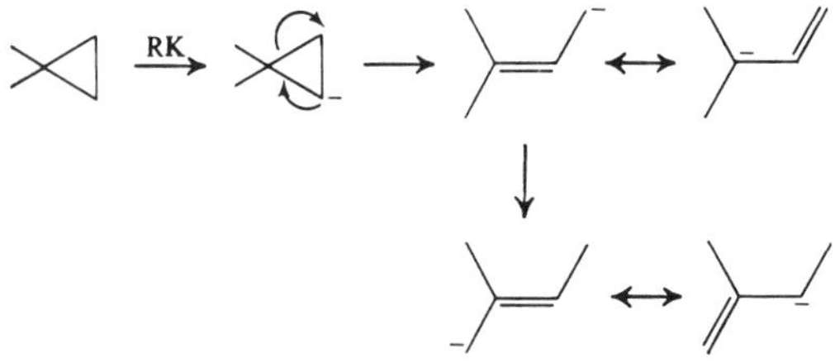

Figure 1-26   Opening of cyclopropane by alkylpotassium

The minor products must arise from fragmentation reactions, a number of which may be visualized. The yield of acetylene increased with time, presumably because of the stability of the salt.

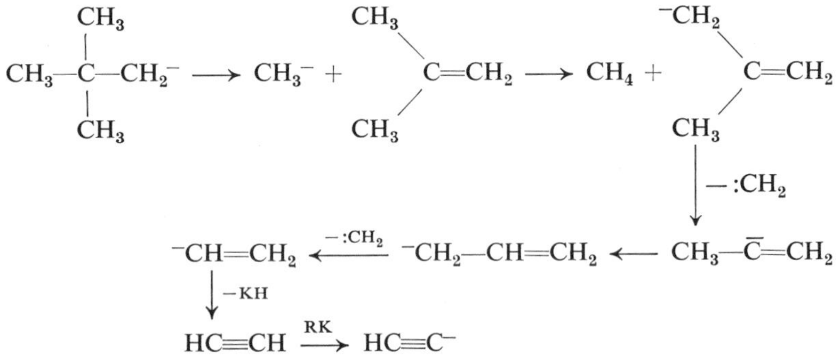

Figure 1-27   Possible fragmentation reactions of alkylpotassiums

Finnegan (reference 17) has also demonstrated that n-butylpotassium prepared in pentane from di-n-butylmercury (to avoid Wurtz coupling) reacts with the solvent rapidly to give amylpotassium derivatives. Analysis involved evaporation of solvent prior to hydrolysis. The results are shown in Table 1-4.

A striking example of the reaction with solvent occurred in cyclohexane, where a 20% yield of benzene was formed after one week. This product presumably results from the sequence

$$C_6H_{12} \rightarrow C_6H_{11}^- \rightarrow C_6H_{10} \rightarrow C_6H_9^- \rightarrow C_6H_8 \rightarrow C_6H_7^- \rightarrow C_6H_6$$

Theilacker and Moellhoff[19] have reported the cleavage of triptycene on

[19] W. Theilacker and E. Moellhoff, *Angew. Chem.*, **74:**781 (1962).

Table 1-4   The metallation of solvent in the preparation of *n*-butylpotassium in pentane

Hydrolysis products	Initial	% comp. 24 hours	1 week
C_4H_{10}	55.8	7.4	0.6
C_4H_8 (1-butene and *cis*- and *trans*-2-butene)	2.3	5.2	8.8
C_4H_6	0.1	0.9	0.5
C_5H_{12}	20.5	10.4	3.8
C_5H_{10} (1-pentene, *cis*- and *trans*-2-pentene)	10.2	9.8	14.3
C_5H_8 (1,4-pentadiene, *cis*- and *trans*-1,3-pentadiene)	4.4	29.7	44.1

treatment with sodium-potassium alloy in diethyl ether to give 9-phenyl-9,10-dihydroanthracene (after quenching with methanol). No reaction took place with sodium metal in di-*n*-butyl ether at 110 to 120°. Triphenylmethane and tetraphenylmethane were also fragmented by potassium to give, after carbonation, di- and triphenylacetic acids, as shown in Figure 1-29. A plausible mechanistic scheme which may account for these products has been suggested by House and Kramer,[20] who examined the reaction of triphenylmethane with potassium in 1,2-dimethoxyethane.[21] Reaction occurred readily at room temperature to give mainly triphenylmethylpotassium, but without the evolution of hydrogen. The various side products and possible modes of formation are shown in Figure 1-30. The fact that hydrogen was not formed indicates that the triphenylmethylpotassium arose from proton abstraction by the various carbanions generated in side reactions as indicated.

Organosodium compounds are far less reactive than their potassium

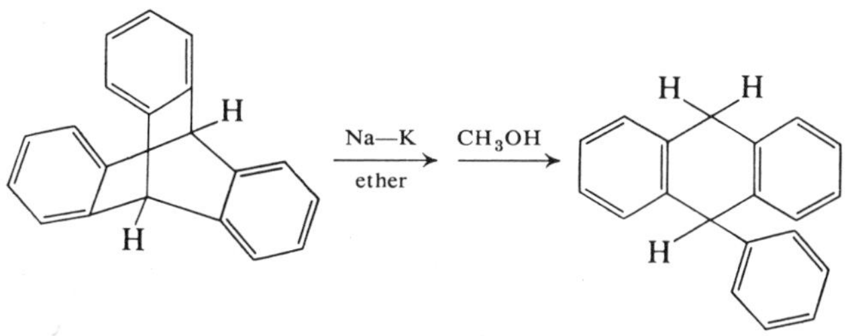

Figure 1-28   Cleavage of triptycene with sodium-potassium alloy

[20] H. O. House and V. Kramer, *J. Org. Chem.*, **27**:4146 (1962).

[21] Potassium is reported to dissolve to a small extent in this solvent: J. L. Downs, J. Lewis, B. Moore, and G. Wilkinson, *J. Chem. Soc.* (*London*) 3767 (1959).

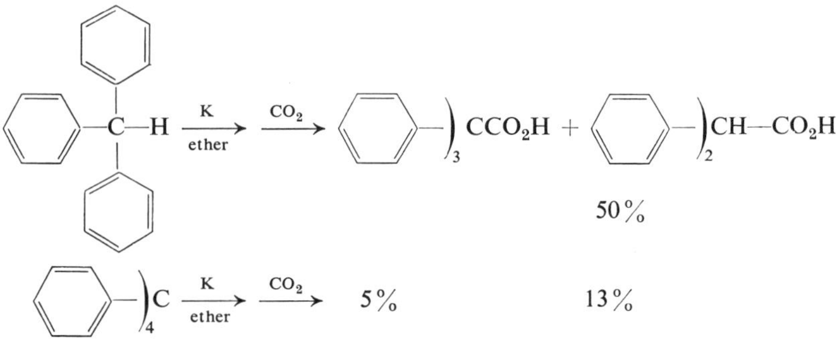

Figure 1-29 Fragmentation of arylmethanes by potassium metal

analogs. Thus Finnegan (reference 17) has reported that amylsodium, after standing several weeks at room temperature, showed only a few percent conversion to pentenylsodium. Sodium compounds can be prepared and used with fair assurance that extreme structural changes have not occurred. Rearrangement is seldom observed in the Wurtz reaction of alkyl halides with sodium. It is in the context of this reaction that most of the information regarding sodium derivatives has been obtained.

The mechanism of the Wurtz reaction has been the subject of speculation for some time. When an optically active halide is treated with an organometallic, the normal course of coupling product formation involves inversion of configuration with varying amounts of racemization.[22] The extent of

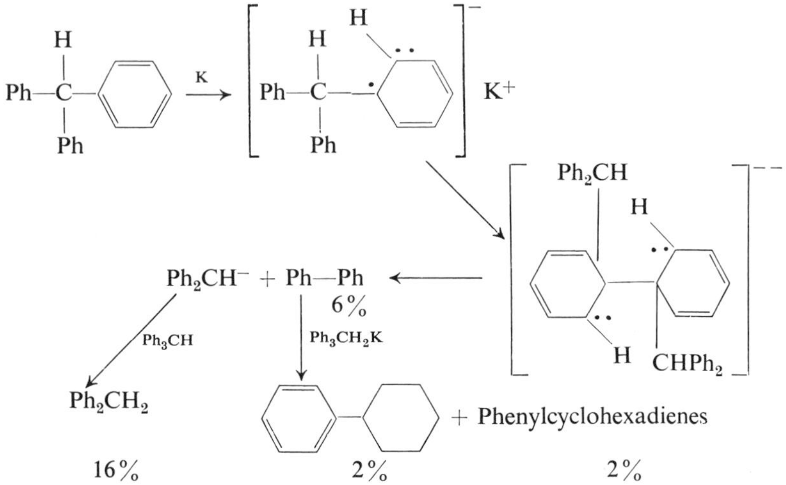

Figure 1-30 The reaction of triphenylmethane with potassium

[22] For a summary of recent work and leading references see E. LeGoff, S. E. Ulrich, and D. B. Denny, *J. Am. Chem. Soc.*, **80**:622 (1958).

racemization is strongly dependent on the structures of the reactants and types of substituents. In general, chlorides give much more stereospecific reactions than do bromides. The inversion specificity also appears to increase with the ionic character of the organometallic, e.g., allyl and benzyl derivatives show less racemization than comparable saturated organometallics. The products of the usual Wurtz coupling process (olefin, hydrocarbon, dimer) can be attributed to either a free radical or an ionic mechanism. The former cannot, of course, explain the formation of active products (assuming a radical process to be completely nonstereospecific). The favored pathway to explain the racemic coupling product is the S_N1 process shown in Figure 1-31, that is, slow ionization of the alkyl halide to a racemic carbonium ion followed by rapid reaction with the organometallic[23] (reference 22). Radical coupling has not been excluded as a competing reaction, however.

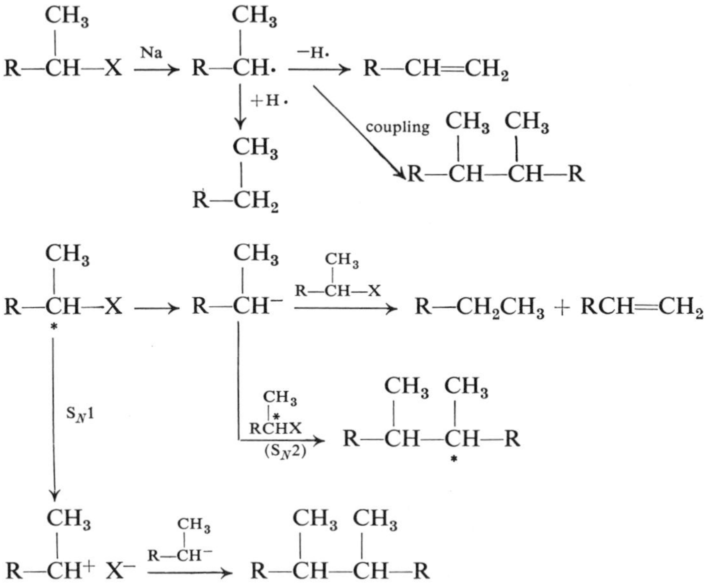

Figure 1-31 Possible free-radical and ionic pathways in a typical Wurtz reaction

1-9 Rearrangements of Organometallics

Carbanionic rearrangement rates depend in a striking manner on the associated metal cation. Although rearrangement to negatively charged carbon is not as broad in scope as migration to electron deficient carbon, certain examples have been substantiated.

[23] J. F. Lane and S. E. Ulrich, *J. Am. Chem. Soc.*, **72**:5132 (1950).

Grovenstein[24] found 2,2,2-triphenylchloroethane to undergo extensive rearrangement when treated with sodium metal in refluxing dioxane.

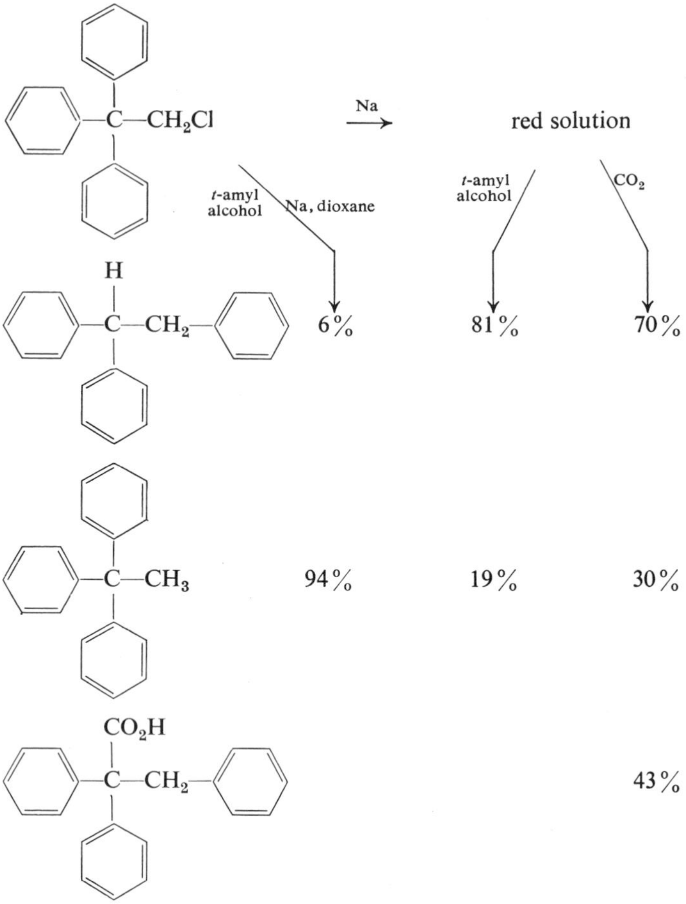

Figure 1-32   Rearrangement of an organosodium compound (hydrocarbon percentages refer to the distributions between hydrocarbons)

The possibility of rearrangement at an intermediate free-radical stage[25] (Figure 1-33) appears to be discounted by the observation that the reaction with sodium in the presence of t-amyl alcohol gives largely unrearranged hydrocarbon. Addition of t-amyl alcohol to the red solution obtained on refluxing, on the other hand, yielded predominately 1,1,2-triphenylethane. In certain instances the organic free radical may be sufficiently long lived to

[24] E. Grovenstein, Jr., *J. Am. Chem. Soc.*, **79**:4985 (1957).
[25] D. Y. Curtin and M. J. Hurwitz, *J. Am. Chem. Soc.*, **74**:5381 (1952).

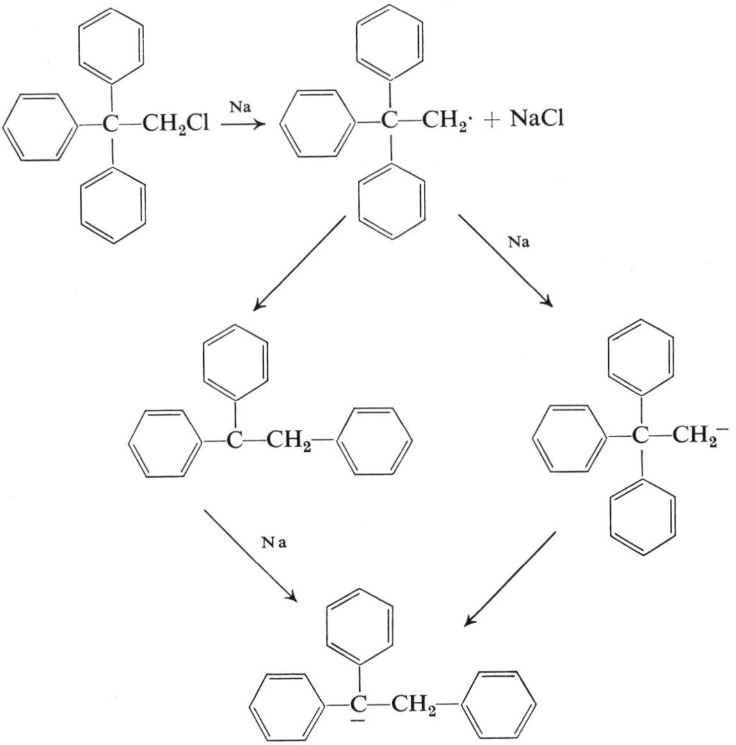

Figure 1-33 Competitive pathways for rearrangement in which metallation of the free radical appears to proceed more rapidly than its rearrangement

be considered an intermediate, and may account for racemization and rearrangement.[26] In the system used by Grovenstein, however, any radical intermediate formed would not be expected to react with *t*-amyl alcohol; thus the unrearranged hydrocarbon formed when the reaction is carried out in the presence of this alcohol clearly implies that the reduction of any free radical intermediate by metal must proceed more rapidly than rearrangement. This may be due to initial reaction at a metallic surface. Additional studies with metals in solution may shed some light on this interesting question.

Zimmerman and Smentowski[27] have observed the same rearrangement with sodium in ether-isooctane at room temperature, and also postulated a

[26] In these discussions it is assumed that the conversion to the anion occurs stepwise by two one-electron transfers through a radical intermediate. A one-step two-electron transfer with direct formation of a carbanion is also plausible. This process could occur by the transfer of two electrons from the electron film on sodium through chloride bridged to carbon and the surface of the sodium with concurrent evolution of two sodium cations from the metallic surface.

[27] H. E. Zimmerman and F. J. Smentowski, *J. Am. Chem. Soc.*, **79**:5455 (1957).

carbanionic rearrangement to account for the formation of triphenylethylene when 2,2,2-triphenylchloroethane was treated with amylsodium (Figure 1-34).

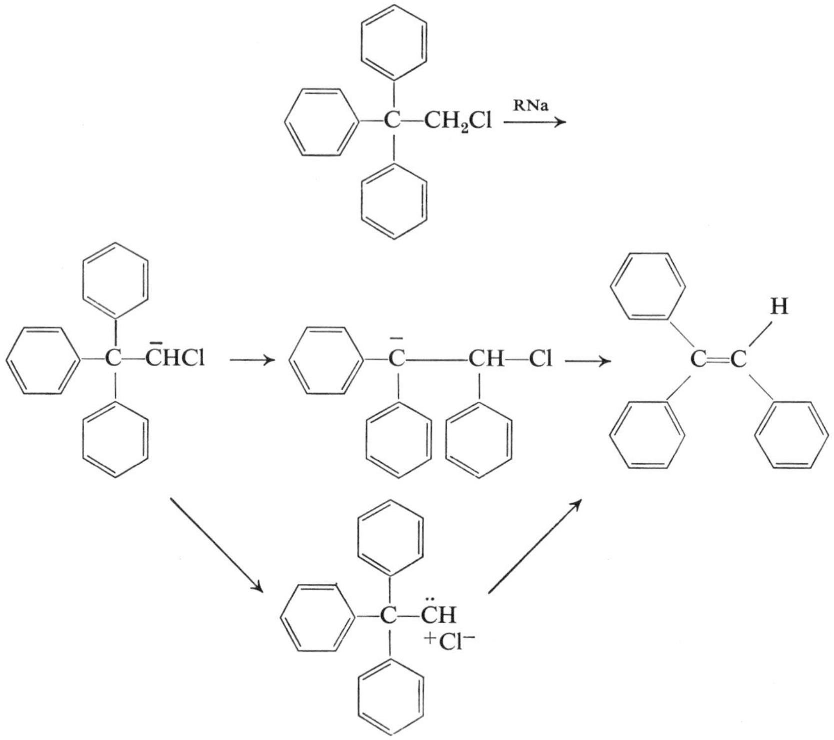

Figure 1-34 The formation of triphenylethylene by anionic rearrangement followed by elimination; a possible alternate mechanism involving carbene intermediate is also indicated

As the first documented examples of carbanion rearrangements,[28] these reactions offered an experimental method to differentiate various organometallics, and this line of research has been pursued by both Grovenstein and Zimmerman and their coworkers with very enlightening results.

The reaction of potassium with 2,2,2-triphenylchloroethane in tetrahydrofuran from 0 to 65° followed by carbonation gave only rearranged acid.

---

[28] This rearrangement was claimed by C. Wooster and N. Mitchell, *J. Am. Chem. Soc.*, **52**:1042 (1930), in the sodium in liquid ammonia reduction of 2,2,2-triphenylchloroethane. However, it was subsequently shown by J. Charlton, I. Dostrovsky, and E. D. Hughes, *Nature*, **167**:987 (1951), that the chloride in this early work had the rearranged structure. The later workers (reference 27) demonstrated that no prior rearrangement of authentic chloride occurred under these reaction conditions.

Competing side reactions presumably did not allow study at lower temperatures in this solvent. The corresponding organolithium, on the other hand, was obtained in unrearranged form at $-60°$, although rearrangement was rapid at $0°$ and above.[29] These results are shown in Table 1-5.

Table 1-5   Metal dependence of a carbanion rearrangement

	72%	—
K, reflux THF		(5% diphenylacetic acid)
Na—K, THF, 20°	53%	—
Na—K, THF, 0°	32%	—
K, $-50°$, dimethoxyethane	some but yield not reported	—
Li, THF, 28°	18%	—
Li, THF, $-60°$	2%	58%
Li, THF, $-60°$ followed by 0°, 1 hour	2 parts	1 part
Li, $-65°$, THF, triethylamine	—	essentially pure

It is worth noting that added triethylamine, which might increase dissociation of the organolithium by solvation of the cation, did not cause rearrangement of this reagent at $-65°$ (last entry in Table 1-5). A study of the effect of added amine on the rearrangement rate at higher temperatures appears to be worthwhile.

Zimmerman and Zweig[30] chose the somewhat less reactive 2,2-diphenyl-1-propyl system for their study of the dependence of carbanion rearrangements on associated metal ion. The results, shown in Figure 1-35, point up the relative stability of the organomagnesium compound. In its lack of rearrangement, the organomagnesium compound more closely resembles the covalent organomercurial than its usual analog, the lithium derivative. This important observation bears on the general question of optical stability of organometallics. Several mechanisms are available for the racemization of stereoisomeric Grignard reagents, but the most attractive appears to be through carbanion formation. Phenyl migration in the species described above reasonably occurs through a carbanion or a species possessing a large amount of carbanionic character. The lack of rearrangement of this Grignard reagent strongly suggests that alkyl Grignard reagents contain *no* carbanions

[29] E. Grovenstein, Jr., and L. P. Williams, Jr., *J. Am. Chem. Soc.*, **83**:412 (1961).

[30] H. E. Zimmerman and A. Zweig, *J. Am. Chem. Soc.*, **83**:1196 (1961).

and that the reagent has low carbanionic nature. This in turn may mean that racemization occurred during formation rather than subsequently, in the many unsuccessful attempts to prepare optically active Grignard reagents.

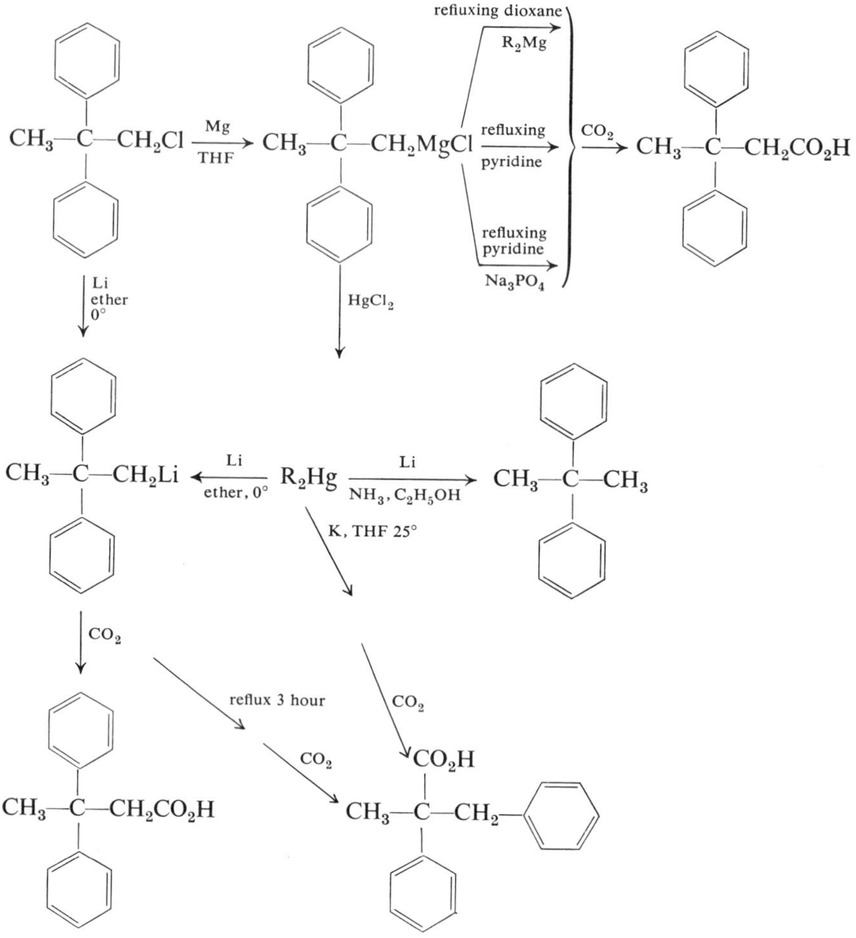

Figure 1-35 Relative ease of rearrangement of 2,2-diphenylpropyl-potassium, lithium, and magnesium derivatives

As with the triphenylethyl compounds, this system upon treatment with potassium gave only rearranged organometallic. The lithium derivative was more stable than the corresponding 2,2,2-triphenylethyllithium, requiring refluxing ether for phenyl migration. Even the use of boiling pyridine and pyridine with added trisodium phosphate (to increase the polarity of the solvent and facilitate dissociation) failed to cause rearrangement of the magnesium derivative.

Whitesides and Roberts[31] have reported that typical secondary Grignard reagents interconvert slowly if at all on the nmr time scale. Further, Jensen and Nakamaye[32] have demonstrated that the exo- and endo-norbornyl Grignard reagents reduce benzophenone at sufficiently different rates that the endo isomer may be preferentially recovered from a reaction with insufficient ketone (Figure 1-36). The endo reagent is slowly converted to the exo isomer at 37° (nmr was used to follow the reaction), with equilibrium established within a day. (This reduction appears to occur by a homolytic process.)

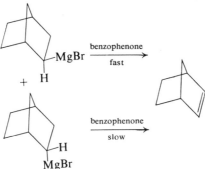

Figure 1-36   The selective destruction of the *exo*-norbornyl Grignard reagent

A plausible mechanistic alternative to intramolecular rearrangement in any of the examples discussed would be elimination of a negatively charged carbon residue to give olefin, with readdition in the reverse direction to give rearranged carbanion. This has been demonstrated to occur more rapidly than intramolecular rearrangement in the 2,2,3-triphenyl-1-propyl system.[33]

When this organolithium reagent was prepared in the presence of benzyl-lithium-1-C^{14}, incorporation of radioactivity in the structurally rearranged product proved that fragmentation had occurred.[34] Elimination of the benzyl carbanion competes very favorably with intramolecular migration of either the phenyl or benzyl group to the anionic center.[35]

A similar fragmentation process in the systems which involve net phenyl migration has been ruled out. Grovenstein and Wentworth (reference 33),

[31] G. M. Whitesides and J. D. Roberts, *J. Am. Chem. Soc.*, **87**:4878 (1965).

[32] F. R. Jensen and K. L. Nakamaye, *J. Am. Chem. Soc.*, **88**:3437 (1966).

[33] a. E. Grovenstein, Jr., and L. P. Williams, Jr., *J. Am. Chem. Soc.*, **83**:2537 (1961).
   b. E. Grovenstein, Jr., and G. Wentworth, *J. Am. Chem. Soc.*, **85**:3305 (1963).
   c. *Ibid.*, **89**:1852 (1967).

[34] The position of the radiolabel has been established (reference 33c).

[35] The conclusion with regard to relative rates of inter- and intramolecular migration of the benzyl group rests on the quantitative data given in reference 33b. The same data establish that the benzyllithium is not in facile equilibrium with either starting material or product, and hence incorporation of radioactivity must occur during the rearrangement process.

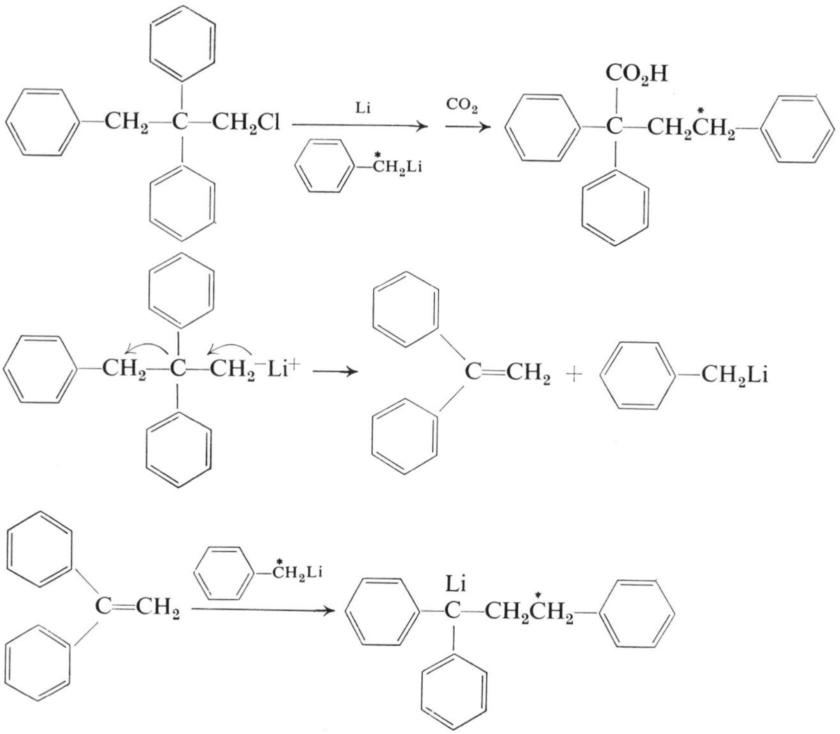

Figure 1-37   The intermolecular nature of a "rearrangement" established by incorporation of radiocarbon fragment

found no radioactivity incorporation in the rearrangement of 2,2,2-triphenyl-ethyllithium in the presence of phenyllithium-C^{14} (Figure 1-38).

Zimmerman and Zweig (reference 30) found the phenyl group to migrate approximately eleven times faster than p-tolyl in 2-phenyl-2-p-tolyl-1-pro-pyllithium (Figure 1-39). This study was complicated by α-proton abstraction; the isotope dilution technique was used (carbon dioxide-C^{14}) to accurately determine the yields of the various products obtained in this reaction.

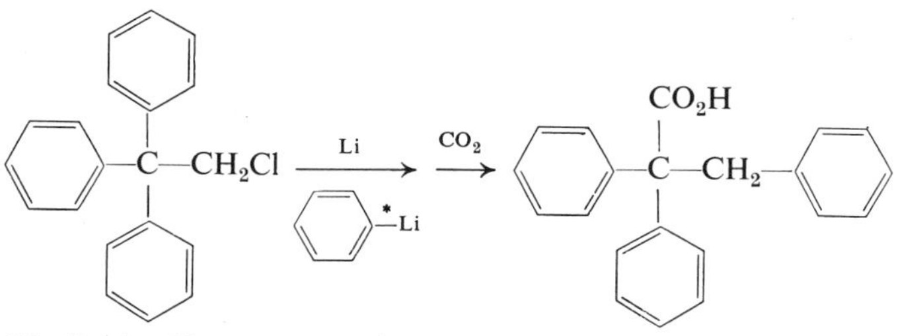

Figure 1-38   Lack of incorporation of radioactivity in the rearrangement of 2,2,2-triphenylethyllithium in the presence of phenyllithium-C^{14}

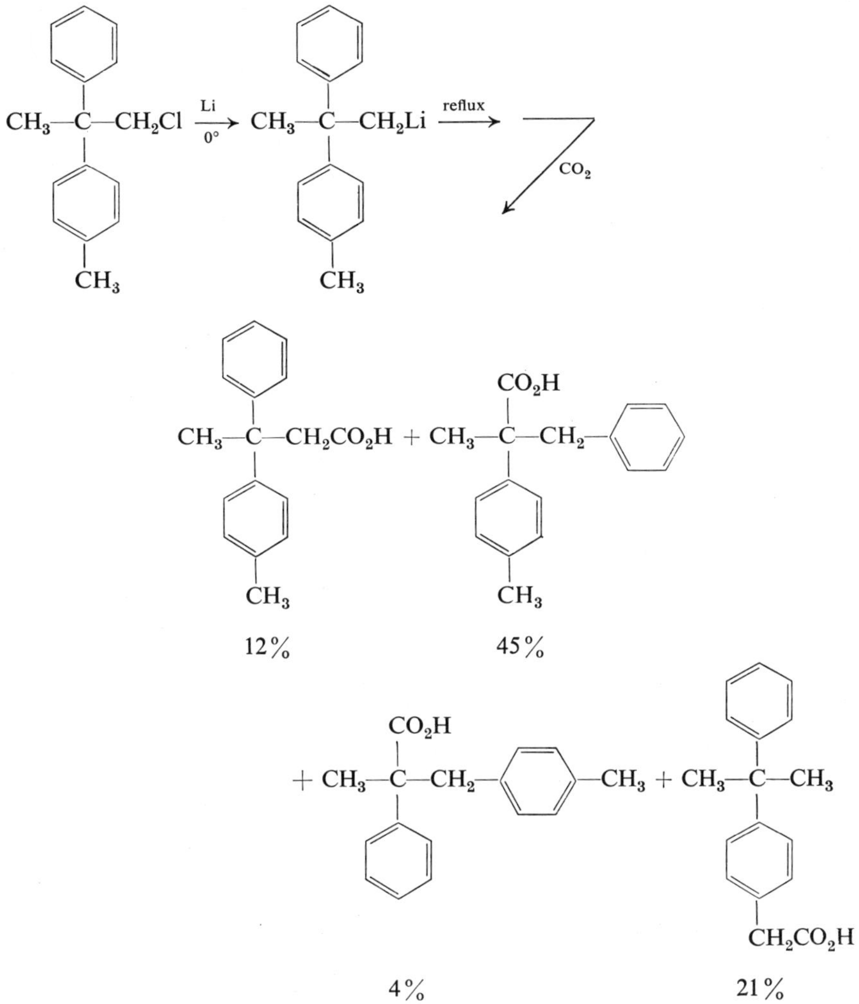

$$CH_3-\overset{\overset{\displaystyle C_6H_5}{|}}{\underset{\underset{\displaystyle C_6H_4CH_3}{|}}{C}}-CH_2Cl \xrightarrow[0°]{Li} CH_3-\overset{\overset{\displaystyle C_6H_5}{|}}{\underset{\underset{\displaystyle C_6H_4CH_3}{|}}{C}}-CH_2Li \xrightarrow{reflux} \quad\xrightarrow{CO_2}$$

$$CH_3-\overset{\overset{\displaystyle C_6H_5}{|}}{\underset{\underset{\displaystyle C_6H_4CH_3}{|}}{C}}-CH_2CO_2H \;+\; CH_3-\overset{\overset{\displaystyle CO_2H}{|}}{\underset{\underset{\displaystyle C_6H_4CH_3}{|}}{C}}-CH_2-C_6H_5$$

12%   45%

$$+\; CH_3-\overset{\overset{\displaystyle CO_2H}{|}}{\underset{\underset{\displaystyle C_6H_5}{|}}{C}}-CH_2-C_6H_4-CH_3 \;+\; CH_3-\overset{\overset{\displaystyle C_6H_5}{|}}{\underset{\underset{\displaystyle C_6H_4-CH_2CO_2H}{|}}{C}}-CH_3$$

4%   21%

Figure 1-39   Rearrangement of the 2-phenyl-2-*p*-tolyl-propyllithium system, with migration of phenyl proceeding more rapidly than migration of the *p*-tolyl group

The facile migration of phenyl relative to *p*-tolyl is in keeping with a transition state involving net electron density increase in the migrating group. The migratory aptitude is opposite that found in comparable carbonium ion rearrangements.

Molecular orbital calculations were carried out (reference 30) to predict relative ease of rearrangement to carbonium ion, free radical, and carbanion centers. For the models chosen (see Figure 1-40), it was concluded that the relative rates would be in the same order for all three electronic states.

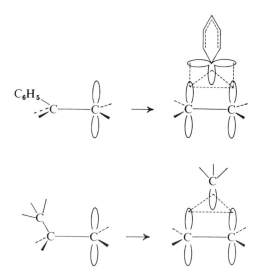

Figure 1-40   Models for ground states and transition states for rearrangement of aryl and alkyl groups to carbonium ion, free radical, or carbanion centers

Experimental evidence is in agreement with this sequence for rearrangement to positive and free radical centers, and the work of Grovenstein and Zimmerman allows some comparison for migration to carbanion centers, where again the sequence is followed.[35a]

Differential reactivities of organometallics have been noted recently in strained-ring-olefinic derivative equilibria, analogous to the cyclopropylmethyl-3-butenyl Grignard reagent interconversion.[36] Hill, Richey, and Rees[37] have reported that cyclobutylmethylsodium, lithium, and magnesium derivatives rearrange to the corresponding acyclic olefinic organometallics, with the Grignard reagent requiring higher temperature (65°).

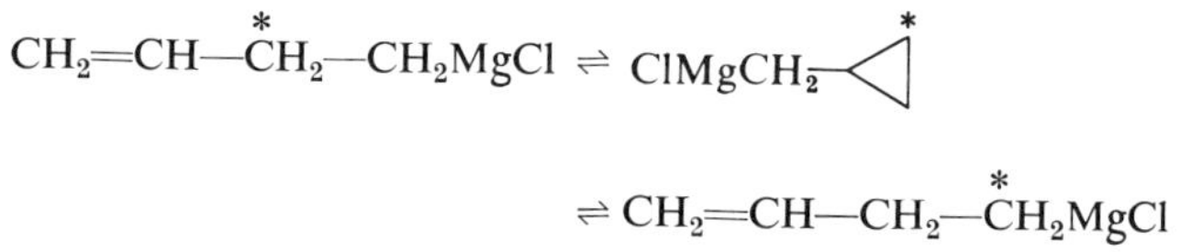

$$CH_2{=}CH{-}\overset{*}{C}H_2{-}CH_2MgCl \; \rightleftharpoons \; ClMgCH_2^*{-}\!\!\triangleleft$$

$$\rightleftharpoons CH_2{=}CH{-}CH_2{-}\overset{*}{C}H_2MgCl$$

Figure 1-41   Rearrangement of the 3-butenyl Grignard Reagent

[35a] A very recent discussion of the nature of the transition state for a carbanionic rearrangement is given by E. Grovenstein, Jr., and G. Wentworth, *J. Am. Chem. Soc.*, **89:**2348 (1967).

[36] M. S. Silver, P. R. Shafer, J. E. Nordlander, C. Ruchlander, C. Ruchardt, and J. D. Roberts, *J. Am. Chem. Soc.*, **82:**2646 (1960).

[37] E. A. Hill, H. G. Richey, Jr., and T. C. Rees, *J. Org. Chem.*, **28:**2161 (1963).

The open-chain system is highly favored over the cyclic structure, although perhaps less so than the cyclopropyl analog. Both the sodium and lithium derivatives rearranged too rapidly to establish that cleavage had not occurred during formation, but this was not the case with the cyclobutylmethyl-magnesium halide.

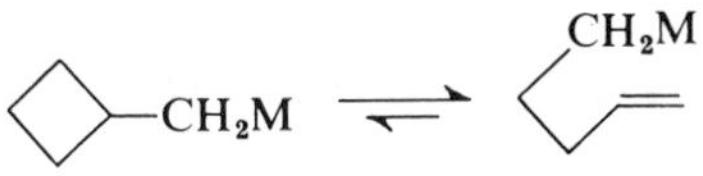

M = Na, Li, MgX

Figure 1-42   Rearrangement of
cyclobutylmethylorganometallics

A cyclobutyl intermediate was also proposed for the rearrangement of the 2-metallo-5-hexenyl system to the 1-metallo-3-methyl-4-pentenyl isomer (Figure 1-43). Again the rearrangement of the Grignard reagent appears to

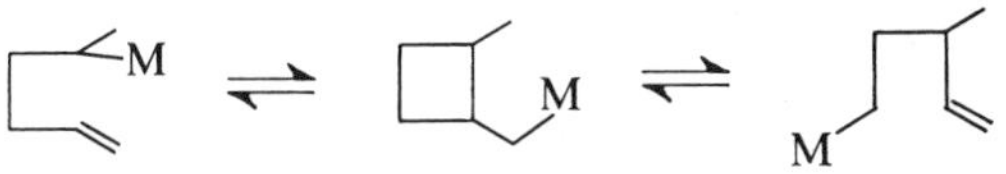

Figure 1-43   Equilibrium between olefinic organometallics
established through a cyclobutylmethyl intermediate

be considerably slower than that of either the organosodium or organo-lithium derivative. An interesting facet of this work was the position of equilibrium in which the primary organometallic was strongly favored over the secondary isomer. With lithium, 99% of 1-lithio-3-methyl-4-pentene was formed (≥ 3 kcal/mole).

In this chapter some of the significant differences in properties of organo-metallics have been discussed; the remaining chapters will deal with various aspects of organomercurial reactions. No attempt has been made here to cover in detail the large volume of interesting work on the "ionic" organo-metallics, or the broad area of carbanion (S_E1) reactions in which the reactive substrate is generated by cleavage of a carbon-hydrogen, carbon-carbon, or other carbon-nonmetal bond. The reader is referred to the recent monograph by Cram[38] for an extensive treatment of this topic.

[38] D. J. Cram, "Fundamentals of Carbanion Chemistry," Academic Press Inc., New York, 1965.

2

THE ORGANOMERCURIALS

2-1 Organomercurials as Models for Stereochemical Studies

The intimate mechanistic details of any reaction are obtained by studying both kinetics and stereochemistry, with full knowledge of both required for determination with certainty. Within the framework of organometallics as models for electrophilic substitution processes, the problems usually associated with stereochemical determination are often compounded to the point that useful results are not obtainable. The numerous attempts to prepare optically active Grignard reagents are illustrative. A primary consideration involved in stereochemical work is the optical stability of the substrate molecule. The trend toward the study of the more covalent organometallics may be viewed as a consequence of this requirement; in fact, the time lapse in making full use of this approach is surprising. The stereointegrity of the carbon-mercury bond, for instance, was established long before any attempts were made to ascertain the specificity of any cleavage of this bond by electrophilic agents.[1] Furthermore, organomercurials are invariably monomeric in solution, thereby avoiding complications (particularly for kinetic studies) which are frequently encountered with more ionic organometallics.

Early work on the nature of and the type of bonding involved in the mercuration products of olefins suggested that isomeric materials were isolable.[2] Definite proof, however, was lacking. In 1926, Sanborn and Marvel[3] isolated two diastereomeric adducts from (−)-menthyl cinnamate. Failure to obtain any other possible diastereomers did not allow a complete demonstration of stereointegrity of the carbon-mercury bond; we recognize this today

---

[1] Drawing analogy between a polar organometallic such as the Grignard reagent and an organomercurial may not seem fully justifiable, but it should be recalled that in general the products given by the two with like reagents are the same, although extreme differences in rate are apparent. For examples of reactions of mercury compounds that will not be specifically discussed here, see H. Gilman and J. F. Nelson, *J. Am. Chem. Soc.*, **61**:743 (1939).

[2] a. W. Schrauth and H. Geller, *Chem. Ber.*, **55**:2783 (1922).

 b. E. J. Van Loon and H. E. Carter, *J. Am. Chem. Soc.*, **59**:2555 (1937).

[3] L. T. Sanborn and C. S. Marvel, *J. Am. Chem. Soc.*, **48**:1409 (1926).

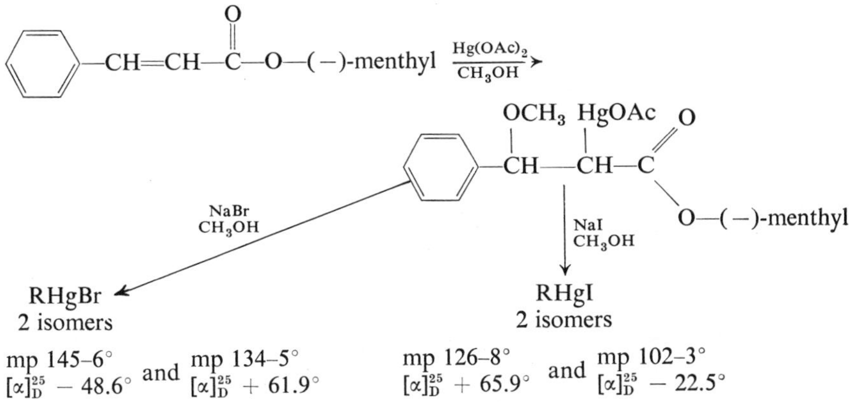

Figure 2-1   Diastereomeric organomercurials

as being a consequence of preferred trans addition of mercuric acetate to the double bond.[4] In later work[5] (+)-bornyl cinnamate was utilized; here again two diastereomers were obtained.

Nesmeyanov, Reutov, and Poddubnaya[6] were able to prepare diastereomeric mercurials by direct mercuration of the diasteriomeric (—)-menthyl ester of α-bromophenylacetic acid.

The isolation of these two materials, which differ only in the configuration of the carbon bearing the metal, clearly illustrates the optical stability of this linkage.[7]

[4] J. Chatt, *Chem. Rev.*, **48**:7 (1951).

[5] E. Griffith and C. S. Marvel, *J. Am. Chem. Soc.*, **53**:789 (1931).

[6] A. N. Nesmeyanov, O. A. Reutov, and S. S. Poddubnaya, *Izy. Akad. Nauk SSSR, Otd. Khim. Nauk*, 649 (1953).

[7] The clear implication exists in this report, in spite of the subsequent recrystallization of product, that the mercuration reaction is stereospecific. The degree of specificity has not been established. While simple alkyl halides in general are inert to metallic mercury, α-bromo esters react readily in the dark. This may well be associated with a specific mechanism available only to α-carbonyl halide, for example,

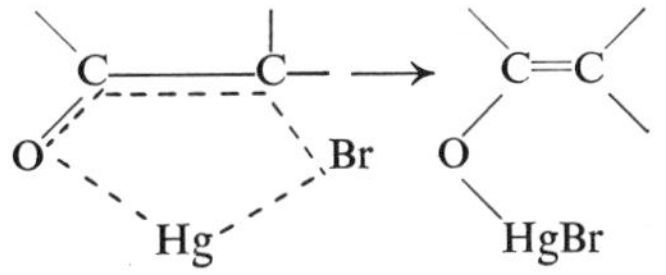

or, to account for stereospecificity.

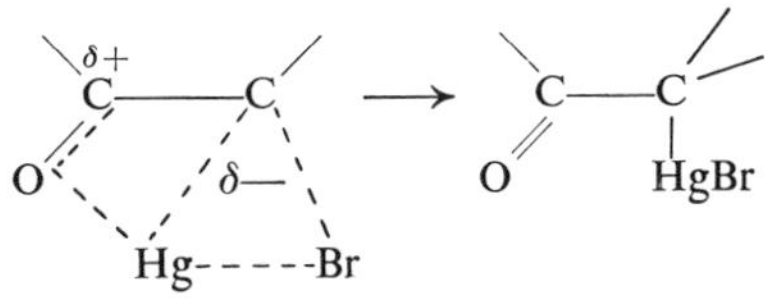

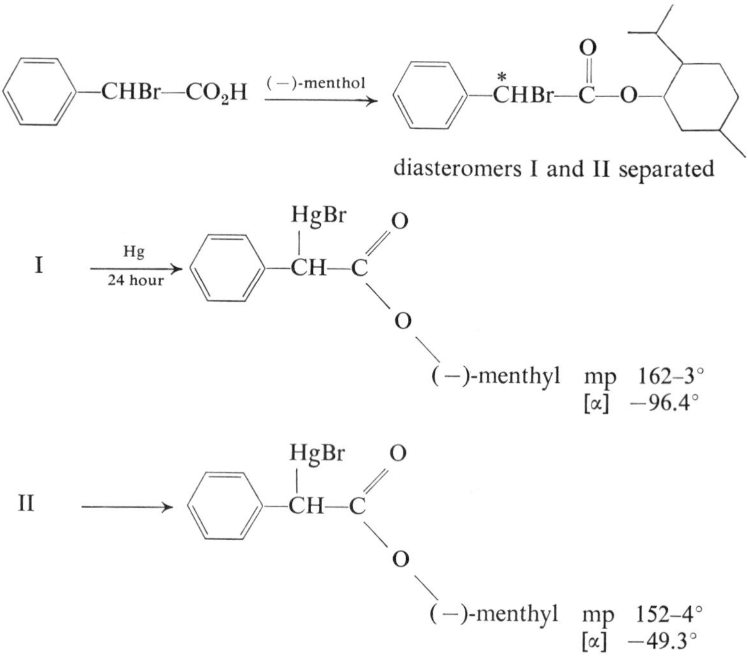

diasteromers I and II separated

Figure 2-2 The formation of diastereomeric alkylmercuric bromides by direct mercuration

All of the optically active mercurials obtained to this point had the disadvantage of containing other asymmetric centers. A stereochemical study of an electrophilic cleavage reaction with these materials would therefore suffer from the possibility of asymmetric induction. The need to overcome this objection by the use of mercurials containing only the asymmetric center associated with the carbon-metal bond was clear. The resolution of organomercurials was accomplished almost simultaneously by three groups.[8] In these studies, *sec*-butylmercuric bromide (reference 8a,b) and 5-methyl-2-bromomercurihexane (reference 8c) were resolved. Facile interconversion of anions utilizing optically active carboxylates permitted resolution of these materials. The geometrical isomers *cis* and *trans*-4-methylcyclohexylmercuric bromide[9] and the related 4-*t*-butyl compounds[10] have been prepared. Synthesis of these materials was especially important for stereochemical studies

[8] a. H. B. Charman, E. D. Hughes and C. K. Ingold, *Chem. & Ind.* (*London*), 1517 (1958).

b. F. R. Jensen, L. D. Whipple, D. K. Wedegaertner and J. A. Landgrebe, *J. Am. Chem. Soc.*, **81**:1262 (1959).

c. O. A. Reutov and E. V. Uglova, *Bull. Acad. Sci. USSR, Div. Chem. Sci.*, 735 (1959).

[9] F. R. Jensen and L. H. Gale, *J. Am. Chem. Soc.*, **81**:1261, 6337 (1959).

[10] F. R. Jensen, A. Wingrove, and J. Rodgers, unpublished results.

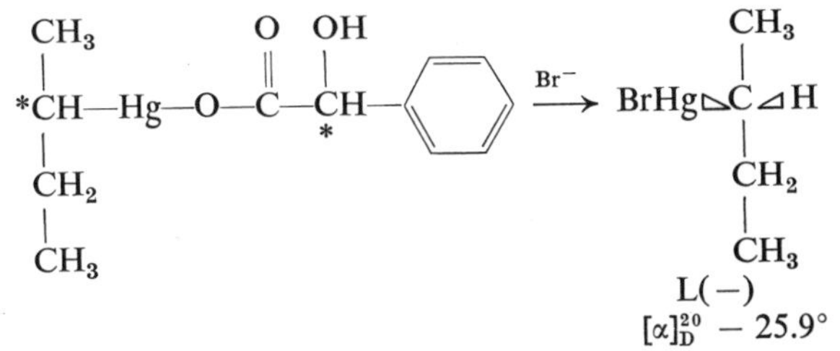

Figure 2-3 The resolution of *sec*-butylmercurial through the mandelate salt; absolute configuration and maximum observed rotation for *sec*-butylmercuric bromide

because of the relative ease of assigning configuration to geometrical as compared to optical isomers. Of interest to subsequent work was the facile free-radical-catalyzed equilibration of the cis-trans isomers (which allowed

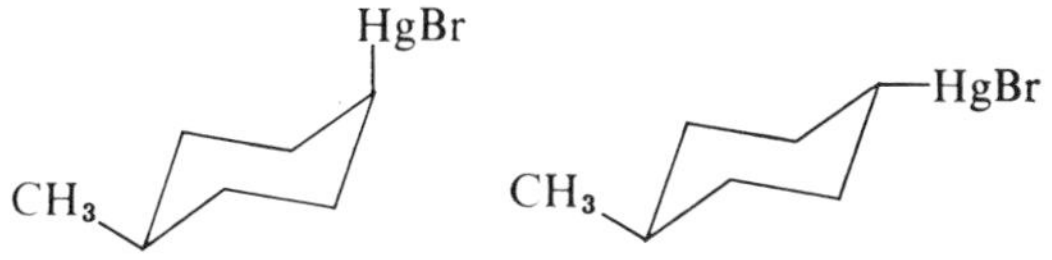

determination of the negligible conformational preference for the large bromomercuri group), indicating a potential source of difficulty in stereochemical studies of electrophilic substitution.

With these types of stereoisomeric organomercurials at hand the stage was set for productive mechanistic study of the numerous electrophilic cleavage reactions which are covered in detail in later sections.

2-2   Complex Formation of Mercury Compounds

It has long been recognized that reagents which interact or complex with the metal atom can play an important role in the reactions of organometallic compounds. Consequently in kinetic investigations, except for very early studies, attempts have been made to determine the relative roles of the electrophile, nucleophile, and solvent in the reaction.

In mercury (II) compounds, the simplest picture of bonding utilizing the lowest available orbitals (with resulting maximum bond strength) is *sp* hydridization; mutually perpendicular to the two resulting linear bonds and each other are the two vacant *p*-orbitals of mercury.

In accord with this bonding picture, mercuric halides do not exhibit a dipole moment in the gas phase.[11] However, in solution, the dipole moments

[11] H. Braune and R. Linke, *Z. Physik. Chem.* (*Leipzig*), **31B:**12 (1935).

Figure 2-4 Orbital picture of mercuric dichloride showing the Cl-Hg bonds formed as a combination of sp(Hg) and p(Cl) atomic orbitals. Also shown are the two vacant p-orbitals of mercury and the occupied p-orbitals of chlorine

of the mercuric halides, dialkyl- and diaryl- mercury compounds and alkyl- and arylmercuric halides indicate that the bonds about mercury are often not linear and vary from 130 to 180°.[12] These deviations from linearity have not been satisfactorily explained in all cases. Since these geometries may be due to solvent effects or interactions between molecules, we will assume for our purposes that the hybridization on mercury is sp, except when direct co-ordination is believed to occur. Such coordination of a nucleophile with covalent mercuric compounds is expected to be accompanied by a change in hybridization to sp^2 (trigonal-planar) leaving an unoccupied p orbital. Further coordination would result in sp^3 hybridization (tetrahedral)[13] and fill the

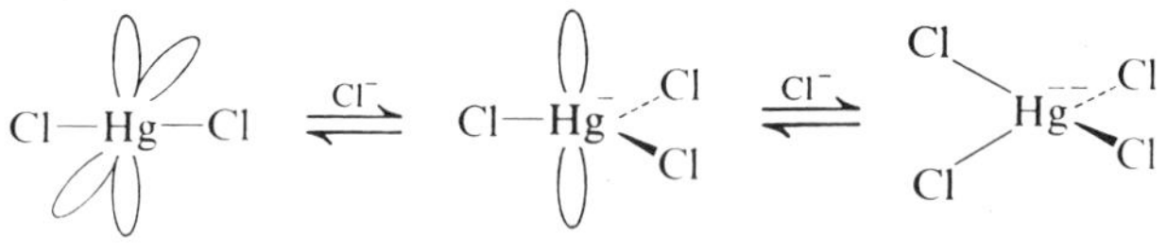

Figure 2-5 Change of hybridization on mercury from linear to trigonal to tetrahedral

outer octet. These reactions are well characterized for the mercuric halides, and the equilibrium constants have been evaluated for the equations as shown in Table 2-1.[14] From these results it is seen that the mercuric halides are essentially nondissociated in solution, but readily coordinate with halide ions to form HgX_3^- and HgX_4^{--}. The tendency to complex increases substantially from chloride to bromide to iodide. Because of the greater dependence on halide concentration for formation of HgX_4^{--} (Table 2-1) as compared to

[12] a. B. C. Curran, *J. Am. Chem. Soc.*, **63**:1470 (1941).

   b. *Ibid.*, **64**:830 (1942).

   c. J. C. Sipos, H. Sawatzky, and G. F. Wright, *ibid.*, **77**:2759 (1955).

   d. H. Sawatzky and G. F. Wright, *Can. J. Chem.*, **36**:1555 (1958); W. C. Horning, F. Lantenschlaeger, and G. F. Wright, *ibid.*, **41**:1441 (1962).

[13] M. L. Delwaulle, F. Fraveois and J. Wiemann, *Compt. Rend.*, **207**:340 (1938).

[14] Y. Marcus, *Acta Chem. Scand.*, **11**:599 (1957).

Table 2-1   Ionization and complex formation of mercuric halides

$$Hg^{++} + HgX_2 \rightleftharpoons 2HgX^+ \quad (I)$$
$$HgX^+ + X^- \rightleftharpoons HgX_2 \quad (II)$$
$$HgX_2 + X^- \rightleftharpoons HgX_3^- \quad (III)$$
$$HgX_2 + 2X^- \rightleftharpoons HgX_4^{--} \quad (IV)$$

| | \log K | | |
	I	II	III	IV
Chloride	0.26	6.3	0.95	2.00
Bromide	0.94	8.3	2.27	4.02
Iodide	1.91		3.67	6.04

HgX_3^-, the latter will be favored in certain concentration ranges even though its equilibrium constant is lower.

In contrast to the ready formation of complexes of inorganic mercury (II), the available evidence indicates that alkylmercuric salts and dialkylmercury compounds complex to a lesser extent. Indirect evidence that some complex formation occurs is based on the dipole moment studies mentioned previously, in which it was shown that in many instances the bond angles are not linear (reference 12). It is expected that both the nature of the organic substituent and the inorganic moiety in the case of organomercuric salts will substantially affect the ability of the metal to further coordinate. Thus, strong electron withdrawing groups should enhance complex formation, as demonstrated in a study of perfluoroalkylmercurials by Emeleus and Lagowski.[15] The complex ions $CF_3HgI_3^{-2}$ and $(CF_3)_2HgI_2^{-2}$ were isolated, and conductometric titration indicated the formation of CF_3HgBrI^-, $CF_3HgBrI_2^{-2}$, and $CF_3HgBr_3^{-2}$. Conversely $CF_3HgBr_2^-$, $CF_3HgBrCl^-$, and $CF_3HgBrCl_2^{-2}$ appeared to be unstable relative to the uncomplexed mixture. Similarly, *bis*-perfluorophenylmercury has given isolable neutral complexes with 2,2'-bipyridyl and with *bis*-1,2-diphenylphosphinoethane.[16]

Using an oscillometric titration technique, Lagowski and his coworkers found evidence for both 1:1: and 2:1 ligand to diphenylmercury complex formation in benzene solution with several neutral Lewis bases, including piperidine, acetone, ethanol, and dimethyl sulfoxide.[17] Although no quantitative data were obtained, it appeared that, as expected, nitrogen bases tend to coordinate more readily than oxygen bases with mercurials.

The enhanced solubility of simple alkylmercuric thiocyanates in aqueous

[15] H. J. Emeleus and J. J. Lagowski, *J. Chem. Soc.*, 1497 (1959).

[16] R. D. Chambers, G. E. Coates, J. G. Livingstone and W. K. R. Musgrave, *J. Chem. Soc.*, 4367 (1962).

[17] H. B. Powell, M. T. Maung and J. J. Lagowski, *J. Chem. Soc.*, 2484 (1963).

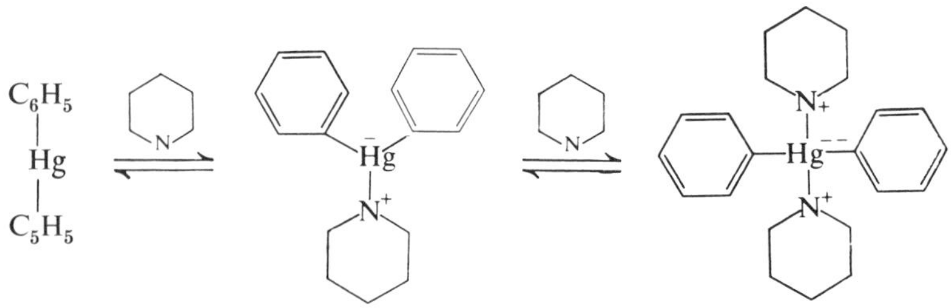

Figure 2-6 Postulated complexes formed from diphenylmercury and piperidine

potassium thiocyanate solution has been cited as evidence for the formation of the monoanion adduct.[18]

In related work, Barbieri and Bjerrum[19] have shown that the solubility of ethylmercuric halide is increased in aqueous iodide solution, while they detected no comparable effect for alkali metal chloride or bromide solutions. Stability constants were determined for both the thiocyanate and the iodide complexes in water and aqueous methanol (Table 2-2). Although the generality

Table 2-2 Complex formation constants for ethylmercuric salts

$$C_2H_5HgX \overset{K_1}{\rightleftharpoons} C_2H_5HgX_2^- \overset{K_2}{\rightleftharpoons} C_2H_5HgX_3^{--}$$

X	Solvent	K_1	K_2
I	H_2O	0.215	5.63
SCN	H_2O	0.80	1.59
SCN	50% aq. CH_3OH	1.73	0.56

of this result was not established, the inversion in magnitude of K_1 and K_2 with the change in solvent is worth noting.

Ultraviolet spectral variations have been cited as evidence of complex formation between phenylmercuric chloride and sodium iodide in 90% aqueous dioxane,[20] in which case the 1:1 adduct was postulated as the predominant species.

While there is no compelling evidence for complex formation of mercurials with many anions, e.g., bromide and chloride, the favorable formation with other ligands, e.g., iodide, suggests that it would be unwise to discount such

[18] V. F. Toropova and M. K. Saikina, *Russ. J. Inorg. Chem.* (*English Transl.*), **10**:631 (1965).

[19] R. Barbieri and J. Bjerrum, *Acta Chem. Scand.*, **19**:469 (1965).

[20] I. P. Beletskaya, A. E. Myshkin, and O. A. Reutov, *Bull. Acad. Sci. USSR, Div. Chem. Sci.*, 226 (1965).

complexes as low concentration reactive intermediates in many electrophilic substitution processes.

In an electrophilic reaction three general rate promoting effects can result from interaction of the nucleophile and the mercury atom. The electron density on carbon should increase and hence promote attack by electrophile. In extreme cases, this interaction may result in formation of a carbanion. A second rate enhancing factor results from the added stability of the (potential) cation by complex formation with the nucleophile. The third effect is the expected weakening of the C—Hg bond as a result of losing *s*-character upon rehybridization. The high ordering of the system tends to cause an overall unfavorable entropy effect. Discounting solvation effects, reactions in which complex formation occurs in small equilibrium concentration and the electrophile reacts preferentially with this material should have large negative entropies associated with them. The loss of one molecule usually results in a decrease of about 20 to 30 eu, which at room temperature contributes towards making the process less favorable by about 6 to 9 kcal/mole. Differential solvation of ions may however cause the overall entropy of activation to be entirely different than that predicted on this basis.

2-3   Mechanisms for Electrophilic Reactions of Organomercurials

A wide variety of reaction pathways are available to organomercurials; some have been observed and documented, others suggested but unproven, while still more are potential mechanisms which may require special forcing conditions to come into play. Orbital pictures, in contrast to dotted line representations, provide better illustrations of the geometrical requirements of the various transition states. In this section the dotted line depiction is used entirely, whereas in later sections both types of pictures are used. (An illustration which contrasts the two representations is given in Sec. 1-6.)

The generation of a fully charged carbanion from an organomercurial may occur in a number of ways. For instance, an anion might by nucleophilic attack displace one of the groups bonded to mercury, expelling RHg^- which could then decompose to R^- and $Hg°$. Alternatively, the attacking anion could bond with the mercury directly, leading to a negatively charged complex which could expel R^-. Instead of an anion, donation of an electron (e.g., by a reducing metal) to a vacant orbital on mercury can also lead to the expulsion of a carbanion. These processes are shown in Figure 2-7.

(A) $R—Hg—R + Y^- \rightarrow R—Hg^- + RY \rightarrow R^- + Hg° + RY$

(B) $R—Hg—R + Y^- \rightarrow R—\underset{\underset{Y}{|}}{Hg^-}—R \rightarrow R^- + RHgY$

(C) $R—Hg—R + e^- \rightarrow R—Hg^-—R \rightarrow R^- + Hg + R$

Figure 2-7   Mercurials as substrates for S_E1 reactions

Of these, the first (A) has not been substantiated, presumably because any reagent nucleophilic enough to give rise to such a displacement would first complex with mercury, as in (B). This latter intermediate, being negatively charged, would not be susceptible to facile nucleophilic attack. Nevertheless, reaction (A) is still plausible, and should be considered particularly in systems involving strong nucleophiles and stabilized anionic products.

Common anions, e.g., halides, acetate, and nitrate, may complex with organomercurials but have not been observed to further cleave the R—Hg bond as in scheme (B). However, two reactions which may be described by this sequence are hydride reductions (treated in Chap. 6), and the alkyl exchange observed when R_2Hg is treated with a polar organometallic compound.

An example of the latter is found in the work of Curtin and Koehl,[21] who made use of the facile cleavage of organomercurials to generate optically active 2-butyllithium in ether-free hydrocarbon solvents. Optically active sec-butylmercuric bromide[22] was treated as a suspension in pentane with sec-butyllithium in the same solvent, to give di-sec-butylmercury of varying degress of activity.[23] The isolated mercurial was subsequently treated with sec-octyllithium in pentane. The effects of temperature, time of reaction, and added ether are shown in Table 2-3. That the reagent once formed is optically unstable is apparent from the diminished specificity associated with increased reaction times. Added ether, in agreement with the observations of

Table 2-3 Preparation and carbonation of optically active sec-butyllithium in pentane

Time, min	Temp.	%2-methylbutanoic Acid	% retention
20	$-8 \pm 2°$	—	30
45	$-8 \pm 2°$	—	20
90	$-8 \pm 2°$	—	13
30	$-8 \pm 2°$	4.7	55
60	$-3°$	31	14
240	$-40°$	24	83
30	$-8°$	52[a]	0[a]

[a] The solvent in this experiment contained 6% diethyl ether.

[21] D. Y. Curtin and W. J. Koehl, Jr., *J. Am. Chem. Soc.*, **84**:1967 (1962).

[22] F. R. Jensen, L. D. Whipple, D. K. Wedegaertner, and J. A. Landgrebe, *J. Am. Chem. Soc.*, **81**:1262 (1959).

[23] Treatment with Grignard reagent would be preferable for the preparation of dialkylmercurials of consistent activity, in view of the absence of (rapid) exchange of the product with organomagnesium halides. In the work of Curtin and Koehl, concern over inclusion of trace amounts of ethereal solvents with the dialkylmercury may have precluded the use of Grignard reagent.

other workers in this field, both increases the rate of exchange[24] and decreases the overall specificity.

While the mechanism of the reaction of dialkylmercurial with organolithium reagent was not discussed in detail, a plausible path would involve a four-center exchange as shown, with racemization of the alkali organometallic

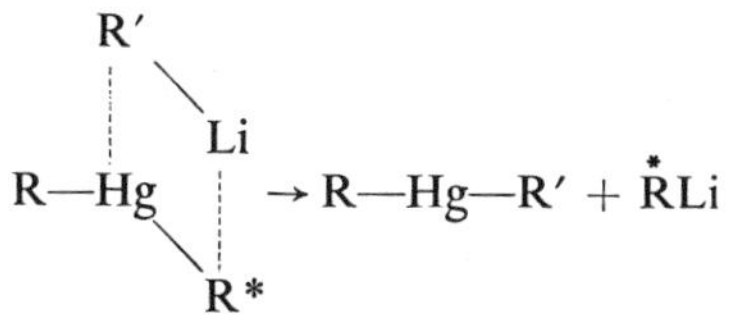

$$R{-}Hg \begin{array}{c} R' \\ \diagdown \\ Li \\ \diagup \\ R* \end{array} \rightarrow R{-}Hg{-}R' + \overset{*}{R}Li$$

through ionization and dissociation.

$$\overset{*}{R}Li \rightleftharpoons \overset{*}{R}{}^-Li^+ \rightarrow R^-Li^+$$

The effects of ether on both exchange and racemization are then explicable in terms of polar transition states demanding solvation (obviously the case for the ionization and dissociation). The alternate S_E1 mechanism involving formation of intermediate lithium trialkylmercury is worth considering, especially in view of the stability of mercuric trihalide and mercuric tetrahalide anions, and the preparation of some analogous adducts of other organometallics by Wittig and his coworkers[25] (e.g., lithium triphenyl-

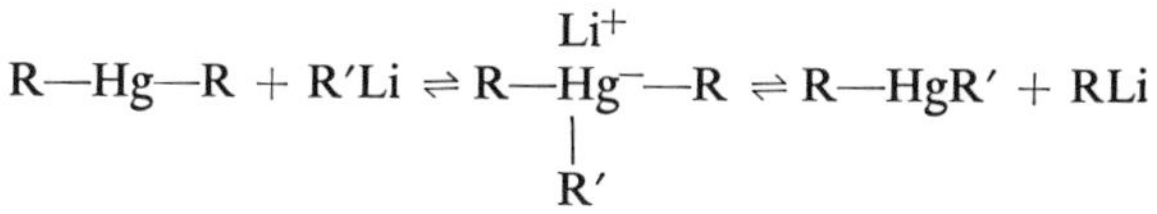

$$R{-}Hg{-}R + R'Li \rightleftharpoons R{-}\overset{\displaystyle Li^+}{\underset{\displaystyle R'}{Hg^-}}{-}R \rightleftharpoons R{-}HgR' + RLi$$

Figure 2-8   Exchange via intermediate complex formation

beryllium, and lithium triphenylcadmium). Conceivably, such an intermediate could build up in solution, and give reactions comparable to those of the free organolithium. If such an intermediate is involved, however, its formation must be relatively slow, as the yield data of Curtin and Koehl indicate that the exchange process is not instantaneous.

The S_E1 cleavage of organomercurials by one-electron addition [path (C) of Figure 2-7; also discussed in Chap. 6] is represented by one of the more

[24] With equivalent amounts of butyl and octyl reagent, an equilibrium distribution close to statistical distribution would be expected. Hence, complete reaction would be indicated by approximately 50% mole ratio of 2-methylbutanoic acid (Table 2-3).

[25] G. Wittig, F. J. Meyer and G. Lange, *Ann. Chem.*, **571**:167 (1951); cf. R. Waack and M. A. Doran, *J. Am. Chem. Soc.*, **85**:4042 (1963). It should be noted that G. Wittig and P. Hornberger, *Ann. Chem.*, **577**:11 (1952), found no evidence for stable complex formation between phenyllithium and diphenylmercury.

widely used reactions of these materials. The alkali metal scission of dialkylmercury is the method of choice for preparing RK, RNa, and RLi in the
absence of halide ion.

There is no substantiated example of a pure S_E2 reaction of an organomercurial. As pointed out in Chap. 1, this same statement may be made with
regard to any organometallic; consequently, the stereochemical course of
such a mechanism is currently in the realm of speculation. If, however,
inversion of configuration is ruled out or considered improbable, the S_E2,
S_Ei, and four-center mechanisms for electrophilic substitution of an organomercurial by a reagent X—Y may be defined as shown in Figure 2-9.

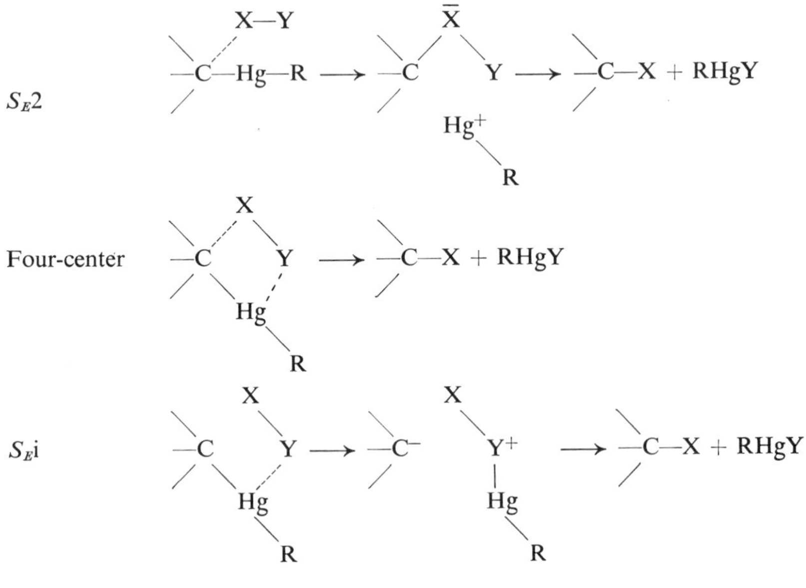

Figure 2-9 Mechanisms for concerted electrophilic
substitution of an organomercurial

The S_E2 and S_Ei mechanisms may thus be viewed as limiting pathways,
perhaps unfavorable relative to the four-center mechanism because of charge
separation. A variation of the S_E2 scheme involving attack of electrophile on
complexed mercurial avoids this difficulty and in fact appears to be a highly
reasonable mechanism.

The problem of distinguishing between these mechanisms, involving subtle
differences in bond making and breaking, has been one of major interest in
the field of organomercury electrophilic substitution. Most of the known
reactions of these materials, treated in subsequent chapters, fall into this
broad general mechanistic classification.

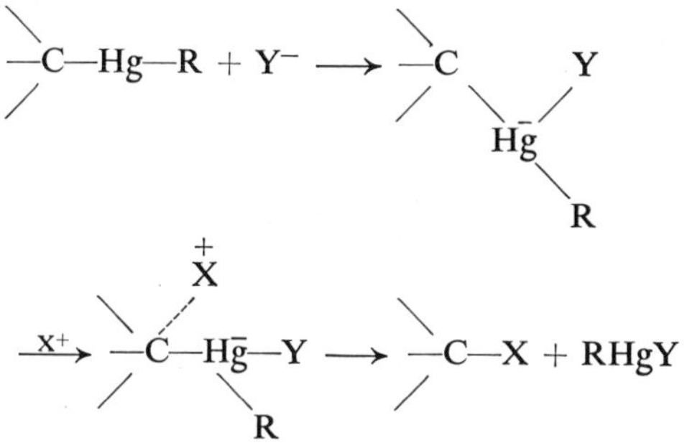

Figure 2-10   The S_E2 cleavage
of a complexed organomercurial

2-4   Nonelectrophilic Reactions of Mercurials

No discussion of the electrophilic cleavage reactions of organomercurials would be complete without including some known nonelectrophilic processes. Mercurials undergo such a wide variety of reactions that they may be justifiably described as versatile intermediates, and yet this same versatility often complicates mechanistic studies.

To illustrate, free-radical sources are known to racemize optically active mercurials. A reasonable pathway for this process involving a tricovalent intermediate is shown in Figure 2-11. This intermediate is expected to be symmetrical and requires resonance contributions from one- and two-electron bonds.

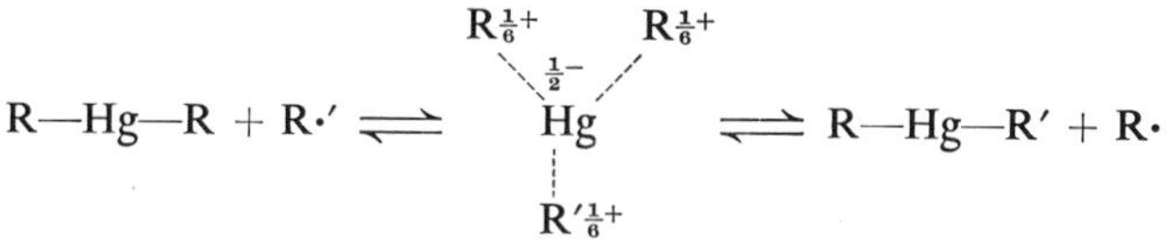

Figure 2-11   A plausible mechanism for free-radical racemization of organomercurials

The more "anionic" ligands bonded to mercury are known to exchange rapidly. Conversion to the more stable halide derivative is a standard technique, as we have seen, in acetoxymercuration.

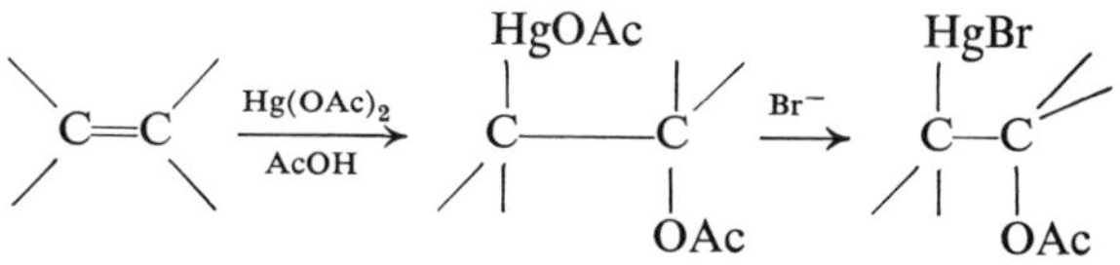

Figure 2-12   Ligand exchange in acetoxymercuration

This facile exchange has also been utilized in preparing the optically active mercurials mentioned previously.

When the mercury-ligand bond becomes particularly ionic, a complication arises from the standpoint of electrophilic cleavage of organomercurials. Certain types of alkylmercuric salts have been shown to undergo demercuration to form carbonium ions[26]

$$R—Hg—Y \rightleftharpoons R—Hg^+ + Y^-$$
$$R—Hg^+ \longrightarrow R^+ + Hg°$$
$$R^+ \longrightarrow \text{solvolysis products} + H^+$$

Figure 2-13   Solvolysis of alkylmercuric salts

This reaction is of course very dependent on the nature of the anion in RHgY, as well as the nature of the alkyl group. With HSO_4^- and ClO_4^-, demercuration is very rapid; with acetate the rate is moderate, and with halide ion the reaction occurs very slowly, if at all. The striking dependency on structure is illustrated by the fact that for a given salt $k_{t\text{-butyl}} \sim 10^{13}k_{\text{methyl}}$.

Failure to recognize this demercuration reaction at an earlier date beclouds a substantial amount of electrophilic substitution work on mercurials, particularly in the protic acid cleavage reaction discussed in the following chapter.

[26] a. F. R. Jensen and R. J. Ouellette, *J. Am. Chem. Soc.*, **83:**2277, 4478 (1961).
   b. *Ibid.*, **85:**363 (1963).

3

PROTIC ACID CLEAVAGE OF THE CARBON-MERCURY BOND

3-1 Characteristics of the Cleavage Reaction

The initial studies of Frankland[1] on the preparation of organomercurials have been followed by an ever-increasing interest in the properties and reactions of these materials. An account of the early history and important developments in organomercury chemistry can be found in Whitmore's treatise.[2] The protic acid cleavage of the carbon-mercury bond was one of the earliest reactions of these compounds investigated; Schorlemmer,[3] in 1864, recommended the sulfuric acid treatment of diethyl mercury as a method of preparing pure ethane. The analogous acid cleavage of diarylmercurials was demonstrated shortly thereafter by Otto,[4] who also examined the reactions of several other reagents with the arylcarbon-mercury bond.

In general the cleavage of dialkyl compounds occurs much more readily than the corresponding reaction of the alkylmercuric salt. This supports the

$$R—Hg—R + HY \xrightarrow{\text{facile}} RH + RHgY$$
$$RHgY + HY \xrightarrow[\text{slow}]{\text{very}} RH + HgY_2$$

Figure 3-1 Hydrocarbon formation from alkyl- and dialkylmercury compounds

view that these reactions truly involve electrophilic cleavage of the carbon-mercury bond, since electronegative elements attached to mercury would tend to lower the electron density at the carbon reaction site.

A number of kinetic investigations and a stereochemical study have been reported for the protic acid cleavage of alkylmercuric compounds. In connection with the stereochemical work, a detailed investigation of the

---

[1] E. Frankland, *Ann. Chem.*, **85**:361 (1953); solid methylmercuric iodide was prepared by the action of sunlight on methyl iodide and mercury.

[2] F. C. Whitmore, "Organic Compounds of Mercury," Reinhold Publishing Corporation, New York, 1921.

[3] C. Schorlemmer, *Ann. Chem.*, **132**:243 (1864).

[4] R. Otto, *Ann. Chem.*, **154**:188 (1870).

45

$$R_2Hg \xrightarrow{HY} RH + RHgY \longrightarrow RHg^+ \longrightarrow R^+ \longrightarrow solv. \ prod. + HY$$

Figure 3-2 A side reaction leading to regeneration of acid in the cleavage of organomercurials

reaction and products was carried out,[5,6] disclosing the complicating side reaction of carbonium ion formation from the product alkylmercuric salts. It is clear that the regeneration of cleaving acid due to carbonium ion solvolysis can severely confuse a kinetic study of the reaction in question. The relative rates of cleavage and solvolysis are very sensitive to the nature of the cleavage reagent and the structure of the alkylmercurial (cf. Chap. 2). Compared to the rate of cleavage of di-*t*-butylmercury by acid, the demercuration of the *t*-butylmercuric cation is exceedingly rapid, while the corresponding reactions of secondary alkyl compounds occur at comparable velocities.

Solvolysis and other possible complicating side reactions were not recognized at the time that many of the earlier kinetic studies of protic acid cleavage of mercurials were accomplished; consequently much of this work must be viewed with suspicion. In many instances, more work is needed to clarify the validity of reported cleavage results since there is some uncertainty regarding the relative velocities of competing reactions. In general, results with acids other than hydrogen halides, excepting those for primary and aromatic systems, must be regarded as tentative.

In the single stereochemical study reported to date, protic acid cleavage was shown to occur with retention of configuration (this work is discussed in detail later in this chapter). It should be noted that in nearly all of the kinetic studies treated here, a four-center mechanism has been proposed or strongly implied by the investigators. Such a mechanistic pathway would necessarily involve complete retention of configuration. Although the available evidence indicates that this is the preferred stereochemistry under certain sets of conditions, more stereochemical studies are needed to determine the generality of this result.

3-2 Relative Rates by Competition Studies

An important and extensive study of the acid cleavage of unsymmetrical organomercurials was instituted by Kharasch[7] in 1925. In these experiments,

[5] L. H. Gale, F. R. Jensen, and J. A. Landgrebe, *Chem. & Ind.*, 118 (1960).

[6] F. R. Jensen and R. J. Ouellette, *J. Am. Chem. Soc.*, **83**:4477, 4478 (1961).

[7] a. M. S. Kharasch and M. W. Grafflin, *J. Am. Chem. Soc.*, **47**:1948 (1925).

b. M. S. Kharasch and R. Marker, *ibid.*, **18**:3130 (1926).

c. M. S. Kharasch and A. L. Flenner, *ibid.*, **54**:674 (1932).

d. M. S. Kharasch, H. Pines, and J. H. Levine, *J. Org. Chem.*, **3**:347 (1938–1939).

e. M. S. Kharasch and S. Swartz, *ibid.*, **3**:405 (1938–1939).

f. M. S. Kharasch, R. R. Legault, and W. R. Sprowls, *ibid.*, **3**:409 (1938–1939).

the authors determined the relative ease of cleavage of mixed alkyl and aryl organomercurials by hydrogen chloride.[8]

While actual rate constants were not determined (the reaction proceeds quite rapidly under the conditions employed), the isolation and characterization of the chloromercurial product was used to measure relative rate. Groups were interrelated directly in some cases, but more frequently they were interrelated by relation to a third substituent. Thus from the reactions in Figure 3-3, the relative order of cleavage of methyl and *t*-butyl was established as methyl > benzyl > *t*-butyl.

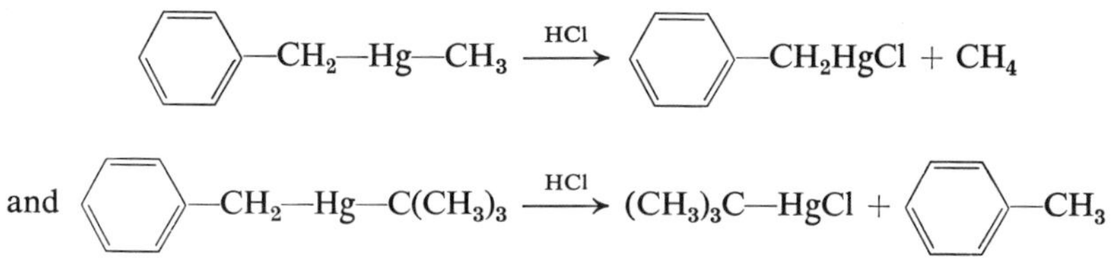

Figure 3-3   Example of sequence for determining relative ease of cleavage

Most of the groups which were examined are shown in Table 3-1 in order of decreasing rate of cleavage. Several important aspects were pointed out by Kharasch and Flenner (reference 7c): (a) the arylcarbon-mercury bond is broken much more readily than the alkylcarbon-mercury bond; (b) the positions of the tolyl, phenyl, and chlorophenyl groups parallel their respective rates of nitration; (c) any substituent replacing a hydrogen of the methyl group causes a decrease in relative rate. Note that the position of the benzyl group in the series led to the (erroneous) predicted order of relative electronegativity benzyl > benzhydryl > triphenylmethyl (reference 7b); (d) chain branching and increasing chain length lead to a decreased relative rate of cleavage, as shown by the positions of isoamyl and cyclohexyl, and by the ethyl, *n*-propyl, and *n*-butyl compounds, respectively.

The effect of chain branching was further elucidated by Whitmore and Bernstein,[9] who, using the method of Kharasch and Marker (reference 7b),

---

[8] Kharasch's original purpose was to determine the relative "electronegativity" of various groups, using as the operational definition for electronegativity the affinity of the organic substituent for "the pair of valence electrons." The cleavage reaction was in fact pictured as occurring by prior dissociation of the mercurial followed by reaction with a

$$R-Hg-R' \rightarrow R^-Hg^+R \xrightarrow{HCl} \text{products}$$

proton source (reference 7b-f). However, Corwin and Naylor (reference 10) have shown that the rate of reaction is dependent on the concentration of acid, indicating that prior dissociation of the organomercurial is not rate-determining. Today, with our knowledge of the high reactivity of carbanions, this proposal would be immediately untenable.

[9] F. C. Whitmore and H. Bernstein, *J. Am. Chem. Soc.*, **60:**2626 (1938).

Table 3-1 The order of decreasing ease of cleavage of groups in unsymmetrical organomercurials by hydrogen chloride according to Kharasch and coworkers (reference 7)

Aryl	Alkyl[a]
p-anisyl	methyl
o-anisyl	ethyl
α-naphthyl	n-propyl[b]
p-tolyl	n-butyl
m-tolyl	isoamyl
phenyl	benzyl[c]
p-chlorophenyl	cyclohexyl[d]
o-chlorophenyl	
m-chlorophenyl	

[a] All the alkyl substituents were found to be cleaved less readily than the aryl substituents.
[b] The isopropyl group fell below n-propyl in this series, but its relationship to n-butyl was not definitely established.
[c] Both t-butyl and β-phenethyl fell below benzyl, but were not further interrelated.
[d] The effect of increasing chain length is shown by the relative position of n-$C_{16}H_{33}$, which was found to be comparable to cyclohexyl.

determined the order: n-butyl ∼ 3,3-dimethylbutyl ∼ n-hexyl ∼ 4,4-dimethylpentyl > 2-butyl > 3,3-dimethyl-2-butyl. These workers also placed the neopentyl group as being approximately equal to t-butyl for relative rate of cleavage. Hence, α and β carbon substitution was shown to have a larger effect than γ substitution on the rate of breaking of the carbon-mercury bond.

Kharasch had originally proposed that the acid cleavage of dialkylmercury compounds occurs through formation of carbanions (footnote 8). However, it is well known that dialkylmercury compounds are stable to water and alcohol and, since carbanions would be expected to react immediately with these solvents, it is clear that such ionization cannot be occurring. Corwin and Naylor,[10] by varying the amounts of acetic and formic acid in dioxane, demonstrated that the cleavage reaction was dependent on the concentration and nature of the acid. Interpretation of the actual rates obtained by these workers is somewhat obscured by the gross solvent changes involved (i.e., high acid concentrations).

[10] A. H. Corwin and M. A. Naylor, *J. Am. Chem. Soc.*, **69**:1004 (1947).

3-3   Kinetics of the Acid Cleavage of Dialkyl and Diarylmercurials

A systematic study of the acid-cleavage reaction in acetic acid solvent was reported in 1955 by Winstein and Traylor.[11] Pseudo first-order rate constants were found for the compounds shown in Table 3-2. Note that the

Table 3-2   Acetolysis of organomercurials (reference 11)

	k(rel) 25°
diphenylmercury	14×10^3
di-*sec*-butylmercury	6.4×10^2
di-*n*-butylmercury	65
dineophylmercury	1

relative rate order *sec*-butyl $>$ *n*-butyl is opposite to that found (reference 9) for the cleavage of the unsymmetrical dialkylmercury, illustrating the dependence of this reaction on the second substituent attached to mercury.

$$RHgR \xrightarrow{\text{HOAc (solvent)}} RH + RHgOAc$$

$$Rate = k[RHgR]$$

Figure 3-4   Stoichiometry and rate expression
for acetolysis of dialkylmercury compounds

The effect of added sodium acetate was investigated in the dineophyl-mercury cleavage. No change in rate was observed, which was taken as evidence that neither nucleophilic attack of acetate ion on mercury nor reaction with the conjugate acid of acetic acid is important.   However, the relative nucleophilicities of acetic acid and sodium acetate in acetic acid are unknown and, since sodium acetate is not dissociated in this solvent and was present in relatively low concentration, it is possible that the reaction *is* assisted by nucleophile under these conditions. Added perchloric acid (again using the dineophylmercury system) gave greatly enhanced rates, and under these conditions, second-order kinetics were obeyed. The magnitude of the second-order rate constant allowed little interference from the pseudo first-order reaction with solvent even at low perchloric acid concentrations.

The mechanism proposed for the acetolysis reaction was classified as $S_E i$, involving molecular acetic acid. The $S_E 2$ mechanism using protonated acetic acid was suggested for the bimolecular reaction which occurred with added

[11] S. Winstein and T. G. Traylor, *J. Am. Chem. Soc.*, **77**:3747 (1955).

perchloric acid, but it was pointed out that several alternatives (e.g., ion pair involvement) had not been ruled out.

$$RHgR + HClO_4 \xrightarrow{\text{HOAc (solvent)}} RHgClO_4 + RH$$
$$\text{rate} = k[HClO_4][RHgR]$$
$$= k[CH_3CO_2H_2^+][RHgR]$$

Figure 3-5 Equation and rate expression for the perchloric acid-catalyzed reaction

During the course of this work, it was noted that the alkylmercuric cation was undergoing decomposition to yield metallic mercury and acid. Although this reaction was attributed to oxidation of the solvent by the alkylmercuric cation, it has since been shown to be a simple solvolysis proceeding through carbonium ions (references 5, 6, Figure 3-2). The re-formation of perchloric acid caused complications in determining the rate constants (Figure 3-5); however, the difficulty was believed to be circumvented by obtaining data only over the first fourth of the reaction.

Further insight into the course of this reaction was provided by the work of Kaufman and Corwin,[12] who examined the perchloric acid cleavage of diphenylmercury in a variety of solvent mixtures. In aqueous dioxane solvent, the effect of increasing the water concentration was to decrease the rate. The change in rate was not very large, e.g., a factor of approximately 9 in going from 70 to 97% aqueous dioxane. This solvent effect is qualitatively in agreement with the acidity of HCl in dioxane and ethanol, which Braude[13] has shown to be diminished by small amounts of added water.

Of particular interest is the effect of added salt on the perchloric acid cleavage reaction. While potassium perchlorate had no effect, potassium chloride caused a significant rate increase. Direct nucleophilic attack on mercury by the chloride ion to give carbanion was ruled out, as the salt gave no reaction in the absence of acid. Complexing of the organomercurial by chloride ion to give a more reactive species was regarded as improbable in view of the observation that neither chloride, iodide, nor cyanide ion affect the solubility of another organomercurial (see, however, Sec. 2-2). It was suggested that the observed rate increase was due to formation of undissociated HCl, which has been shown to be a weak acid in dioxane (reference 13).

In related work, Zimmer and Makower[14] found that HBr reacted approximately twice as fast as HCl with diphenylmercury in approximately 5% aqueous methanol. Under these conditions sulfuric, perchloric, nitric,

[12] F. Kaufman and A. H. Corwin, *J. Am. Chem. Soc.*, **77**:6280 (1955).

[13] E. A. Braude, *J. Chem. Soc.*, 1971 (1948).

[14] H. Zimmer and S. Makower, *Naturwissenschaften*, **41**:551 (1954).

hydrofluoric, acetic, and trichloroacetic acids reportedly did not cause cleavage of the mercurial. In view of the results of other workers with perchloric acid, it appears probable that many of these acids do in fact cause reaction, although at diminished rates.

Nerdel and Makower[15] have examined the scission of a series of dialkyl- and diarylmercurials by HCl in aqueous tetrahydrofuran and dioxane solvents, and have stated that in all cases a simple second-order rate law is obeyed. They determined the sequences

$$\text{di-}p\text{-tolyl} > \text{di-}o\text{-tolyl} > \text{di-}m\text{-tolyl} > \text{diphenyl}$$

and   di-(γ-phenylpropyl) > di-β-phenylethyl) > dibenzyl

Experimental details regarding precise conditions and kinetic techniques are lacking.

Recently Reutov and his coworkers[16] reported the results of their studies of the cleavage of dibenzylmercury by HCl in a variety of solvents. Contrary to the report of Nerdel and Makower (reference 15), Reutov claims that this reaction is first-order in dibenzylmercury and first-order overall. This report is clouded, to say the least, by statements that HCl catalyzes the reaction, is complexed with the mercurial in the transition state, and yet does not appear in the kinetic formulation. From the data presented, no definite conclusions can be drawn, and it appears that errors in both experimental technique and interpretation are involved. The behavior noted is similar to results obtained in the air oxidation of mercurials.

Dessy, Reynolds and Kim have investigated the kinetics of the cleavage of dialkyl- and diarylmercury compounds by hydrogen chloride in dimethyl sulfoxide-dioxane (10:1) solution.[17] These results and their interpretation have been widely quoted as evidence for a four-center mechanism; therefore, the data will be scrutinized in detail.

It was reported that the conductance of a solution of hydrogen chloride in dimethyl sulfoxide-dioxane (10:1) is a linear function (not simply a proportional function) of added hydrogen chloride over the concentration range employed (0.01 to 0.08 M). The linear relationship was stated to be due to either complete dissociation of the hydrogen chloride, or to very low dissociation, where the deviation from linearity is smaller than experimental

[15] F. Nerdel and S. Makower, *Naturwissenschaften*, **45**:491 (1958).

[16] I. P. Beletskaya, L. A. Fedorov, and O. A. Reutov, *Proc. Acad. Sci. USSR Chem. Sect.*, **163**:794 (1965).

[17] a. R. E. Dessy, G. F. Reynolds, and J. Kim, *J. Am. Chem. Soc.*, **81**:2683 (1959).
   b. *Ibid.*, **82**:686 (1960).
   c. R. E. Dessy and J. Kim, *ibid.*, **83**:1167 (1961).
   d. The data used in the discussion for the system with added water was taken from the Ph.D. Thesis of G. F. Reynolds, University of Cincinnati, 1959, rather than reference 17a.

error.[18] Considering the behavior of the acidity function in the concentration range employed, it was concluded that the degree of dissociation of hydrogen chloride in the solvent system is small, i.e., the equilibrium of Figure 3-6 lies far to the left at concentrations above 0.01 M.

$$HCl \rightleftharpoons H^+ + Cl^-$$

Figure 3-6 Proposed position of equilibrium in 10:1 DMSO-dioxane

Since this work appeared, the behavior of various acids in dimethyl sulfoxide solution has been investigated in detail by Kohltoff and Reddy.[19] Hydrochloric and sulfuric acids were found to be completely dissociated (below 0.0089 M) in dimethyl sulfoxide solutions containing 0.1 M sodium perchlorate. The concentrations of hydrogen chloride in the HCl, R_2Hg reactions were considerably larger (greater than 0.01 M), and therefore the results are not necessarily conflicting. In addition, the cleavage studies were carried out in the presence of dioxane (10%), which could reasonably decrease dissociation; the physical studies were carried out with 0.1 M sodium perchlorate, which should increase dissociation.

During the course of individual cleavage reactions with $[R_2Hg] = [HCl]$, the resistance of the solution increased approximately linearly with time. Since conductance was found to vary linearly with concentration of added hydrogen chloride, these results were taken to be indicative of a second-order reaction. Upon observing that changing the initial concentration of the dialkylmercury compound (twentyfold) and hydrogen chloride (twofold) produced essentially no change in rate constant, it was concluded that the reaction is first-order in each reagent. Second-order fits were reported to be obtained for over 66% of the reaction with a variation in k of $\pm 2\%$ between

---

[18] The term linear was not meant to imply that the line intersects the origin. A single set of conductivity versus N_{HCl} data was given, which upon plotting shows curvature from the indicated relationship. However, when these data are treated by the proper function for a weak electrolyte,

$$\frac{1}{\Lambda} = \frac{1}{\Lambda^\circ} + \frac{\Lambda N_{HCl}}{K(\Lambda^\circ)^2}$$

(H. S. Harned and B. B. Owen, "The Physical Chemistry of Electrolytic Solutions," p. 286, Reinhold Publishing Corporation, New York, 1958) an excellent fit of the data is obtained, giving a curve which intersects the origin. The value of the equilibrium constant thus obtained indicated that 0.08N HCl is about 37% dissociated in this solvent system. However, this treatment is inconsistent with the claim in the paper that the actual kinetic plots were linear for the reported relationship. Unfortunately, no kinetic data were reported.

[19] a. I. M. Kolthoff and T. B. Reddy, *J. Electrochem. Soc.*, **108**:980 (1961).

   b. *Ibid.*, *Inorg. Chem.*, **1**:189 (1962).

runs. In the kinetic expression, given in Figure 3-7, the [HCl] term is equal to the total hydrogen chloride concentration.

In order to study the effect of medium on the rate of reaction, dioxane was systematically added to dimethyl sulfoxide. With diethylmercury, substitution of dioxane until its mole fraction was 0.5 resulted in an 89.8% increase in rate; with diphenylmercury, substitution of dioxane until its mole fraction was 0.729 resulted in a 147% increase in rate. Although the conclusion had been given earlier in the paper that the degree of dissociation of hydrogen

$$R_2Hg + HCl \longrightarrow RH + RHgCl$$
$$Rate = k[HCl][R_2Hg]$$

Figure 3-7   Equation and kinetic expression
for the cleavage by hydrogen chloride

chloride must be very low, it was suggested that the effect of dioxane was to increase the amount of undissociated hydrogen chloride present. A more cautious view is that such a small change in rate with drastic change in solvent is not readily subject to interpretation.

Next these workers investigated the effect on rate of substituting water for organic solvent. From the data given (reference 17d), the total volume of reaction mixture is calculated to be 33.0 ml in all cases. The water was changed from 0.0 M to 3.4 M (i.e., to about 2 of the 33.0 ml of solution). This change in composition of the reaction mixture resulted in a decrease in rate by a factor of 2.42. This was regarded (reference 17a) as a marked change in reaction rate and the authors proposed "that this effect must be due to a shift in the dissociation equilibria of the hydrogen chloride in solution."

In the present authors' opinion, if hydrogen chloride is only slightly dissociated in 10:1 DMSO-dioxane as claimed by Dessy and coworkers, the addition of water to the extent of 3.4 M should cause the hydrogen chloride to dissociate to a substantial extent. Then, if the reactive species is undissociated HCl, the rate constant would reasonably be expected to decrease by a larger factor than 2.42. In any event, the proposed explanation requires more complex kinetics than those reported in the paper. For example, if the hydrogen chloride is greatly dissociated and the rate expression is

$$Rate = k[R_2Hg][HCl]_{undissoc.}$$

the $[HCl]_{undissoc.}$ term must be expressed in terms of a known concentration, namely, that of the added HCl.

$$HCl \rightleftharpoons H^+ + Cl^-$$
$$[HCl]_{undissoc.} = K[H^+][Cl^-]$$

In the absence of added chloride ion,

$$[H^+] = [Cl^-] \simeq [HCl]_{added}$$

and
$$[HCl]_{undissoc.} = K[HCl]_{added}$$

so that the expected rate expression in terms of known quantities is

$$Rate = kK[R_2Hg][HCl]_{added}$$

Since second-order kinetics were reported, the actual data fit neither dissociated nor undissociated hydrogen chloride alone as reactive intermediate. The complexity of the kinetic picture required for complete acid dissociation has been illustrated for only one assumed rate expression. Equally severe difficulties would be experienced if the cleavage were catalyzed by hydrogen ion alone, since results, given in Table 3-3, show that added chloride ion greatly accelerates the rate of reaction.

To investigate the role of added salts, the hydrogen chloride cleavages were carried out in the presence of sodium chloride and sodium sulfate. As noted by Dessy and coworkers, adding a small amount of sodium chloride was found to have a marked effect on the reaction rate.[20] They concluded that the chloride effect is mainly due to a shift in the hydrogen chloride dissociation, and that this indicates that undissociated hydrogen chloride is an attacking species. However, this is contrary to the earlier conclusion in the same paper that the hydrogen chloride must be largely undissociated. The maximum possible effect of added chloride ion on rate, assuming the only reactive species is the undissociated hydrogen chloride, is equal to the ratio

$$\frac{[HCl] + [Cl^-]}{[HCl]}$$

and this maximum effect would be obtained only if the hydrogen chloride is largely dissociated. The data of Dessy, Reynolds and Kim for the effect of added chloride ion are presented in Table 3-3. The last column gives the maximum possible rate constant obtainable in the presence of added chloride ion assuming the hydrogen chloride is completely dissociated. ([HCl] = added acid.)

The observed and calculated (maximum possible) rate constants are comparable for diethylmercury. For diphenylmercury the effect is greater than attributable to a change in the $[HCl]_{undissoc.}$ even under the most favorable conditions. If the hydrogen chloride is essentially undissociated, as concluded by Dessy (reference 17a), this phenomenon can have little effect on the rate. It is not possible from these data to assign the exact role of the chloride ion. It may be due to a combination of factors, including activation

[20] However, see reference 17a, p. 2686 and reference 17b, p. 688.

Table 3-3   Cleavage of dialkylmercurials by hydrogen chloride in
DMSO-dioxane (10:1) (reference 17)

	[HCl] = [R_2Hg] = 0.07 M		
		Rate constants, (1 m^{-1} sec^{-1}) $\times 10^2$	
	[NaCl]	k, observed	$k \dfrac{[HCl] + [Cl^-]}{[HCl]}$
($C_6H_5)_2$Hg	0.0	0.93	
	0.01	1.08	1.06
	0.02	1.38	1.19
($C_2H_5)_2$Hg	0	5.3	
	0.01	6.0	6.1

of the mercurial by complex formation or increasing the amount of undissociated hydrogen chloride; it may be simply a salt effect.

Dessy et al. (reference 17a) reported that the addition of sodium sulfate
to the reaction mixture of HCl, R_2Hg in DMSO-dioxane (10:1) had no effect
on rate, but no experimental details were given. This result is very surprising
in view of the finding by Kohltoff and Reddy that in dimethyl sulfoxide
solution, sodium bisulfate has a much smaller ionization constant (pK_a
9.1) than hydrogen chloride. A mixture of hydrogen chloride and sodium
sulfate can be expected to react and form sodium chloride and sodium
bisulfate (Na$^+$ HSO$_4^-$) in dimethyl sulfoxide solution. Therefore, these
results of Dessy and coworkers appear to be anomalous.

Sulfuric acid does not react noticeably with diphenylmercury according to
this study[21]; it was further stated that adding an equimolar amount of sulfuric
acid to the HCl, R_2Hg reaction mixture caused only a small increase in rate.
However, no product studies were reported even though sulfuric acid has been
used by other workers to cleave dialkylmercury compounds. Although these
data were taken to support the view that undissociated hydrogen chloride
is the attacking agent, a decision, in our opinion, is not warranted until
more complete information is available.

In the above discussion the available kinetic data for the hydrogen chloride
cleavage of dialkylmercurials have been harshly, but not exhaustively, scrutinized. The broad implications which have been drawn in references to this
work are in our opinion not warranted. Although a four-center mechanism
is reasonable a priori for this reaction, our view is that no firm mechanistic
conclusions can be drawn from the published results.

[21] The apparent lack of reaction with sulfuric acid may have been due to conductance by
the products, RHg$^+$ and HSO$_4^-$, in the reaction medium, since the conductivities of these
ions were not commented upon.

Table 3-4 Cleavage of organomercurials by hydrogen chloride in DMSO-dioxane (10:1) at 25°

Mercurial	Relative rate	$E_{act,}$ kcal/mole	$\Delta S^{\ddagger}$, eu
Diethylmercury	1	15.5	−27
Diphenylmercury	1200	12.2	−29
Ethylphenylmercury	5600	—	—
Dicyclopropylmercury	8200	16.5	−11
Divinylmercury	1800	13.6	−23

Table 3-4 gives the rates of hydrogen chloride cleavage of a series of mercurials (reference 17). The position of the unsymmetrical compound, ethylphenylmercury, in this series is of interest, as it is cleaved faster than either of its component symmetrical analogs. Thus, the original work of Kharasch and his coworkers, in attempting to establish an electronegativity series by cleaving unsymmetrical mercurials, gave results which are not necessarily indicative of the rate sequences for the symmetrical compounds. The simplest, and probably correct, explanation for the finding that the unsymmetrical mercurial (ethylphenylmercury) reacts faster than the symmetrical materials is that the inductive effect of each substituent affects the rate of cleavage of the other. The effect is pronounced and illustrates again the electrophilic nature of these reactions.

The question of the direction of cleavage of unsymmetrical mercurials had received relatively little attention since the work of Kharasch. Recently, Dessy[22] has reported that the materials shown in Figure 3-8 cleave in the direction anticipated for an electrophilic reaction.

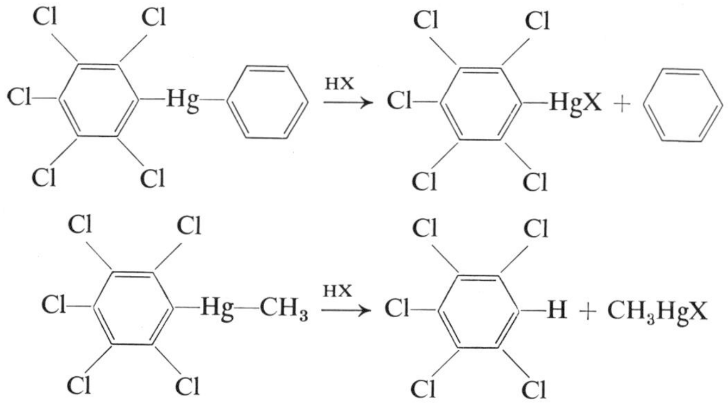

Figure 3-8 Direction of cleavage of some unsymmetrical mercurials

[22] F. E. Paulik, S. I. E. Green and R. E. Dessy, *J. Organometal. Chem.*, **3**:229 (1965).

The very rapid cleavage of dicyclopropylmercury relative to the cleavage observed for the other systems was attributed to the more positive entropy of activation. The products were determined for this reaction and were the normal expected materials—cyclopropane and cyclopropylmercuric chloride. One simple explanation for these results is that, whereas ordinary electrophilic cleavages by acid are concerted, in the cyclopropyl case an unstable protonated intermediate is formed which is free of other ligands. Thus, freeing the proton of nucleophiles in an equilibrium rather than concerted manner makes the entropy more favorable.

The relative rate of cleavages of a series of dialkylmercury compounds in DMSO-dioxane with HCl followed the order diethyl-> di-isopropyl-> di-n-propyl->dimethylmercury. Structural effects are not as pronounced under these conditions as under the acetolysis conditions employed by Winstein and Traylor (reference 11). For instance, the cleavage of di-isopropylmercury was only about 10% faster than the cleavage of di-n-propylmercury, while di-sec-butylmercury reacts nearly ten times faster than di-n-butylmercury with acetic acid (Table 3-2).

A variety of acids and solvent systems were used by Dessy and Kim (reference 17c) for the cleavage of diphenyl mercury. The dielectric constant of the medium does not correlate well with the reaction rates. A linear relationship exists between E_{act} and $\Delta S^{\ddagger}$ (over a wide range of values), implying a very similar role for both solvent and proton source for the various substrates in the mechanism of the cleavage reaction. A similar linear relationship was reported for the HCl scission of a series of symmetrically substituted diphenylmercurials in DMSO-dioxane solvent (reference 17b). The large

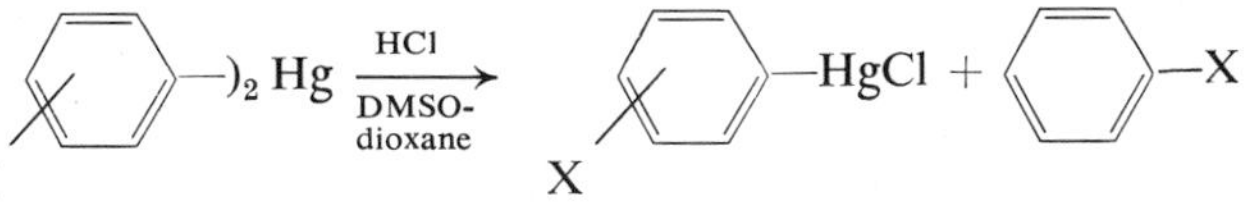

Figure 3-9   Cleavage of symmetrically substituted diarylmercury compounds

variation in $\Delta S^{\ddagger}$ in this series (-3 eu in the p-methoxy case, -10 eu for m-nitro) was attributed to variations in ground-state solvation for the mercurial. As the transition state for the reaction is probably highly polar and solvated, the extent of solvation should be enhanced by electron-withdrawing substituents such as the nitro group. The importance of such solvent interactions is demonstrated in the work of Sawatzky and Wright,[23] who calculated C—Hg—C bond angles from dipole moment measurements. Values considerably lower than that for a normal sp hybrid ($180°$) were obtained. Further, the existence of ions such as HgI_4^{--}, with known tetrahedral configurations,[24]

[23] H. Sawatzky and G. F. Wright, *Can. J. Chem.*, **36**:1555 (1958).
[24] M. L. Delwaulle, F. Fraveois, and J. Wiemann, *Compt. Rend.*, **207**:340 (1938).

shows clearly the ability of mercury to rehybridize. In the substituted di-phenyl compounds, sp^3 hybridization of the metal should block electronic interactions between the rings. The uv spectrum of diphenylmercury in ethanol suggests that such interactions are not important.[25] While neither σ nor σ^+ gave a linear Hammett plot, (σ and σ^+)/2 vs log k_2 gave a straight line with $\rho = -2.8$, according to Dessy and Kim.

Similar results were obtained by Nesmeyanov and his coworkers,[26] who examined the HCl cleavage of a number of symmetrically substituted aryl- and vinylmercurials in 90% aqueous dioxane. Second-order kinetics were observed.

3-4 Cleavage of Organomercuric Halides

The greatly decreased reactivity of alkylmercuric halides relative to dialkyl-mercurials towards electrophilic cleavage is evident from the earliest studies, e.g., Kharasch's work, where the halides were often isolated in high yield. One notable exception to the general stability of alkylmercuric halides is shown in the cleavage of methylmercuric iodide by acids to yield methane.[27] Kreevoy has examined the kinetics of this reaction with aqueous sulfuric and perchloric acid solutions at temperatures of about 100°.[28] The reaction was followed spectrophotometrically by measurement of the HgI_2 formed accord-ing to the indicated stoichiometry. In subsequent papers, the reactions were

$$CH_3HgI + H^+ \xrightarrow{H_2O} CH_4 + HgI^+$$
$$HgI^+ + CH_3HgI \longrightarrow CH_3Hg^+ + HgI_2$$

Figure 3-10 Stoichiometry of cleavage
of methylmercuric iodide

investigated with other alkyl groups.[29] However, considerable doubt is placed on these latter results because the expected solvolysis of the alkyl-mercuric cations[30] (references 5, 6) should bring about the conversion of mer-curic iodide to mercurous iodide. From the reported kinetic data, the relative rates at 110° of solvolysis of RHg^+ to acid cleavage of $RHgI$ are: for methyl, 0.02; for ethyl, 1.6; for isopropyl, 10^7; and for t-butyl, 10^{12}. Therefore the

[25] B. G. Gowenlock and J. Trotman, *J. Chem. Soc.*, 1454 (1955).

[26] A. N. Nesmeyanov, A. E. Borisov, and I. S. Saveleva, *Proc. Acad. Sci. USSR Chem. Sect.*, **155**:280 (1964).

[27] C. R. Crymble, *J. Chem. Soc.*, **105**:658 (1914); H. Framherz and K. Lih, *Z. Physik. Chem. (Leipzig)*, **A167**:103 (1933).

[28] M. M. Kreevoy, *J. Am. Chem. Soc.*, **79**:5927 (1957).

[29] a. M. M. Kreevoy and R. L. Hansen, *J. Am. Chem. Soc.*, **83**:626 (1961).
     b. *Ibid.*, *J. Phys. Chem.*, **65**:1055 (1961).

[30] F. R. Jensen and R. J. Ouellette, *J. Am. Chem. Soc.*, **85**:363, 367 (1963).

$$RHg^+ \rightarrow R^+ + Hg^\circ$$
$$R^+ \rightarrow \text{solvolysis products}$$
$$Hg^\circ + HgI_2 \rightarrow Hg_2I_2$$

Figure 3-11 Probable solvolysis
and conversion of HgI_2 to Hg_2I_2

concentration of mercuric iodide should be correct only for the methyl compound. Results with other alkyl groups are not included in the present discussion.

The reaction of methylmercuric iodide and a large excess of sulfuric or perchloric is first-order in methylmercuric iodide. From the dependence of the rate constant on the perchloric acid concentration, it was shown that the rate depends (approximately) on the molar concentration of the acid and not on H_0.[31] Combination of these results gives the overall expression of Figure 3-12.

$$\text{Rate} = k_2[H_3O^+][CH_3HgI]$$

Figure 3-12 Kinetic expression for
cleavage of methylmercuric iodide

The failure of the reaction to follow H_0 indicates that the proton transfer to carbon must not be reversible and that a water molecule is tightly held in the transition state.

Change of solvent from water to deuterium oxide caused no measurable change in reaction rate, indicating that the proton bonding is not greatly affected in progressing from initial state to transition state. The thermodynamic parameters $\Delta H^\ddagger = 22.2 \pm 0.3$ kcal/mole and $\Delta S^\ddagger = -29 \pm 1$ eu were obtained. It was proposed that these results could best be accounted for by a transition state in which the oxygen-hydrogen bond is only slightly disturbed and the hydrogen-carbon bond is just beginning to form, but in which the carbon-mercury bond is almost completely broken. This description of the relative amount of bonding in the transition state, without specifying stereochemistry, is probably the most detailed for any electrophilic substitution which has appeared in the literature.

Brown, Buchanon and Humffray[32] have recently examined the HCl cleavage of various arylmercuric chlorides in 90% aqueous ethanol. They found the reaction to be first-order in the mercurial, first-order in acid (proton), and zero-order in chloride ion, although the latter was required for the reaction to proceed. No cleavage was observed with either perchloric or sulfuric acid. They proposed the mechanism shown in Figure 3-13. Lack of

[31] For a discussion of this concept, see F. A. Long and M. A. Paul, *Chem. Rev.*, **57**:935 (1957).

[32] a. R. D. Brown, A. S. Buchanon, and A. A. Humffray, *Aust. J. Chem.*, **18**:1507 (1965).
b. *Ibid.*, p. 1513.

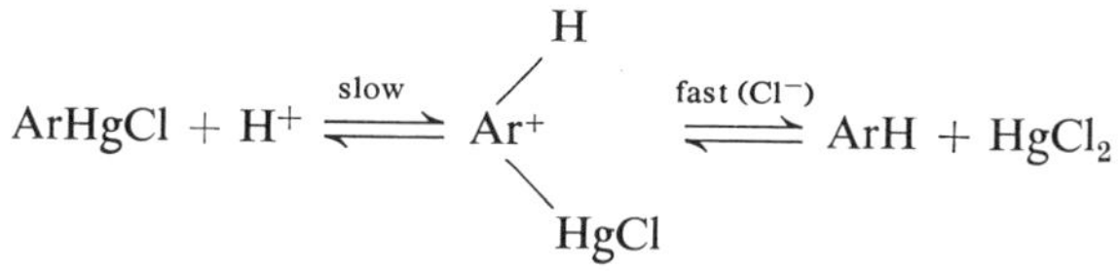

$$ArHgCl + H^+ \underset{slow}{\rightleftharpoons} \overset{\displaystyle H}{\underset{\displaystyle HgCl}{Ar^+}} \underset{fast\,(Cl^-)}{\rightleftharpoons} ArH + HgCl_2$$

Figure 3-13 A proposed mechanism for protic acid cleavage of arylmercuric chlorides

reaction in the absence of halide ion was explained on the basis of an unfavorable equilibrium for the second step of the proposed scheme. Data for a number of *m*- and *p*-substituted phenyl-mercuric chlorides gave a linear correlation with σ^+; analysis of thermodynamic parameters suggested that the dominant effects were on entropies of activation.

The effect of chloride ion concentration was studied in detail with the 3-furylmercuric chloride system; with a mercurial concentration of 5×10^{-4} and constant acid and ionic strengths (0.10), variation of chloride ion from 0.02 to 0.10 M caused no variation in rate constant. Higher chloride ion concentrations (using a different mercurial) caused increased rates, although comparable effects with perchlorate ion suggested that this is a salt effect rather than a specific function of the halide.

An alternate explanation of the effect of chloride ion on the cleavage, namely, by complex formation with the arylmercuric chloride, would appear to be ruled out by the zero-order relationship with salt at lower concentrations. In addition, attempts (reference 32a) to detect such complexes with mixtures of RHgCl and LiCl in dimethylformamide by ^{199}Hg nmr gave no evidence for their existence.[33]

The kinetics of HCl cleavage of benzylmercuric chloride in nearly anhydrous dioxane (70°) have been examined; the reaction was found to be first-order in each reactant and the rate was depressed by added water.[34a] It should be noted, however, that attempts to reproduce this work by others have failed; it has in fact been claimed that the reaction medium described by Reutov is a two-phase system (reference 32a).

Subsequent work[34b] with DCl in dry dioxane at 120 to 140° indicated that the product toluene contained considerable *o*-deuterium, with incorporation exceeding that in recovered starting material. A cyclic transition state was proposed to account for the preference for ortho exchange; an attractive intermediate for the cleavage is 1-methylene-2,4-cyclohexadiene.

---

[33] It was pointed out, however, that the unusually high solubility of the mercurials in dimethylformamide may indicate the formation of a complex with solvent, with which the chloride ion may not compete effectively.

[34] a. O. A. Reutov, I. P. Beletskaya, and M. Y. Aleinikova, *Russ. J. Phys. Chem.* (*English Transl.*), **36**:256 (1962).

b. Y. G. Bundel, N. D. Antonova, and O. A. Reutov, *Dokl. Akad. Nauk SSSR*, **166**:1103 (1966).

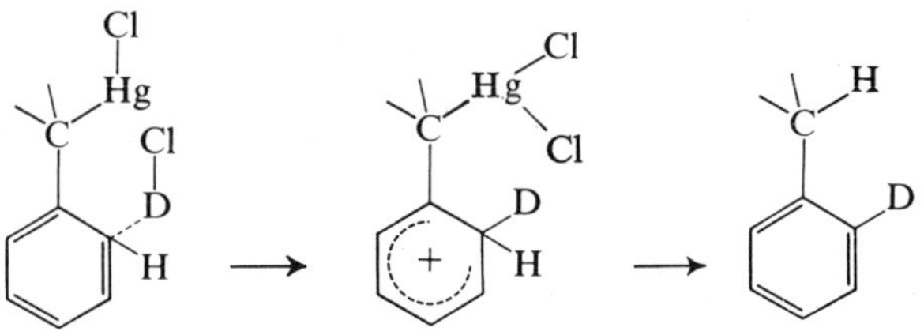

Figure 3-14   Cyclic mechanism proposed to account for preferential *o*-deuteration under DCl cleavage conditions

A fairly extensive study of the reaction of phenylmercuric bromide with HCl in 95% aqueous dioxane has also been reported by Reutov and his co-workers.[35] The second-order rate constant was found to decrease with time, falling to about one-half its original value during the course of the reaction. This phenomenon was ascribed to inhibition by the product HgBrCl; addition of one mole of HgBrCl per mole of mercurial gave a time-invariant second-order rate constant, with a magnitude about one-fourth the value in the absence of added mercuric salt.[36]

While this apparent inhibition by product could be caused by any of several mechanisms, reasonable processes are complexing of halide ion by the product mercuric halide, or exchange of phenylmercuric bromide to form phenylmercuric chloride, or a combination of both. It is expected that ability to complex will decrease in the order

$$HgX_2 > RHgX > R_2Hg$$

for normal alkyl and aryl mercurials. If the cleavage reaction involves the species $RHgX_2^-$ wholly or in part, then it is conceivable that, depending on the degree of dissociation of HCl under the reaction conditions, salt effects and the magnitude of the equilibrium constants involved for complex formation, the formation of HgX_3^- would cause the observed rate depression.

Covalent radii considerations suggest that the relative rates of cleavage of organomercuric halides should be in the order

$$RHgI > RHgBr > RHgCl$$

although rate differences may not be large.

There is no direct evidence bearing on the question of halide exchange between phenylmercuric bromide and HCl under the reaction conditions used

[35] I. P. Beletskaya, A. E. Myshkin, and O. A. Reutov, *Bull. Acad. Sci. USSR, Div. Chem. Sci.*, 226 (1965).

[36] The HgBrCl was added as an equimolar mixture of HgBr₂ and HgCl₂; the authors apparently assumed that these materials would equilibrate readily, although the same behavior was not ascribed to the organomercuric halide.

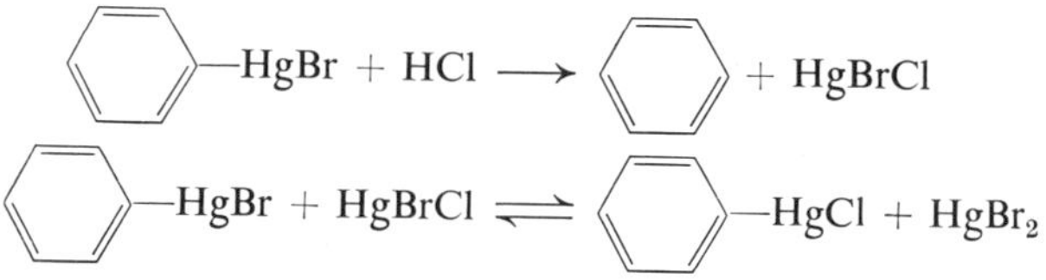

Figure 3-15 Halide exchange of an organomercurial

in this kinetic study. If this exchange were rapid, too many equilibria would be involved to allow a simple prediction of the effect on reaction rate with time. However, even if this direct exchange is negligibly slow, organomercuric chloride formation might be anticipated through the exchange of the organic salt with the HgBrCl that is formed during the course of the reaction (footnote 36). Thus, the observed decrease in rate constant may be due to formation of phenylmercuric chloride.

The addition of sodium iodide to the phenylmercuric bromide, HCl system in 90% aqueous dioxane caused a very large rate enhancement.[37] The reaction was reported to follow clean second-order kinetics with molar ratios of NaI to phenylmercuric bromide of 3.5 and greater. The rate constant increased with increasing ratio, although over a wide range of NaI concentrations the relationship was not directly proportional.

Reutov considered five factors which might explain this phenomenon (Figure 3-16). Of these, the first appears to be unreasonable on the basis of the magnitude of the rate enhancement, i.e., an increase to a value no greater

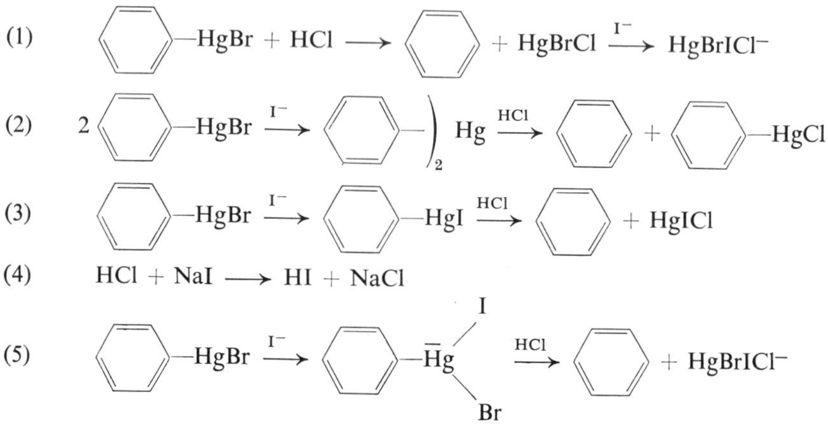

Figure 3-16 Possible mechanisms responsible for the NaI-induced rate enhancement of phenylmercuric bromide cleavage

[37] A factor of 10^4 was estimated; the reaction of phenylmercuric bromide with HCl was shown to occur about seven times faster in 98.5% than in 95% aqueous dioxane.

than the initial rate in the absence of NaI would be anticipated if the entire effect were due to complex formation of the inorganic mercuric halide.

The possibility of symmetrization by iodide (a known reaction; cf. Chap. 6) was ruled out by examining the rate of cleavage of diphenylmercury, both with and without added NaI, under the reaction conditions. Interestingly, these rates were both lower (although not a great deal lower in the case of diphenylmercury with NaI) than the NaI catalyzed reaction of phenylmercuric bromide.

Mechanism (3) was discarded by examining the rate of cleavage of phenylmercuric iodide with HCl; the rate constant was reported to be of the same order of magnitude (no numerical details were given) as that of phenylmercuric bromide. The rate again drifted downward as the reaction progressed.

The possibility that HI might prove a much stronger cleaving reagent than HCl was ruled out by examining the rate of cleavage of both phenylmercuric bromide and iodide with the former material. Again, although no details were given, it was reported that the rate with HI was very close to the rate observed with HCl. Unfortunately, here the authors did not comment on any drift in the rate constant. If this drift had been due to halide exchange in the phenylmercuric bromide—HCl cleavage, no such behavior should have been seen in the phenylmercuric iodide system.

Reutov has thus concluded that the rate enhancement by NaI is due to complex formation with phenylmercuric bromide. In support of this conclusion he has shown that a new band appears in the uv spectrum of mixtures of the mercurial and NaI, at 303 mu. In agreement with this suggestion is the known (cf. Chap. 2) greater tendency for iodide, compared with bromide and chloride, to complex with mercurials. It is interesting that although no spectrophotometric evidence was found for complex formation between diphenylmercury and iodide in 90% aqueous dioxane, iodide did enhance the rate of this cleavage to a substantial degree.

Anomalous results have been reported recently by Reutov and his co-workers[38] for the reaction of *cis-* and *trans-β*-chlorovinylmercuric chloride with HCl and DCl. In anhydrous dioxane, second-order kinetics (first-order in each reactant) were observed for both HCl ($k = 7.9 \times 10^{-4}$ liter/mole-sec) and DCl ($k = 7.1 \times 10^{-4}$ liter/mole-sec) for the trans isomer at 60°. The cis material reacted somewhat more rapidly ($k = 8.8 \times 10^{-4}$ liter/mole-sec) under these conditions.

In dimethyl sulfoxide, however, it was reported that the reaction followed first-order kinetics, with the rate constants for HCl and DCl being identical, 1.86×10^{-3} sec^{-1}, for the *trans*-mercuric chloride (35°), and the cis isomer reacting somewhat more slowly (1.70×10^{-3} sec^{-1}).

[38] I. P. Beletskaya, V. I. Karpov, V. A. Moskalenko, and O. A. Reutov, *Proc. Acad. Sci. USSR, Chem. Sect.*, **162**:414 (1965).

Reutov has claimed that the cleavage in both solvents occurs with complete retention of configuration, although his description of the experimental procedure used to prepare products for determining stereochemistry is very different than his kinetic conditions, which does not allow a direct correlation.

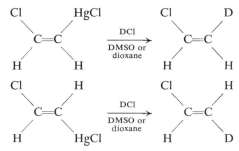

Figure 3-17 Cleavage of a vinylmercurial with retention of configuration as reported by Reutov et al. (reference 35)

The mechanism of the first-order reaction in dimethyl sulfoxide was postulated (reference 35) to involve dissociation of vinylmercurial to a carbon ion-pair (Figure 3-18); this seems unlikely in view of the fact that there are no special carbanion stabilizing effects in this system. Additional work is clearly needed before this and other related examples of $S_E 1$ reactions are accepted.*

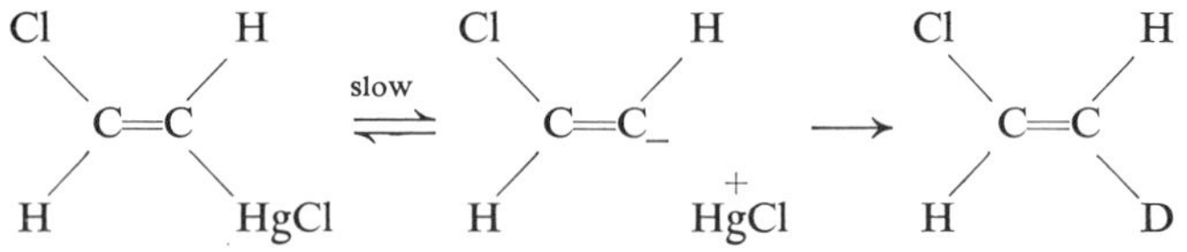

Figure 3-18 Mechanism postulated by Reutov to account for first-order kinetics and retention of configuration

Kreevoy studied the acid cleavage of vinylmercuric iodide[39] and allylmercuric iodide[40] in aqueous solution (second-order kinetics) in which large $(k_H/k_D \sim 5$ to $7)$ isotope effects were observed, indicating rate-determining proton transfer. His studies imply a very different mechanistic situation than suggested by Reutov et al. Unfortunately, substrate and solvent differences do not permit a direct comparison of these studies.

3-5 Stereochemistry of Acid Cleavage

While the mechanism most frequently suggested for the electrophilic substitution of organomercurials (the four-center concerted pathway)

---

* Substantial parts of the work in reference 38 have been shown to be incorrect: P. J. Banney, W. Kitching, and P. R. Wells, *Tetrahedron Letters*, 27 (1968).

[39] M. M. Kreevoy and R. A. Kretchmer, *J. Am. Chem. Soc.*, **86**:2435 (1964).

[40] M. M. Kreevoy, P. J. Steinwand, and W. V. Kayser, *J. Am. Chem. Soc.*, **88**:124 (1966).

implies retention of configuration at the carbon atom formerly bearing the metal, actual stereochemical results have been obtained in only a few cases.

As noted in Chap. 2, the general configurational stability of the carbon-mercury bond has led to the preparation of several pairs of such compounds which are related diastereomerically. More recently materials such as the *sec*-butylmercurials have been obtained in optically active form. With one exception, stereochemical studies utilizing these materials have centered around cleavage by reagents other than protic acids; these will be covered in detail in subsequent chapters.

The absence of rigid configurational requirements appears to be a general aspect of the scission of the carbon-mercury bond by a variety of reagents. While ring size (in the few cases for which data are available) can appreciably affect the relative rate of reaction (references 5, 17) there is no evidence which suggests that gross mechanistic changes are involved. The acid cleavage of a bridgehead mercurial, which must necessarily occur with retention of configuration, has been demonstrated by Winstein and Traylor.[41] Both acetic acid and perchloric acid in acetic acid solvent were used with this

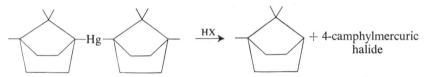

Figure 3-19 A cleavage reaction which must occur with retention of configuration

compound, and the relative rates were compared with those obtained previously by these authors (reference 11) with open chain systems. It was pointed out that if a different mechanism were involved for the bridgehead system due to its restrictive geometry, a decreased rate would be expected. In fact, the relative rate for the reaction with acetic acid at 25° was fourteen, compared to one for dineophyl mercury and sixty-five for di-*n*-butylmercury. While it was concluded that the camphyl system was "not especially un-reactive," no simple tertiary system was available for comparison. Actually, the rate change found in progressing from *n*-butyl to *sec*-butyl (a factor of ~10; see Table 3-2) suggests that the cleavage of di-4-camphylmercury may be considerably slower than that of an open-chain tertiary analog. It is clear, however, that the very large factors involved in S_N1 reactions are not noted here.

In this connection, Nesmeyanov and Kritskaia[42] have stressed the extreme stability of the carbon-mercury bond in α-chloromercuricamphenilone (Figure 3-20). Although alkylmercuric halides in general are less reactive than

[41] S. Winstein and T. G. Traylor, *J. Am. Chem. Soc.*, **78:**2597 (1956).

[42] A. N. Nesmeyanov and I. I. Kritskaia, *Proc. Akad. Sci. USSR, Chem. Sect.*, **121:**569 (1958).

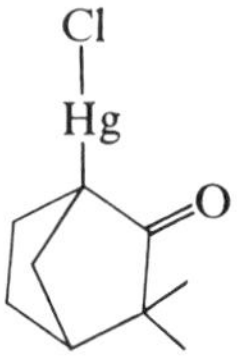

Figure 3-20   α-Chloromercuricamphenilone,
a very stable mercurial

dialkylmercurials in electrophilic substitution reactions, an α-carbonyl group has long been known to greatly enhance the rate of acid cleavage of the carbon-metal bond.[43] Clearly the bridgehead position in camphenilone is not typical of α-keto-compounds for electrophilic reactions; camphenilone-carboxylic acid (bridgehead carboxyl) can be distilled at 312° without decomposition (reference 42), and camphenilone itself does not undergo base-catalyzed deuterium exchange.[44] This inertness clearly indicates the necessity of forming an enolic intermediate and the difficulties of including bridgehead atoms (small rings) in the enolic system. However, it appears that chloro-mercuricamphenilone is much more resistant to acid cleavage than an analogous system lacking the carbonyl group, as exemplified by Winstein's 4-camphyl derivative (reference 41). An explanation of this result has been offered (reference 44), involving increased angle strain in the transition state for the ketomercurial relative to the noncarbonyl containing compound. In spite of the fact that the bridgehead bond and the carbonyl group are not suitably oriented for π-overlap, the residual electronic effect of the carbonyl dipole cannot be discounted. By analogy with the increased reactivity of mixed dialkylmercury compounds (Table 3-4) and the unreactivity of alkyl-mercuric halides towards acids, this inductive effect is expected to cause a depression in rate.

Observation of the stereochemistry of the protic acid cleavage of the carbon-mercury bond was accomplished by Gale, Jensen and Landgrebe in 1960.[45] Di-L-(−)-sec-butylmercury was subjected to reaction conditions similar to those discussed earlier in this section, with the proton source replaced by a deuterio acid.

The results, shown in Table 3-5, illustrate an important difficulty in the study of organomercurials. This is the apparently facile racemization of starting material observed under all of the conditions examined. While the mechanism of this racemization is not known with certainty, free radicals

---

[43] Whitmore (reference 2, p. 45) states that loss of mercury can occur with cold dilute HCl in the case of α-halomercuriketones.

[44] A. N. Nesmeyanov, D. N. Kursanov, K. A. Pechenskaia, and Z. N. Parnes, *Bull. Acad. Sci. USSR, Div. Chem. Sci.*, 592 (1949).

[45] L. H. Gale, F. R. Jensen, and J. A. Landgrebe, *Chem. & Ind.*, 118 (1960).

$$\underset{*}{\overset{\overset{\displaystyle CH_3}{|}}{CH_3CH_2CH}} \text{—Hg—} \underset{*}{\overset{\overset{\displaystyle CH_3}{|}}{CH}} \text{—CH}_2CH_3 \xrightarrow{\ SD\ } CH_3CH_2CHDCH_3$$

$$[\alpha]_D{}^{25}\ -20.9°$$

$$+\ CH_3\text{—}\overset{\displaystyle |}{CH}\text{—CH}_2CH_3$$
$$\overset{|}{Hg}$$
$$\overset{|}{S}$$

Figure 3-21   Cleavage by deuterio acid

have been shown to racemize mercury compounds (for further discussions see Sec. 6-3 and Sec. 7-2)[46] (reference 45).

Since the absolute configuration of 2-deuterobutane is known,[47] it is possible to conclude that the positive rotation of RD (Table 3-5) was caused by retention of configuration at the seat of electrophilic substitution. However, the concurrent racemization of starting material does not allow the calculation of the exact degree of stereospecificity with which the protic acid cleavage occurs. Consequently, the higher retention observed with dioxane-DCl relative to deuterioacetic acid may only reflect the relative rates of cleavage and racemization of starting material. It is clear in the perchloric acid-deuterioacetic acid cleavage that no evidence regarding the stereochemistry of the carbon-mercury bond scission was obtained, due to the very rapid loss of activity of the dialkylmercury compound.

Table 3-5   Stereochemistry of the acid cleavage
of di-L-(−)-*sec*-butylmercury at 25° (reference 42)

		$[\alpha]$		
		Recovered[a]		
Solvent	Acid	R_2Hg	$RHgI^b$	RD
DOAc	DOAc	−5.26	−2.51	0.085
DOAc	$HClO_4$	−.008	0.00	−0.003
Dioxane	DCl	−6.23	−9.56	0.135

[a] Starting material has $[\alpha]_D{}^{25}$ −20.9° in each case. Specific rotations are given in all instances.

[b] Isolated as the iodide for reasons of solubility.

[46] The racemization of mercury compounds by radicals could reasonably occur by α-hydrogen abstraction, or by addition (and reversal) of radicals to the compounds,

$$R_2{}^*Hg + R\cdot \rightleftharpoons [R_2{}^*HgR]\cdot \rightleftharpoons R^*HgR + R\cdot \rightleftharpoons [R^*HgR_2]\cdot \rightleftharpoons R_2Hg + R\cdot$$

[47] G. K. Helmkamp, C. D. Joel, and H. Sharman, *J. Org. Chem.*, **21**:844 (1956).

Table 3-6

$$CH_3-\!\!\left\langle\right\rangle\!\!-Hg-\!\!\left\langle\right\rangle\!\!-CH_3 \xrightarrow{SD} CH_3-\!\!\left\langle\right\rangle\!\!-D + CH_3-\!\!\left\langle\right\rangle\!\!-Hg-S$$

| | | | % trans | | | |
| | | | Initial | Recovered | | |
Solvent	Acid	Temp. °C	R_2Hg	R_2Hg	RHgX	RD
DOAc	DOAc	75	100	37	37	95
DOAc	DOAc	75	18	37	37	95
Dioxane	D_2SO_4	15	100	41	41	95
Dioxane	D_2SO_4	15	16	34	31	95
Dioxane	DCl	25	100	99	98	80
Dioxane	DCl	15	18	15	14	36

Comparable results were obtained using both *cis-* and *trans-*di-4-methylcyclohexylmercury as substrates. Table 3-6 lists values from three different solvent-acid systems. Several points are worth noting. The higher temperature required for electrophilic substitution of the di-cyclohexylmercurial (relative to the di-*sec*-butyl system) apparently allows the racemization (isomerization of starting material) mechanism to control the reaction. The relatively invariant constitution of recovered R_2Hg from the first four entries in the table suggest that steady state concentrations have been attained in these cases.[48] The similar cis-trans distribution of RHgX implies that interconversion is very rapid under these conditions. The large preponderance of

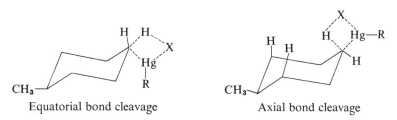

Equatorial bond cleavage   Axial bond cleavage

Figure 3-22   Illustration of steric hindrance to axial reaction

*trans-*4-methylcyclohexane-1-*d* is apparently due to a more rapid cleavage of the equatorial over the axial carbon-mercury bond, indicating an appreciable steric requirement of the transition state for this reaction.

Only in the DCl-dioxane case is direct evidence of stereospecificity obtained, and as in the open-chain case retention of configuration occurs. Very

[48] There is no axial-equatorial conformational preference for the substituent —Hg—X. F. R. Jensen and L. H. Gale, *J. Am. Chem. Soc.*, **81**:6337 (1959).

little isomerization of starting material was observed in this solvent-acid system, and consequently the stereochemical values, 80% retention in the case of *trans*-di-4-methylcyclohexylmercury and 73% retention for *cis*-di-4-methylcyclohexylmercury, should represent well the specificity of the protic acid cleavage reaction.

Indirect evidence dealing with the stereochemistry of electrophilic substitution by acids is found in a variety of sources. For instance, in the work of Reutov and Uglova,[49] the rotational values observed in the HBr scission of di-5-methyl-2-hexylmercury imply that no significant racemization of starting material occurred.[50] The possibility of asymmetric induction in the preparation of dialkylmercury appears to be excluded by the rotation of the product of $HgBr_2$ cleavage, a reaction which is known to occur with a high degree of specificity (Sec. 5-4).

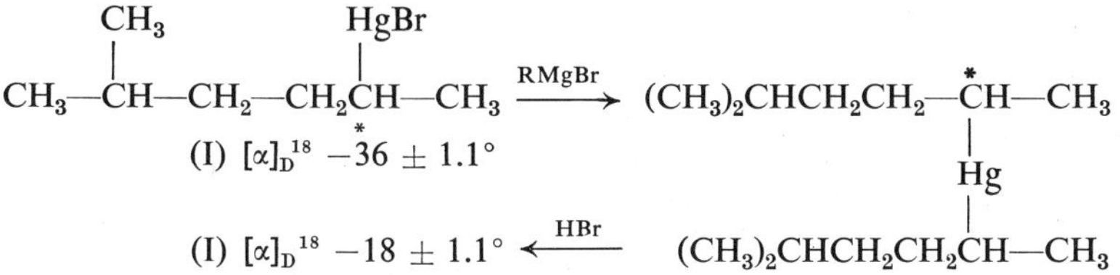

Figure 3-23   Cleavage of a dialkylmercurial without racemization of the alkylmercuric salt

From the foregoing it is clear that in systems which have been investigated stereochemically, retention is the preferred course of the acid cleavage of the alkyl carbon-mercury bond. At the present time, it is not possible to state the degree of specificity because of interfering side reactions.

3-6   Mechanisms of Acid Cleavages of Mercurials

Evidence exists that mercurials undergo acid-cleavage, e.g., with hydrogen bromide, by radical pathways (reference 11). Little information is available concerning these reactions, but it is likely that the details are similar to those presented in Sec. 4-2 for homolytic cleavage by halogens. The discussion in this section will be limited exclusively to polar cleavage mechanisms.

Although the stereochemical results (Sec. 3-5) are far from conclusive, it will be assumed for simplicity that all cleavages proceed with retention of configuration. It has been commonly proposed that these reactions proceed

[49] O. A. Reutov and E. V. Uglova, *Bull. Acad. Sci. USSR, Div. Chem. Sci.*, 1628 (1959).

[50] Winstein and Traylor reported that the reaction of alkylmercuric bromides with HBr in acetic acid solvent proceeds entirely by a radical path. The solvent was not specified in reference 49.

by four-center or similar mechanisms. Since four-center mechanisms of necessity require retention of configuration, the stereochemical course for a "pure" S_E2 reaction, i.e., where the free, uncomplexed, electrophile undergoes reaction with carbon, is then open to question. Uncoordinated protons occur in prohibitively small concentrations; therefore, in the acid-cleavage reaction, the electrophile is always bonded to a group which may potentially serve as a nucleophile on mercury. At some future time, a sufficiently selective complexing agent may be found which can fully coordinate mercury, for example, $R_2HgY_2^{--}$, and thereby greatly decrease the probability of a four-center pathway. The stereochemistry of various electrophilic reactions with compounds of mercury having this degree of coordination should be exceedingly interesting.

It does not appear possible at the present time to ascribe exact mechanisms to any of the acid scission reactions. Transition states are presented below for a few of the possible types of cleavages, but the reader is referred to Chap. 1 for a general discussion of mechanisms which may operate for concerted electrophilic cleavage.

In considering the charge density at the central carbon atom in the transition state, it is clear that for aryl compounds electron-donating groups on the ring facilitate the rate of reaction. It appears that cleavage of aryl compounds is closely related to aromatic substitution and proceeds through a σ-complex. For aliphatic compounds, the relative rate sequence depends on the cleaving reagent. Thus, for hydrogen chloride cleavage, n-butyl > cyclohexyl (reference 7), n-butyl > sec-butyl (reference 9), and isopropyl is slightly slower than n-propyl (reference 17c). However, in the cleavage by acetic acid sec-butyl is about ten times faster than n-butyl (reference 11). These limited data indicate that in dialkylmercurials the effect of structure on rate is difficult to predict and may vary considerably with reagent. Little evidence regarding the influence of steric effects is available.

As noted by Winstein and Traylor (reference 11), there are many possible combinations of electrophilic and nucleophilic reagents in the acetolysis of dialkylmercury compounds. Although it was not thought possible to distinguish between these, an S_Ei mechanism was selected as the most likely for the cleavage by acetic acid, and S_E2 mechanism for the mineral acid-catalyzed cleavage by protonated acetic acid (Figure 3-22).

The electron movements for the reaction with molecular acid shown in Figure 3-24 are actually arbitrary. When the electron transfers occur simultaneously and concertedly, electrophilic or nucleophilic classification as discussed earlier becomes diffuse. Classification of this reaction as S_Ei is meant to indicate that coordination of oxygen with mercury and breaking of the carbon-mercury bond (with partial carbanion formation) is well along the reaction pathway before bonding of carbon to hydrogen becomes appreciable. However, it should be emphasized that nucleophiles alone do not cleave

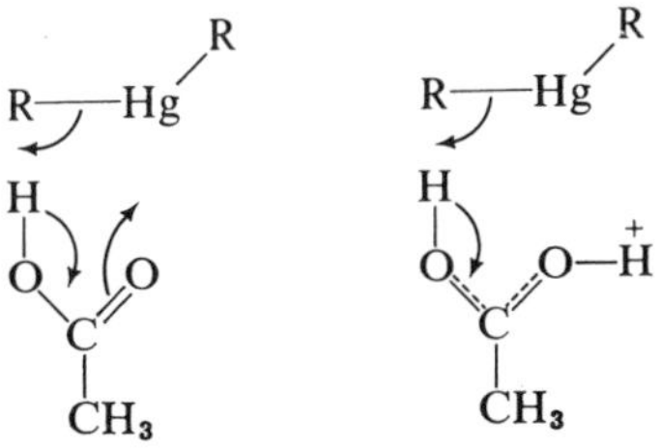

R—Hg   R—Hg

Molecular acid   Protonated acid

Figure 3-24 $S_E i$ (molecular acid) and $S_E 2$
(protonated acid) cleavage mechanism

mercury compounds of this type to produce carbanions. The $S_E 2$ mechanism
depicted in Figure 3-24 is the simplest type of electrophilic reaction which can
be envisioned. It should again be pointed out that the above assignments of
mechanism were tentative.

Pictures such as those shown in Figure 3-24 do not give a definite indication
of bonding changes which occur during the reaction. Several different
combinations of orbitals can be used to represent either transition state.

An orbital (partial) picture for a concerted cleavage of a mercurial by
acetic acid is shown in Figure 3-25. Only the bonds which undergo changes
during the course of the reaction are represented as a combination of atomic
orbitals; a mercury vacant p orbital which enters into the reaction is also
included. Omitted from the picture is the π-molecular orbital (perpendicular
to the plane of the drawing) of the carboxyl group. In the transition state (II),
the origin of the electrons in the resulting orbitals is irrelevant. This picture
as shown implies no separation of charge. Therefore, classification of this
reaction as electrophilic is at least partially arbitrary. In the drawings, the
position of acetic acid and the mercury atom are held essentially constant,
while the alkyl groups attached to mercury show considerable movement.

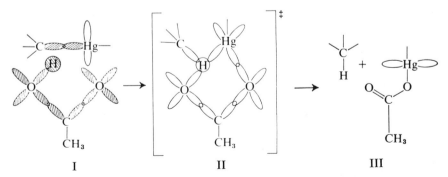

Figure 3-25   Orbital picture (partial) for a concerted acetic acid cleavage of a
mercurial

This relative representation of movement is again, of course, arbitrary. Hybridization of carbon remains unaffected, but the bonding on mercury undergoes changes. In the transition state (II), the two bonds to mercury which are being varied are shown to each have about $\frac{1}{4}$ and $\frac{3}{4}$ p character. However, it is possible that the hybridization on all three bonds to mercury are nearly equivalent in the transition state and are more nearly sp^2. It should be noted that this cleavage in Figure 3-25 is formally almost identical with that of a four-center reaction because of the interplay of the π bond in the carboxyl group.

The hydrogen chloride cleavage has been postulated to occur through molecular acid by Kaufman and Corwin (reference 12) and Dessy, Reynolds and Kim (reference 17). The evidence was examined in detail in Sec. 3-3,

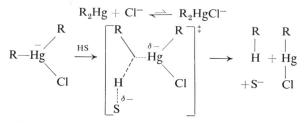

Figure 3-26 $S_E 2$ Cleavage of an activated mercurial

and in the present authors' opinion it is not possible to draw a definite conclusion at this time regarding the validity of this assumption. Of the possible mechanisms, only two are presented here. The argument was advanced (references 12, 17) that the rate-accelerating effect of added chloride ion is probably not due to complex formation of this anion with mercury because chloride ion has no measurable effect on the solubility of organomercurials. However, such an intermediate would be expected to be very reactive and its presence in low concentration could easily account for the increase in rate. A possible way of picturing this reaction is shown in Figure 3-26. Mercury, originally with sp hybridization, undergoes a change upon complex formation to sp^2, but upon cleavage reverts to the initial configuration. The reaction of the electrophile is shown occurring on the carbon-mercury bond both in Figures 3-24 and 3-25. The role of the alkyl group in the reaction could be described as a "hinged action" on the sp^3 orbital, or if the charge on carbon is large, as a "hinged action" of a carbanion.

Reaction of molecular hydrogen chloride is readily pictured as occurring through a four-center mechanism. This representation can be described in terms of several orbital pictures. For each orbital portrayal, many variations in the relative amounts of bond making and bond breaking are possible, and under certain conditions the reaction may be described as a "no-mechanism" process. One possible depiction is very similar to that shown in Figure 3-25

$$
\begin{array}{ccccc}
\text{R—Hg—R} & & \text{R}\cdots\text{Hg}\diagup^{\text{R}} & & \text{R} \\
+ & \longrightarrow & \vdots\quad\vdots & \longrightarrow & | + \text{Hg} \\
\text{H—Cl} & & \text{H}\cdots\text{Cl} & & \text{H}\quad | \\
& & & & \text{Cl}
\end{array}
$$

Figure 3-27   Four-center cleavage

for molecular acetic acid wherein reaction of electrophile again occurs on the carbon-mercury bond.

An interesting orbital portrayal for this reaction, which resembles the usual dotted line picture (Figure 3-27), includes rehybridization of carbon. In the transition state for this depiction, carbon has undergone a change in hybridization from sp^3 to sp^2 and p. (The structure designated as the transition state

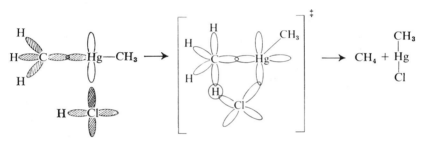

Figure 3-28   Four-center mechanism with attack of electrophile on carbon with resulting rehybridization of carbon

could actually be a reaction intermediate.) The transition state can be constructed with one-electron bonds[51] or as a resonance hybrid (Figures 3-29 and 3-30, respectively).

This mechanism, which demands extensive changes in the bond angles on carbon, cannot be universally applicable since it has been shown that bridgehead mercurials cleave with acetic acid and protonated acetic acid at rates not substantially depressed from those of open-chain compounds (reference 41). The necessary rehybridization would be improbable with these compounds.

$$
\begin{array}{ccc}
 & & \text{CH}_3 \\
 & & \diagup \\
\text{H}_3\text{C} & \times & \text{Hg} \\
\bullet & & \bullet \\
\text{H} & \times & \text{Cl}
\end{array}
$$

Figure 3-29   Transition state as in Figure 3-27 constructed with one-electron bonds

[51] J. W. Linnett, *J. Am. Chem. Soc.*, 83:2643 (1961).

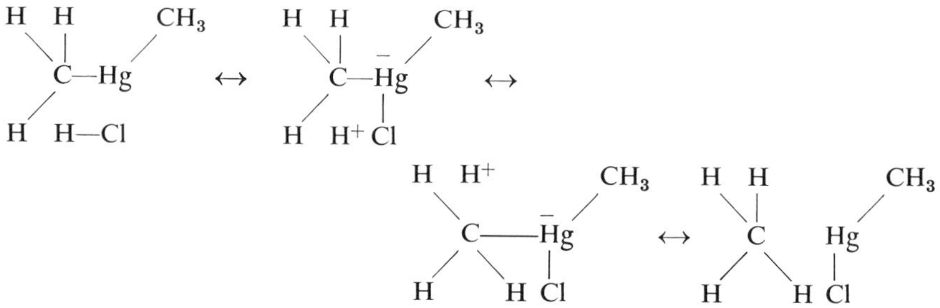

Figure 3-30 Resonance forms of the transition state of Figure 3-27

From the available data it appears unlikely that a single mechanism will be found to hold for all acid cleavage reactions. Clear pictures of the details await combined studies of the kinetics, products, and stereochemistry of individual reactions.

4

HALOGEN AND FREE RADICAL
CLEAVAGES OF MERCURIALS

4-1 Halogen Cleavage of Mercurials

One of the problems presented by a study of electrophilic substitution is the limited number of easily accessible electrophiles (discounting the surfeit of proton sources). The positive or potentially positive halogen ion represents a valuable class of electrophilic agents which can be generated under a variety of conditions. The reaction of dialkylmercurials with the halogens[1] was examined shortly after the discovery of this class of organometallics, and the general course was established (Figure 4-1).

$$R_2Hg + X_2 \rightarrow RX + RHgX$$

Figure 4-1 Halogen cleavage of dialkylmercurials

The isolation of the alkylmercuric halide has been regarded as demonstrating that, as with the protic acid cleavage, the second carbon-mercury bond is broken less readily than the first (Figure 4-2). In fact, these results have no

$$RHgX + X_2 \rightarrow RX + HgX_2$$

Figure 4-2 Halogen cleavage of alkylmercuric salts

bearing on the relative rates of reaction shown in Figures 4-1 and 4-2. It is well known that dialkylmercury compounds are rapidly cleaved by mercuric salts (Figure 4-3); therefore, the same products would be obtained with stoichiometric quantities of mercurial and halogen even if the reaction of

$$R_2Hg + HgX_2 \rightarrow 2RHgX$$

Figure 4-3 Mercuric halide cleavage of dialkylmercurials

[1] F. C. Whitmore, "Organic Compounds of Mercury," Reinhold Publishing Corporation, New York, 1921, has reviewed the early work in this field.

halogen with alkylmercuric halide were much faster than the initial cleavage of dialkylmercurial.

Considerable variation in reactivity has been noted depending on the halogen and other reaction conditions employed, but these differences have not been put on a quantitative basis (reference 1). To date, no comprehensive study of the halogen cleavage reaction has been published. Most of the pertinent literature deals with isolated examples, and consequently this reaction remains one of the least understood of the organomercurial cleavage processes.

One may well question consideration of the scission by halogen of the carbon-metal bond as an electrophilic substitution reaction. In fact, many of the early studies probably involved free-radical intermediates, and the suppression of this path has been a major problem faced by later workers.

In addition to detecting the intervention of radical reactions, kinetic-order determinations are important, since the symmetrization process (Sec. 6-1) may occur if metal-complexing agents are present (Figure 4-4). The

$$2RHgI + 2I^- \rightarrow RHgR + HgI_4^-$$

Figure 4-4 Symmetrization by complex ion formation

existence of this equilibrium has been demonstrated by Whitmore and Sobatzki for a variety of arylmercuric iodides and for benzylmercuric iodides with sodium or potassium iodide in ethanol solution.[2] However, these workers were unable to show the existence of the equilibrium for cyclohexyl- or phenylethylmercuric iodides even in the presence of a large excess of iodide ion. It was found that in refluxing solution the arylmercuric halide often predominates, but on cooling the less soluble diarylmercurial precipitates, illustrating the ease with which equilibrium is attained with many of these systems.

In general, the equilibria appear to be rapidly established for bromomercuri groups on aromatic rings, benzyl positions, and active methylene groups (ketones and esters). There is no evidence that dialkylmercury compound is formed when any simple, saturated aliphatic mercuric salt is treated with iodide ion or with other complexing agents. (Dialkylmercury compounds are readily prepared by reduction of alkylmercuric salts.) Nevertheless, if the dialkylmercury compounds possess the same higher degree of reactivity in the halogen cleavage as observed in the reaction with protic acids (Sec. 3-4), trace amounts formed in rapid equilibrium could account for the major portion of the product. In a kinetic study of electrophilic cleavage by halogen, the possible more rapid scission of the dialkyl material could result in a third-order reaction which is bimolecular in the alkylmercuric halide and which is inhibited by mercuric halide. An order intermediate between second and

[2] F. C. Whitmore and R. J. Sobatzki, *J. Am. Chem. Soc.*, **55**:1128 (1933).

third may also be found, depending on the position of equilibrium and the relative cleavage rates of the two mercurials.

4-2 Homolytic Halogen Cleavage of Mercurials

Although discussion of free-radical reactions of mercurials is outside the intended scope of this book, the frequent competition of radical and electrophilic cleavages in many systems makes it desirable to include the details of several homolysis reactions.

The interplay of radical and polar cleavages of mercurials was first noted by Keller,[3] who observed that the rate of reaction of alkylmercuric iodides with iodine in dioxane is sensitive to light and peroxides, and is strongly retarded by oxygen. This reaction is approximately second-order in iodine and independent of alkylmercuric iodide concentration, with a rate $= k[I_2]^2$. The exact dependence of oxygen was not determined, but the rate was roughly inversely proportional to its concentration.

Reutov and coworkers[4] obtained evidence indicating the occurrence of homolytic iodine cleavage of benzylmercuric bromide and ethyl α-bromomercuriphenylacetate. In the absence of added cadmium iodide, the reaction is instantaneous with the benzyl compound, while the α-phenylacetate reacts at a measurable rate.[5] For the latter, first-order kinetics in halogen and zero-order in organometallic were established. Although there is some question regarding the order in halogen, both this work and the work of Keller (reference 3) are in agreement that the rate for the radical reaction is independent of the concentration of mercurial.

Further evidence supporting a radical pathway was obtained by Jensen and Gale.[6] The geometrical isomers *cis*- and *trans*-4-methylcyclohexylmercuric bromide were prepared and subjected to a variety of halogen scission conditions, the results of which are discussed in detail in Sec. 4-3. Depending on conditions, complete loss of configuration or intermediate stereospecificity results. The degree of loss of configuration depends markedly on the atmosphere in the vessel, the reaction being more stereospecific in the presence of oxygen. In nonpolar solvents such as carbon tetrachloride or carbon disulfide,

---

[3] J. Keller, doctoral dissertation, University of California, Los Angeles, 1948, as quoted by S. Winstein and T. G. Traylor, *J. Am. Chem. Soc.*, **78**:2596 (1956).

[4] a. O. A. Reutov and I. P. Beletskaya, *Bull. Acad. Sci., USSR, Div. Chem. Sci.*, 1958 (1960).

b. I. P. Beletskaya, O. A. Reutov, and T. P. Guryanova, *ibid.*, 1463 (1961).

c. *Ibid.*, p. 1863.

[5] This radical reaction was described in the English translation as occurring by a photochemical process, but specific conditions were not included in the paper.

[6] a. F. R. Jensen and L. H. Gale, *J. Am. Chem. Soc.*, **81**:1261 (1959).

b. *Ibid.*, **82**:145, 148 (1960).

the identical isomeric mixtures of 52.6% *trans*- and 47.4% *cis*-4-methyl-cyclohexyl bromides are obtained from either *cis*- or *trans*-4-methylcyclo-hexylmercuric bromide. This loss of configuration and low selectivity, i.e., about statistical distribution of products, indicates the intervention of a common, reactive intermediate such as a free radical. More importantly, a closely similar distribution of products (50 ± 2% *trans*) is obtained from the corresponding carboxylic acids in the Hunsdiecker reaction,[7] which is generally regarded as occurring with intervention of radical intermediates.[8]

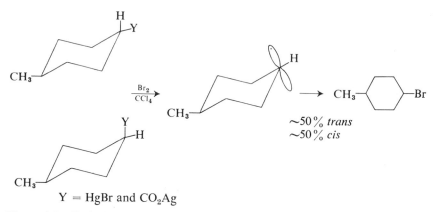

Y = HgBr and CO₂Ag

Figure 4-5 Similarity of the Hunsdiecker reaction and the homolytic cleavage of mercurials

It is reasonable to expect that the transition state for the reaction of an alkyl radical with halogen occurs early along the reaction coordinate, i.e., with little bond making, at appreciable C—Br distance and with small disturbance of the structure of the radical.[9] Product stabilities should therefore have small influence on transition state stabilities. However, when the product distributions are about 50:50, relatively small reflected energies can have an appreciable influence on the product ratio.

It is interesting to note that very similar product distributions are obtained

[7] F. R. Jensen and L. H. Gale, unpublished results.

[8] C. V. Wilson, *Org. Reactions*, **9**:332 (1957).

[9] For the corresponding Hunsiecker reactions with *cis*- and *trans*-4-*t*-butylcyclohexane-carboxylic acids, E. L. Eliel and R. V. Acharya, *J. Org. Chem.*, **24**:151 (1959), have reported distributions of products from 57 to 68% *trans*- and 43 to 32% *cis*-alkylhalides. These results were interpreted on the assumption that the product determining step has an appreciable activation energy, so that product stabilities will influence the transition states. However, the reactions were carried out in refluxing carbon tetrachloride, conditions where some isomerization of product was observed by Eliel and Acharya. These reactions have been repeated at low temperature (0 to 25°) under nonisomerizing conditions and *cis*-4-*t*-butylcyclohexyl bromide was obtained in at least 50% yield from each isomer (unpublished results of F. R. Jensen and J. Rodgers).

from "radical" cleavages of *cis-* and *trans-*4-methylcyclohexylmercuric salts by various halogens (Table 4-1).[10] In the radical intermediates from these compounds, the conformational preference of methyl is sufficiently large (about 1.8 kcal/mole) that this group will be largely equatorial. It is to be expected that the product distributions will be very similar

Table 4-1 Product distributions from radical
cleavages of mercurials by halogens

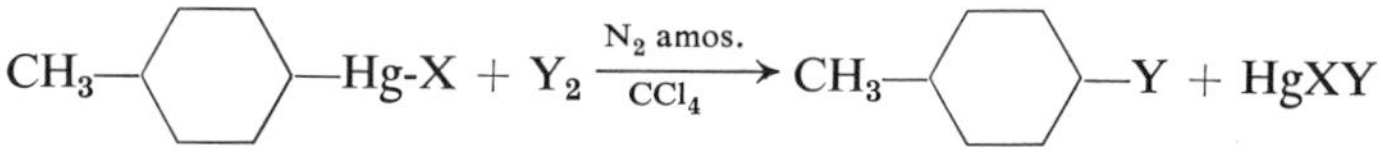

$$CH_3-\langle\ \rangle-Hg\text{-}X + Y_2 \xrightarrow[CCl_4]{N_2 \text{ amos.}} CH_3-\langle\ \rangle-Y + HgXY$$

Isomer	X	Y_2	% *trans*-RY
cis or trans	Cl	Cl_2	$49 \pm 2\%$
cis or trans	Br	Br_2	$52.6 \pm 1\%$
cis or trans	I	I_2	$50.5 \pm 1\%$
trans	Cl	I_2	$50.3 \pm 1\%$
trans	OAc	Br_2	$52 \pm 1\%$

for the 4-*t*–butylcyclohexyl compounds wherein the *t*-butyl group almost entirely assumes the equatorial position. Cleavage of *cis-* or *trans-*4-*t*- butyl-cyclohexylmercuric bromide by bromine in carbon tetrachloride solutions yield $50 \pm 2\%$ of each alkyl halide.[11]

In contrast to the above results, Greene and his coworkers[12] have reported that decomposition of dimethyl-(*trans-*4-*t*-butylcyclohexyl)-carbinyl hypo-chlorite in carbon tetrachloride solution yields, in addition to acetone, *cis-* (67%) and *trans-* (33%) 4-*t*-butylcyclohexyl chloride (Figure 4-6). Identical results are obtained starting with the cis-isomer.

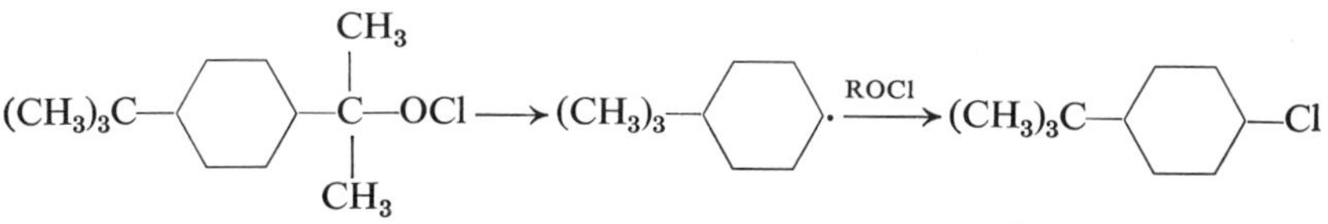

$$(CH_3)_3C-\langle\ \rangle-\overset{\overset{\displaystyle CH_3}{|}}{\underset{\underset{\displaystyle CH_3}{|}}{C}}-OCl \longrightarrow (CH_3)_3-\langle\ \rangle\cdot \xrightarrow{ROCl} (CH_3)_3C-\langle\ \rangle-Cl$$

67% *cis*
33% *trans*
+ R· + acetone

Figure 4-6 Stereochemistry of the reaction of the 4-*t*-butylcyclohexyl radical with hypochlorites

[10] F. R. Jensen and J. Miller, unpublished results.
[11] F. R. Jensen and J. Rodgers, unpublished results.
[12] a. F. D. Greene, C. Chu, and J. Walia, *J. Am. Chem. Soc.*, **84:**2463 (1962).
  b. *Ibid., J. Org. Chem.*, **29:**1285 (1964).

At the present time there seems to be no reason to question that the cleavage of mercurials cited above, the Hunsdiecker reaction and the decomposition of hypochlorites all involve radical intermediates. Assuming that the various forms the radical may take are identical from each isomer or interconvert rapidly, the differences may lie in the step in which the radical reacts with the halogenating agent. Perhaps the reaction of the radical with the hypochlorite occurs with less bond making and earlier along the reaction coordinate, since the trans-isomer is thermodynamically favored over the cis.[13] Alkyl radicals have been shown to be planar or nearly planar,[14] but deviations from planarity may be sufficient to result in higher "axial" electron density and consequently preferred attack from this direction in reactions which have neglible activation energies. Further research is necessary to understand the product distributions in reactions of this type.

It is possible to envision a number of mechanisms for homolytic cleavage of organomercurials. Indeed, it would not be unreasonable to expect that a radical reaction could give retention of configuration. To date, however, there is no conclusive demonstration of the occurrence of such a pathway.

No detailed information with regard to chain initiation is currently available. The radical reaction appears to occur rapidly in the dark; however, no kinetic data are available regarding the influence of light on the reaction rate. The kinetic investigations in which the rates were found to be independent of mercurial concentration indicate the initial step of the reaction is homolytic scission of halogen. At least part of the reaction may be self-initiating according to the scheme in Figure 4-7.

$$RHgX + X_2 \rightarrow R\cdot + HgX_2 + X\cdot$$

Figure 4-7 Possible chain-initiating step for the cleavage of mercurials by halogen-free radicals

For the chain-propagating steps, it is necessary that loss of configuration occurs during the course of the reaction. A reasonable scheme is shown in Figure 4-8. The electron deficient species $[RHgX_2]\cdot$ is included as a possible

$$R\cdot + X_2 \rightarrow RX + X\cdot$$
$$X\cdot + RHgX \rightleftharpoons [RHgX_2]\cdot$$
$$[RHgX_2]\cdot \rightarrow R\cdot + HgX_2$$

Figure 4-8 Chain propagation

[13] a. A. J. Berlin and F. R. Jensen, *Chem. & Ind.*, 998 (1960).

  b. L. W. Reeves and K. O. Strømme, *Can. J. Chem.*, **38**:1241 (1960).

[14] a. T. Cole, H. O. Pritchard, N. R. Davidson, and H. M. McConnell, *Mol. Phys.*, **1**:406 (1958).

  b. S. Ogawa and R. W. Fessenden, *J. Chem. Phys.*, **41**: 994 (1964).

intermediate in the reaction, although there is no direct evidence in support of its existence. It is included because the reversible formation of such an intermediate could account for the racemization, or interconversion, of mercurials by alkyl or aryl radicals.[15,16]

$$R\cdot + R^*HgX \rightleftharpoons [RR^*HgX]\cdot \rightleftharpoons R\cdot + RHgX$$

Figure 4-9   Possible mode of radical-catalyzed
interconversion of mercurials

Figure 4-10 contains a possible chain-propagating step for radical reaction of mercurials which could lead to a stereospecific cleavage (either inversion or retention of configuration).

$$Y\cdot + RHgX \rightarrow R{-}Y + \cdot HgX$$
$$\cdot HgX + YZ \rightarrow HgXZ + Y\cdot$$

Figure 4-10   Possible stereospecific radical
cleavage of mercurials

From consideration of bond energies[17] for the stereochemistry-controlling steps of Figures 4-8 and 4-10, it can be seen that there is not a substantial energy favoring the former reaction sequence. The energy differences for the two pathways with the various halogens are presented in Figure 4-11. Since both ΔH_A and ΔH_B are positive, a negative difference is taken to indicate a preference for reaction A. With the chlorine radical ($Cl\cdot$) the difference is

$$(A) \qquad X\cdot + RHgCl \rightarrow R\cdot + XHgCl$$
$$(B) \qquad X\cdot + RHgCl \rightarrow RX + \cdot HgCl$$
$$\Delta H_A - \Delta H_B = -D(X{-}HgCl) + D(R{-}X)$$

$$\Delta H_A - \Delta H_B \cong \begin{cases} 0 & \text{for } X = Cl \\ -5 \text{ kcal/mole} & \text{for } X = Br \\ -12 \text{ kcal/mole} & \text{for } X = I \end{cases}$$

Figure 4-11   Preference of halogen radicals
for reaction at carbon or mercury

[15] F. R. Jensen and L. H. Gale, *J. Am. Chem. Soc.*, **81**:6337 (1959); see also R. E. Rebbert and P. Ausloos, *ibid.*, **85**:3086 (1963), **86**:2068 (1964).

[16] For the reactions listed in Table 4-1, racemization of starting material has been shown not to occur in the bromine cleavage of the alkylmercuric acetates. Unchanged starting material was also recovered from the cleavage of the chloride by chlorine, but this result is not necessarily significant, since the alkylmercuric halides were only partially soluble under the reaction conditions.

[17] T. L. Cottrell, "The Strengths of Chemical Bonds," Butterworth Scientific Publications, London, 1958.

approximately zero. For this reagent one might expect reaction by both pathways, but path *A* must predominate since the same distribution of chlorides is obtained from both *cis-* and *trans-*4-methylcyclohexylmercuric chlorides.

4-3 Kinetic Evidence for Polar Halogen Cleavage of Mercurials

In his investigation of the cleavage of mercurials by iodine, Keller (reference 3) found that in the presence of iodide ion (excess lithium iodide in 90% aqueous dioxane was used) the radical reaction was suppressed and a study of electrophilic cleavage was feasible. This latter reaction was shown to be first-order in mercurial and first-order in triiodide ion. Except with compounds which react very slowly, the radical reaction does not compete appreciably when triiodide ion is used as the cleavage agent.

Using this method, the rate sequence (25°) was established for the alkyl-mercuric iodide series: neophyl, 1; *n*-butyl, 115; *sec*-butyl, 807; phenyl, 1.34×10^5. The substituent order and magnitude of rate differences are very similar to those found for the protic acid cleavage reaction of the corresponding disubstituted mercurials, suggesting a similarity in mechanism.

A related kinetic investigation by Reutov and coworkers (reference 4) also revealed the intervention of a polar reaction in the presence of iodide ion. As noted previously, the radical-iodine cleavage of benzylmercuric bromide occurs instantly, while ethyl α-bromomercuriphenylacetate reacts slowly. However, electrophilic scission in the presence of excess cadmium iodide shows the opposite structural dependence. The ester reacts instantaneously, in keeping with the very facile acid cleavage of α-carbonylmercurials, while benzylmercuric bromide obeys measurable second-order kinetics.

	Nature of scission	
	Radical	*Electrophilic*
⬡—CH₂HgBr	Instantaneous	Rate $= k_2[I_3^-][RHgBr]$
⬡—CH—CO₂C₂H₅ ∣ HgBr	Rate $= k_2[I_2]$	Instantaneous

Figure 4-12 Dependence of structure on relative rate of radical and electrophilic cleavage by iodine

α-Halomercuri esters in general readily undergo the symmetrization reaction (Figure 4-4) when treated with iodide ion. Reutov and coworkers (reference 4) claimed to have circumvented this difficulty by avoiding the use of Group I metal halides; cadmium iodide was reported to not cause symmetrization because of the low concentration of free iodide ion in its solutions.

As indicated in Sec. 4-1, the intervention of the symmetrization reaction would probably lead to a kinetic behavior other than first-order in the alkylmercuric halide. It is probable that both alkylmercuric bromides and alkylmercuric iodides are involved in this cleavage study due to halide exchange between the starting mercurial and iodide ion in solution, but this aspect was not discussed by Reutov and coworkers. In general, a large excess of cadmium iodide was used in these kinetic studies.

The rate of electrophilic cleavage was examined in four media: methanol > 70% aqueous dioxane > ethanol > dimethylformamide. The rate variation was rather small, with a factor of approximately four between the two extremes at 20° (reference 4c). Large variations in activation parameters were noted, with a linear, compensating relationship between enthalpy and entropy. Complex formation between solvent and organomercurial was suggested to account for this behavior.

Table 4-2   Activation parameters for the iodine-cadmium
iodide cleavage of benzylmercuric bromide

Solvents	E_{act}, kcal/mole	$\Delta S^{\ddagger}$, eu
Methanol	9.6	−26.0
70% Aq. Dioxane	10.8	−23.3
Ethanol	11.6	−19.6
Dimethylformamide	15.3	−7.8

Although α-bromomercuriphenylacetate underwent reaction with iodine (in the presence of cadmium iodide) in polar solvents at rates too fast to measure, a kinetic study has been accomplished in toluene containing 1.5% methanol.[18] The second-order rate constants for various compounds with substituents in the aromatic ring are shown in Table 4-3; the Hammett equation was obeyed, with $\rho = 2.3$.

The rate-enhancing effects of electron withdrawing substituents lead to the conclusion that considerable carbanionic character is developed in this cleavage reaction.

Although benzylmercuric halide was reported to undergo free-radical cleavage by halogen in nonpolar solvents, Reutov has shown that small amounts of oxygen-containing additives (e.g., water, alcohols, and esters in concentrations comparable to those of the reagents used) changed the kinetic behavior such that the reaction became first-order in bromine and first-order in benzylmercuric chloride. Furthermore, the rate was no longer affected by illumination. The second-order rate constant with a variety of additives

[18] G. A. Artamkina, I. P. Beletskaya, and O. A. Reutov, *Proc. Acad. Sci. USSR, Chem. Sect.*, 939 (1963); the methanol was needed to solubilize the cadmium iodide.

Table 4-3   Rates of iodine-cadium iodide
cleavage of some substituted ethyl
α-bromomercuriphenylacetates

Substituent	k_2 (liters/mole-sec)
p-NO_2	615 (calcd.)
p-Br	79
p-Cl	33.5
p-F	14
H	10.1
m-CH_3	7
p-isoC_3H_7	4
p-t-C_4H_9	3.5

within a homologous series was shown to be proportional to the dielectric constant of the added material. Reutov has suggested[19] that the attacking reagent under these conditions is a complex of bromine with the oxygen-containing molecule.

The cleavage of substituted benzylmercuric chlorides by iodine and cadmium iodide has been studied in both methanol and dimethylformamide solvents.[20] The results are shown in Table 4-4. In methanol, the p-nitro

Table 4-4   Rates of cleavage of substituted
benzylmercuric chlorides by iodine-cadmium
iodide (20°)

Substitutent	k (liters/mole-sec)	
	Methanol	DMF
p-OCH_3	8.33	2.78
p-CH_3	1.93	0.51
m-CH_3	0.83	0.23
o-CH_3	1.75	0.45
p-F	0.84	0.19
m-F	0.42	0.12
o-F	0.22	0.08
H	0.75	0.25
p-Cl	0.71	0.16
o-Cl	0.23	0.08
m-Br	0.46	0.12

[19] I. P. Beletskaya, T. A. Azizyan, and O. A. Reutov, *Bull. Acad. Sci., USSR, Div. Chem. Sci.*, 1208 (1963).

[20] I. P. Beletskaya, T. P. Fetisova, and O. A. Reutov, *Proc. Acad. Sci., USSR, Chem. Sect.* **55**:347 (1964).

compound reportedly was cleaved at a rate too rapid to measure. Clearly, no linear free-energy relationship holds in this reaction, in which both electron withdrawing and electron donating groups, e.g., methyl, cause a rate enhancement relative to the unsubstituted compound. Activation parameters were determined for the reaction in dimethylformamide solution. It was found that the various substituents caused essentially no change in activation energy; the rate differences are associated with changes in the entropy of activation. Differences in solvation of the ground and transition states may well account for the observed effects. It also appears from the relatively large rate enhancement caused by the *p*-nitro substituent that a gradual mechanistic change may be involved, with more carbanionic character in the transition states substituted in such manner to best disperse this charge.

In a more recent study, Reutov and his coworkers[21] have examined the effect of iodide concentration on the rate of cleavage of phenylmercuric chloride by iodine in methanol. At low levels, cadmium iodide, sodium iodide,

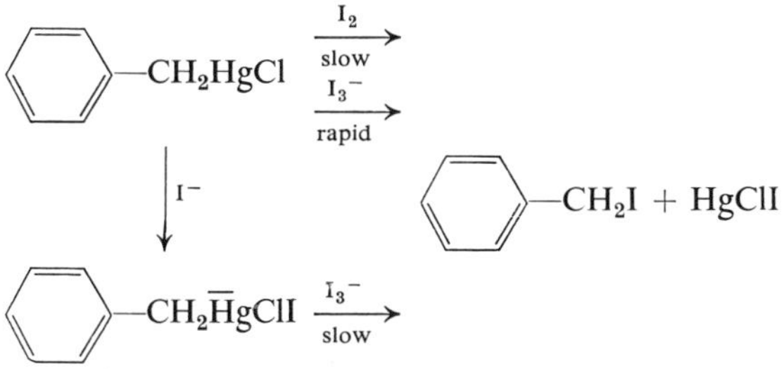

Figure 4-13 Effect of various concentrations of iodide on the rate of cleavage of benzylmercuric chloride

and tetrabutylammonium iodide caused an increase in the rate of cleavage. Reutov has concluded, in agreement with earlier workers (reference 3), that the reactive species under these conditions is the triiodide ion. Large excesses of these salts (except cadmium iodide) caused the rate to decrease, leading to the proposed scheme outlined in Figure 4-13. Thus, subsequent to complexing the available iodine (as triiodide), formation of the trivalent mercurial complex should occur. Although normally this species would be very susceptible to electrophilic attack, the absence of uncharged electrophile was postulated to lead to rate depression. Lack of a similar rate-lowering effect with a large excess of cadmium iodide may be ascribed simply to a low dissociation constant for this salt. In fact, cadmium iodide itself may compete effectively with the mercurial for free-iodide ion, as expressed in the equilibrium shown in Figure 4-14.

[21] I. P. Beletskaya, T. P. Fetisova, and O. A. Reutov, *Dokl. Akad. Nauk SSSR*, **166**:681 (1966).

$$RH\overline{g}I_2 + CdI_2 \rightleftharpoons RHgI + CdI_3^-$$

Figure 4-14   Postulated competition for
iodide ion by a mercurial and cadmium
iodide

The work of Beletskaya, Ermanson, and Reutov[22] allows some interesting
comparisons of the rates of cleavage of phenylmercuric bromide by iodine
and by bromine (Table 4-5). These second-order reactions were carried out in
the presence of an excess of cadmium iodide or ammonium bromide with the
corresponding halogen. The rate constants are similar in magnitude for both
reactants, with the iodine cleavage being somewhat faster in DMF and

Table 4-5   Solvent effects and activation parameters for the cleavage of phenylmercuric bromide by bromine and iodine (20°)

Solvent	Halogen	k_2 (liters/mole-sec)	E_{act} (kcal/mole)	$\Delta S^{\ddagger}$ (eu)
dimethylformamide	I_2	20.2	9.8	-20
80% aq. dioxane	I_2	78.0	11.2	-14
methanol	I_2	148.1	11.1	-13
dimethylformamide	Br_2	4.22	13.4	-12
80% aq. dioxane	Br_2	89.4	14.0	-3
methanol	Br_2	129.9	8.2	-22

methanol, and slightly slower in 80% aqueous dioxane. The effect of solvent
on rate was comparable to that observed previously for alkylmercuric halide
cleavages.

First-order (in halogen) kinetics have been reported (reference 22) for the
iodine and bromine cleavage of phenylmercuric bromide in benzene solutions.
Although the reaction was described as being light-catalyzed, no evidence was
presented regarding the rate in the absence of illumination.

4-4   Stereochemistry of Electrophilic Halogen Cleavage of Mercurials

Winstein and Traylor[23] have determined the rate of cleavage of 4-cam-
phylmercuric iodide, in which scission can only occur with retention of configuration. They found that it was intermediate in reactivity between the
rates determined by Keller (reference 3) for n-butyl- and neophylmercuric
iodides. These results show that electrophilic cleavage by iodine *can* occur

[22] I. P. Beletskaya, A. V. Ermanson, and O. A. Reutov, *Bull. Acad. Sci. USSR, Div.
Chem. Sci.*, 218 (1965).
[23] S. Winstein and T. G. Traylor, *J. Am. Chem. Soc.*, **78**:2597 (1956).

with retention of configuration. In carrying out this study with camphyl-mercuric iodide, it was found to be exceedingly difficult to control the radical reaction, as evidenced by erratic kinetic behavior. At very low triiodide concentration under an oxygen atmosphere, satisfactory second-order behavior, first-order in mercurial and first-order in triiodide, was displayed.

A stereochemical study of the triiodide reaction under the conditions used by Winstein and Traylor has been carried out with *trans*-4-methylcyclo-hexylmercuric iodide (reference 11). This work indicated 20% loss of configuration,[24] but kinetic studies were not carried out simultaneously.

Table 4-6 Effect of solvent and atmosphere on the stereochemistry of bromine cleavage of *cis*- and *trans*-4-methylcyclohexylmercuric bromides (reference 6)

Isomer	Solvent	Atmosphere	% retention[a]
trans	CCl_4	N_2	0
trans	CS_2	N_2	0
cis	CCl_4	N_2	8
trans	$CS_2(1\% \text{ EtOH})$	N_2	0
trans	AcOH	N_2	18
cis	AcOH	N_2	11
trans	$CHCl_3(0.75\% \text{ EtOH})$	N_2	31
trans	CS_2	air	0
trans	AcOH	air	80
trans	CH_3OH	air	85
trans	$CHCl_3(0.75\% \text{ EtOH})$	air	92

[a] Calculated on the basis that loss of configuration gives the products obtained in the free-radical reaction, 47.5% *cis* and 52.5% *trans*.

Jensen and Gale (reference 6) established that retention of configuration is the normal course of electrophilic cleavage of the carbon-mercury bond by bromine. The geometrical isomers *cis*- and *trans*-4-methylcyclohexylmercuric bromide were prepared and subjected to a wide variety of halogen scission conditions. Competing radical cleavage was reduced or completely suppressed either by using a more positive bromine source than the halogen itself or by allowing the reaction to proceed in the presence of oxygen. Table 4-6 shows the important effects of solvent and atmosphere on the stereochemistry of cleavage by bromine. Table 4-7 lists the various brominating agents used in this study.

The most striking generalization that can be drawn from these data is that, while retention appears to be the normal course for the reaction, total

[24] Corresponding to 90% *trans*-alkyl iodide, complete loss of configuration by the radical reaction gives 50% *trans*; cf. Table 4-1.

Table 4-7   Effect of brominating agent on the stereochemistry of cleavage of cis- and trans-4-methylcyclohexylmercuric bromides (reference 6)

Reagent	Solvent	Isomer	Atmosphere	% retention[a]
N,N-dibromo-benzenesulfon-amide	AcOH	trans	air	24
Hypobromous acid	50% aqueous dioxane	trans	air	90
Br_2 with $ZnBr_2$	AcOH	trans	air	92
Pyridinium bromide perbromide	AcOH	trans	air	>98
Pyridinium bromide perbromide	AcOH	trans	N_2	73
Bromine-pyridine complex	Pyridine	trans	air	100
Bromine-pyridine complex	Pyridine	trans	N_2	100
HOBr, 0.1 N H_2SO_4	50% aq. dioxane	cis	N_2	0
Br_2 with $ZnBr_2$	AcOH	cis	N_2	18
Pyridinium bromide perbromide	AcOH	cis	air	79
Pyridinium bromide perbromide	AcOH	cis	N_2	60
Bromine-pyridine complex	Pyridine	cis	air	100
Bromine-pyridine complex	Pyridine	cis	N_2	100

[a] See footnote a, Table 4-6.

stereospecificity is observed only with the bromine-pyridine complex. The various extents of isomerization found in all other cases demonstrate the extreme difficulty in suppressing the presumably free-radical mechanism.

Extending this work to include the other halogens (reference 10), it has been shown that electrophilic cleavage of cis- and trans-4-methylcyclohexyl-mercuric chloride by chlorine (complexed with pyridine) occurs stereo-specifically with retention of configuration. Iodine, with its greater tendency

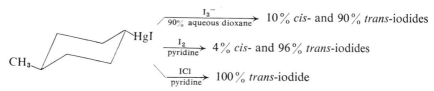

$$\xrightarrow[90\% \text{ aqueous dioxane}]{I_3^-} 10\% \text{ cis- and } 90\% \text{ trans-iodides}$$

$$\xrightarrow[\text{pyridine}]{I_2} 4\% \text{ cis- and } 96\% \text{ trans-iodides}$$

$$\xrightarrow[\text{pyridine}]{ICl} 100\% \text{ trans-iodide}$$

Figure 4-15   Cleavage by iodine and derivatives

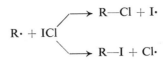

Figure 4-16   Reaction pathways for ICl

for homolysis and relatively weak complex formation with pyridine, reacts through the intermediacy of free radicals. To induce complete electrophilic scission, it is necessary to use iodine in a more electropositive form; iodine monochloride–pyridine complex, for instance, gives alkyl iodide with retention of configuration.

Iodine monochloride (uncomplexed, CCl_4 as solvent) gives an appreciable amount of alkyl chloride, as would be expected in the reaction of R· with ICl. Considerations of carbon-chlorine vs. carbon-iodine bond strengths (81 vs. 52 kcal/mole) as well as the stability of the product halogen radical lead to this conclusion. As anticipated for electrophilic cleavage, the stereospecific reaction with pyridine-complexed ICl gives only alkyl iodide as product.

It is of interest to note that *N*-iodo- and *N*-bromosuccinimide cleave *trans*-4-methylcyclohexylmercuric chloride completely stereospecifically with retention of configuration, whereas *N*-chlorosuccinimide gives 7% *cis*-chloride and 93% *trans*-chloride (reference 10). It appears that the halogens are highly polarized positively in the *N*-bromo and *N*-iodo compounds, and probably in complex formation with pyridine. Lack of such polarization would make the *N*-chloro derivative more susceptible to radical reactions.

The cleavage of organomercurials by bromine when extended to open-chain systems gives results comparable to those found with 4-methylcyclohexylmercuric bromide. Partially resolved D-(+)- and L-(−)-*sec*-butyl mercuric bromides[25] when treated with bromine in a variety of solvents[26] proved to be somewhat more prone to radical reaction than the cyclohexyl system; cleavage with bromine-pyridine complex at 0° occurred with a maximum of 86% retention (Table 4-8). Lowering the reaction temperature increased the specificity of the reaction. Thus, cleavage in pyridine at −45° gave products with a rotation essentially equivalent to that observed when the reaction was carried out at −65° in solvent composed of 70% γ-collidine, 30% pyridine. The degree of stereospecificity obtained using other solvents parallels that found for the 4-methylcyclohexylmercuric bromide systems. In general, the more polar (and more basic) the solvent, the greater the specificity. Either enhancement of the polar electrophilic cleavage, or suppression of the presumed radical pathways, or a combination of both may explain the observed solvent dependency.

[25] F. R. Jensen, L. D. Whipple, D. K. Wedegaertner, and J. A. Landgrebe, *J. Am. Chem. Soc.*, **81**:1262 (1959).

[26] F. R. Jensen, L. D. Whipple, D. K. Wedegaertner, and J. A. Landgrebe, *J. Am. Chem. Soc.*, **82**:2466 (1960).

Table 4-8 Stereochemistry of the bromine cleavage of 2-bromomercuributane in various solvents

Solvent	Temp., °C	$[\alpha]_D^{22}$, start mat.	$[\alpha]_D^{22}$, prod.	% retention
CS$_2$	25	+3.62	0	0
CS$_2$, 10% CH$_3$OH	25	+3.43	+0.24	5
CH$_2$Cl$_2$, 10% CH$_3$OH	25	+3.11	+0.4	11
CH$_2$Cl$_2$, 10% CH$_3$OH	25	−3.28	−0.51	12
pyridine	0	+3.76	+4.15	86
pyridine	−45	−4.94	−6.31	99.7
γ-collidine, 70%; pyridine, 30%	−65	−4.94	−6.33	100

Cleavage of dialkylmercury compounds by iodine (1 mol equiv.) in pyridine solution also has been shown to occur with complete retention of configuration (reference 10). Both the *trans*-4-methylcyclohexyl iodide and *trans*-4-methylcyclohexylmercuric iodide formed in this reaction are free of isomeric materials, within the limits of detection. Under identical reaction conditions, the alkylmercuric iodide gives 4% *cis*-alkyl halide (compare Figures 4-15, 4-17). This limited evidence indicates that alkylmercuric halides, compared to dialkylmercurials, have a relatively greater tendency to react by free-radical pathways. In fact, it is reasonable to expect that radicals react at about the same rate with both classes of compounds, but that electrophiles react much faster with the dialkyl compounds. By analogy with the scheme proposed for the free-radical reaction of alkylmercuric halides (Figure 4-8), it is expected that in the homolytic reaction the alkyl halide would be formed with loss of configuration and the alkylmercuric halide would have retained configuration.

The highest reported rotation for D-(+)-*sec*-butylmercuric bromide is $[\alpha]_D$ 25.8 (reference 26). Evidence is given below which indicates that this

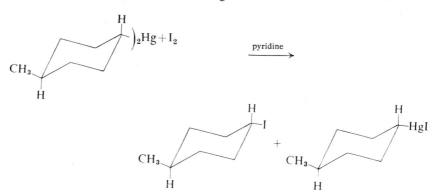

Figure 4-17 Stereochemistry of the iodine cleavage of a dialkylmercury compound

may not be the maximum rotation. Since the report of the resolution, it has become recognized that mercurials are racemized by radicals, and some racemization may have occurred during each crystallization by (small) homolytic decomposition of the mercurial.

Using the rotation relationships given in Table 4-8, D-(+)-*sec*-butylmercuric bromide, $[\alpha]_D$ 25.8, gives D-(+)-*sec*-butyl bromide, $[\alpha]_D$ 33.1. However, two larger values obtained by indirect methods have been reported for D-*sec*-butyl bromide: $[\alpha]_D^{25}$ 35.3[27] and $[\alpha]_D$ 39.4.[28] Both values purportedly represent pure isomer rotations, which illustrates the difficulty of determining this property for alkyl halides. Since the 33.1° value obtained by the mercurials is in essence a direct value it must correspond to an *absolute* lower limit.

Table 4-9   Rotational relationships for alkyl halides
from alkylmercuric halides (references 11, 21)

| D-(+)-*sec*-butylHgX | | Conditions | D-(+)-*sec*-butylX | |
X	$[\alpha]_D^{25}$ (c4,EtOH)[a]		X	$[\alpha]_D^{25}$ (neat)
Br	25.8	Br$_2$, pyridine-γ-collidine, $-65°$	Br	33.1
Cl	26.0	Br$_2$, pyridine-α-picoline, $-75°$	Br	32 6
Cl	26.0	Cl$_2$, pyridine, $-30°$	Cl	36.0
Cl	26.0	ICl, pyridine-DMF, $-10°$	I	33.4

[a] Actual conversions carried out with material of lower activity and then recalculated using the maximum reported value for sec-butylmercuric bromide (25.8°).

Table 4-9 gives the configurations and rotations for halogen cleavages. The chlorine and bromine cleavages are believed to be completely stereospecific, but there is some doubt that this is true for the reaction with iodine.[29] Using these data and the upper limit for 2-bromomercuributane calculated using Letsinger's value for 2-bromobutane (reference 27), upper limits for 2-chloromercuributane of $[\alpha]_D$ 28.2, for 2-chlorobutane of $[\alpha]_D$ 39.0,[30] and 2-iodobutane of $[\alpha]_D$ 36.2[31] are obtained.

[27] R. L. Letsinger, *J. Am. Chem. Soc.*, **70**:406 (1948).

[28] P. S. Skell, R. G. Allen, and G. Helmkamp, *J. Am. Chem. Soc.*, **82**:410 (1960).

[29] Letsinger and coworkers (reference 27) and R. L. Letsinger, L. G. Maury, and R. L. Burwell, Jr., *J. Am. Chem. Soc.*, **73**:2373 (1951), have reported upper limits for 2-chlorobutane, $[\alpha]_D$ 38.4 and 2-bromobutane, $[\alpha]_D$ 35.3. The ratio of these rotations is identical with the ratio of the rotations given in Table 4-9.

[30] In good agreement with the literature upper limit, reference 29.

[31] Maximum observed value, $[\alpha]_D^{28}$ 33.6 (neat), unpublished results of F. R. Jensen and W. N. Smith, from active 2-butanol and hydrogen iodide.

Reutov[32] and his collaborators have studied both the kinetics and the stereochemistry of the first-order (in halogen), light-catalyzed reaction of bromine with optically active *sec*-butylmercuric bromide in benzene solution. Although these authors reported that the reaction occurred with 30% retention of configuration, the low yield of product bromide (30%) and its observed rotation ($[\alpha]_D^{20}$ 0.86), as well as the fact that the rotation of starting mercurial was not stated, leave the validity of this value in question. Retention of activity, while a possible consequence of a free-radical cleavage reaction (Sec. 4-2), is not in agreement with other work using the 4-methylcyclo-hexylmercury system (Table 4-1). It appears that a reinvestigation of the *sec*-butylmercuric halide cleavage in benzene is in order.

When methanol was added to the benzene solution, a light-insensitive second-order reaction occurred, in agreement with the previously reported (reference 19) effect of small amounts of an added polar solvent on rate. Under these conditions, 80% retention of configuration was reported.[33]

4-5   Mechanisms of the Polar Cleavages by Halogens

Evidence has been presented previously for the polar cleavage of alkyl-mercuric halides by triiodide ion (Secs. 4-3 and 4-4), and by bromine, chlorine, and iodine monochloride when polarized by pyridine. Other reagents also give stereospecific or partially stereospecific reactions, but only the four reagents listed above will be discussed here.

A number of mechanistic possibilities exist and no attempt will be made to select the correct pathway for each reaction. Instead, a limited discussion will be presented in the hope that the problems illustrated will stimulate research in this area. For a general discussion and description of other types of electro-philic mechanisms which apply here, see Chap. 2.

The triiodide ion is linear; its structure can be represented by two canonical forms,[34] or by the bonding picture of Linnett involving two one-electron bonds.[35,36] In the ion, the negative charge is divided equally between the terminal atoms with a small increase in the charge density of the central atom by induction. It is reasonable to expect that, except for effects due to metal complexing, electrophilic reactions of I_3^- should be slower than similar reactions of I_2. The greater stereospecificity of the I_3^- cleavage of the

---

[32] O. A. Reutov, E. V. Uglova, I. P. Beletskaya, and T. B. Svetlanova, *Bull. Acad. Sci. USSR, Div. Chem. Sci.*, 1297 (1964).

[33] The value $[\alpha]_D^{20}$ 39.4 was used as the rotation of optically pure 2-bromobutane, al-though no reference to its derivation was given. As in the homolytic reaction, the rotation of starting material was not reported.

[34] G. C. Pimental, *J. Phys. Chem.*, **19**:446 (1951).

[35] J. W. Linnett, *J. Am. Chem. Soc.*, **83**:2643 (1961).

[36] Alternate structures which utilize *d*-orbitals have been proposed, but the available evidence supports the structures shown in Figure 4-18.

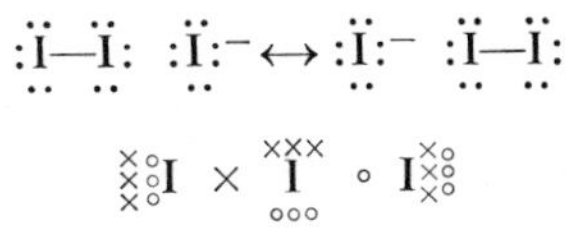

$$\ddot{\mathrm{I}}{-}\ddot{\mathrm{I}}: \quad :\ddot{\mathrm{I}}:^- \leftrightarrow :\ddot{\mathrm{I}}:^- \quad :\ddot{\mathrm{I}}{-}\ddot{\mathrm{I}}:$$

Figure 4-18 Alternate but equivalent
pictures of the structure of the
triiodide ion

alkylmercuric halide could thus result from an even greater decrease in reactivity of I_3^- as compared to I_2 in radical reactions.

From the reported data the triiodide reaction appears to be independent of the concentration of (excess) added iodide ion[37] (reference 3). Since the rate $= k[I_3^-][RHgI]$, it is possible that the reactive materials are either the triiodide ion acting as a unit or the iodide ion and iodine (formed in small equilibrium concentration) acting individually but simultaneously. Excess iodide ion would have no influence on this latter pathway, since it would suppress the concentration of free iodine by a factor equivalent to the rate acceleration provided by the excess free iodide ion. In contrast to the mercurial results, the cleavage of tetraalkyltin compounds by bromine is not assisted by excess bromide ion.[38] This reaction has been studied in detail, and even though Br_3^- is the predominant species in solution, no evidence was found to indicate that it serves as an electrophilic cleaving agent. Rather, the small equilibrium concentration of bromine reacts to yield alkyl halide in a second-order process.

Winstein and Traylor have pictured the iodine cleavage as occurring through separate action of iodide ion and iodine and have labelled the process as $S_E i$. In the original paper, only the transition state was shown and the additional steps are presumed from context.

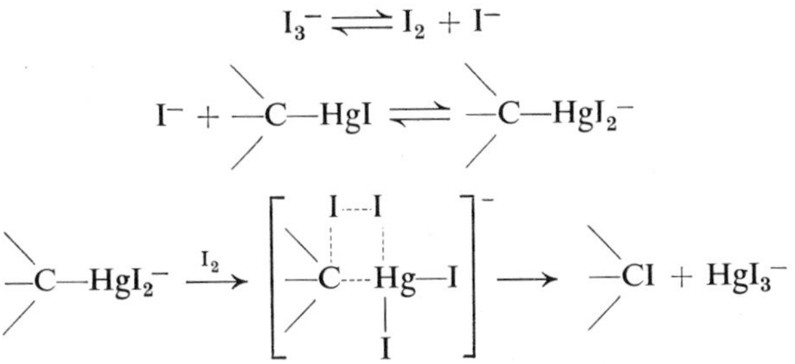

$$I_3^- \rightleftharpoons I_2 + I^-$$

$$I^- + {-}\overset{\textstyle |}{\underset{\textstyle |}{C}}{-}HgI \rightleftharpoons {-}\overset{\textstyle |}{\underset{\textstyle |}{C}}{-}HgI_2^-$$

$$-\overset{\textstyle |}{\underset{\textstyle |}{C}}{-}HgI_2^- \xrightarrow{I_2} \left[\begin{array}{c} I{\cdots}I \\ -\overset{\textstyle |}{\underset{\textstyle |}{C}}{\cdots}Hg{-}I \\ I \end{array} \right]^- \longrightarrow -\overset{\textstyle |}{\underset{\textstyle |}{C}}I + HgI_3^-$$

Figure 4-19 Four-center reaction with
activation by complex formation

[37] However, Reutov (reference 21) has reported rate depression by a large excess of iodide in the cleavage of phenylmercuric chloride.

[38] M. Gielem and J. Nasielski, *Bull. Soc. Chim. Belges.*, **71**:601 (1962).

It is important to note that inhibition of the radical reaction would occur not only because of $RHgI_2^-$ formation, but also because the radical reaction may in some cases have a higher-order dependence in iodine (reference 3).

While complex formation between iodide and iodine should lead to a weaker electrophile, the complex formed between iodide and alkylmercuric iodide, $RHgI_2^-$, is expected to have greatly enhanced reactivity towards electrophiles.

A somewhat simpler but equally attractive four-center mechanism would result by direct reaction of triiodide ion and alkylmercuric iodide. Since the central halogen atom bears the smallest charge (see Figure 4-18), it is presumed to be the atom that attacks carbon. However, an alternate mechanism involving a five-atom cyclic transition state is possible. Although the triiodide

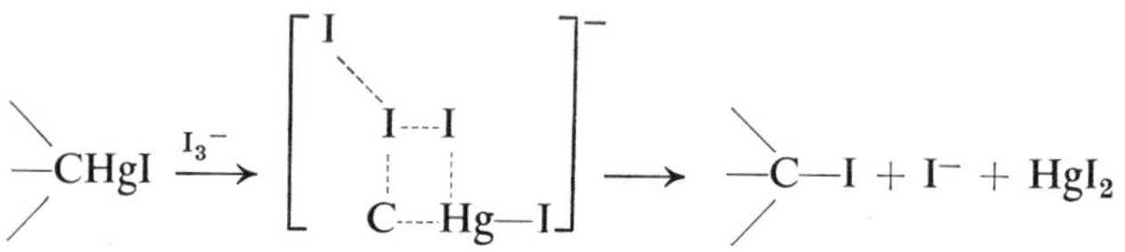

Figure 4-20 Four-center mechanism in which triiodide ion acts as a unit

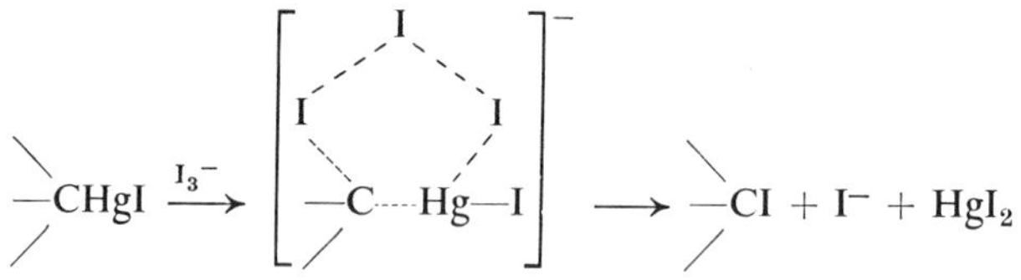

Figure 4-21 Five-atom transition state

ion is linear, it must become bent in the transition state. This may be feasible provided the orbitals on iodine and mercury are not too rigidly oriented; however, the required distortion appears to be so severe that reaction by this mechanism is unlikely.

The S_E2 process (cf. Chap. 2) for attack of electrophile on either $RHgI$ or $RHgI_2^-$ is another mechanism which cannot be discounted by the available data.

Hassel and coworkers[39] have examined the structures of a number of amine-halogen 1:1 compounds by x-ray analysis and in each instance, the crystalline compounds were shown to possess a linear structure with a lengthened halogen-halogen bond. The bond lengths of pyridine·ICl are N-I, 2.26 Å, I-Cl, 2.51 Å, whereas the normal bond length of ICl is 2.32 Å. The compounds, therefore, probably have structures analogous to I_3^-,

[39] For a review of this work, see O. Hassel and C. Rømming, *Quart. Rev. London*, **16**:1 (1962).

ICl_2^- and related materials. Material with the composition pyridine·$2I_2$ was found to be a mixture of an ionic compound, (pyridine)$_2I^+I_3^-$, and free I_2 in crystal form. In solution, the 1:1 compounds may exist both as complexes and in ionic forms (Figure 4-22). (An alternate structure for the complex is

$$\overset{\diagdown}{\underset{\diagup}{N}} \times \overset{\circ\circ\circ}{\underset{\circ\circ\circ}{Br}} \circ \overset{\times\times\times}{\underset{\times\times\times}{Br^\times}}.)$$ While it is anticipated that pyridine·Br^+ has a much

greater electrophilic reactivity than the undissociated complex (pyridine·Br_2), the actual rates also depend on the concentrations of the various species. It is also conceivable that the free halogen (in small equilibrium concentration)

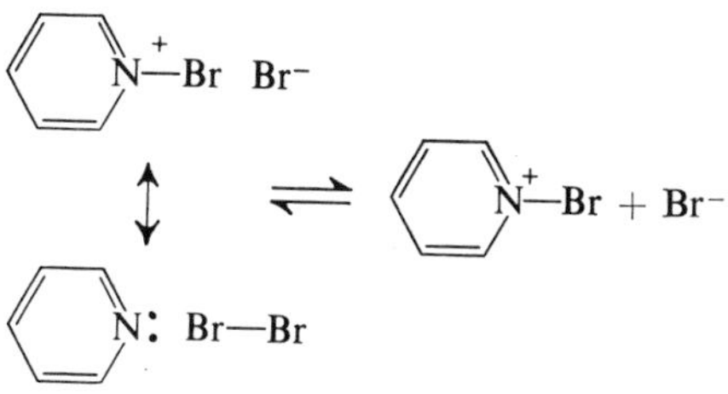

Figure 4-22   Complex and ionic forms of pyridine·Br_2

is the active reagent, and no compelling evidence is available which favors one form over another. The pyridine·X^+ offers promise as an electrophile which should undergo reaction by a "pure" S_E2 reaction. Since amines form complexes with alkylmercury compounds (but ordinarily highly reversibly) and such complex formation should both activate the mercury compounds toward electrophilic reaction and decrease their sensitivity to radical attack, it is reasonable to propose that these complexes have at least partial roles in the reactions.

Pyridine·X_2 may react by any of the possible pathways discussed previously for triiodide ion. As shown in Chap. 2, the usual depiction of a four-center reaction involves attack on carbon; in fact, in an electrophilic reaction the attack occurs more plausibly on the carbon-mercury bond. In other words, the conventional dotted line drawing of a transition state serves well where attention is focused on the action of the nucleophile, but it can be misleading where electrophilic attack is to be stressed. Orbital and conventional bond pictures of four-center electrophilic reaction of bromine on the carbon-mercury are shown in Figure 4-23. These pictures are simplified in that only atomic orbitals which participate in the reaction are included. (It should be noted that these illustrations could easily be modified to represent the reaction with the pyridine·Br_2 complex, where the pyridine is attached to the bromine which becomes bonded to carbon. The pyridine molecule would be parallel to the reaction plane.) This mechanism, like any four-center reaction, entails

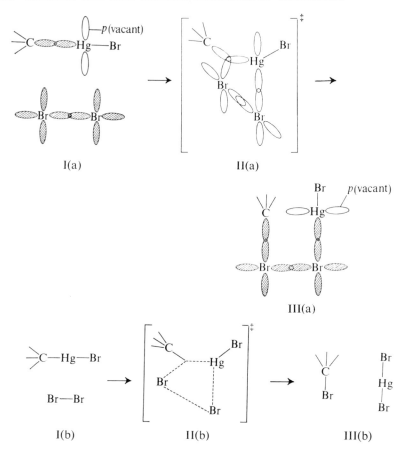

Figure 4-23 Atomic orbital and bond depictions of a four-center mechanism. Only atomic orbitals which participate in the reaction are shown

considerable movement of the atoms comprising the cycle during the course of the reaction.[40]

Of particular interest is the transition state pictured by alternate formulations II(a) and II(b). The fourth "center" is the carbon sp^3 atomic orbital. In structure II(b), this orbital is represented as a line of normal intensity, indicating that its charge density is changed primarily by electronic factors rather than the actual making and breaking of the bond.

Since halogen is highly electronegative, it is reasonable to expect that the central carbon atom bears a partial positive charge in the transition state.

[40] However, the bond angles in alkylmercuric halides need not be linear and are known to undergo changes in various solvents. H. Sawatzky and G. F. Wright, *Can. J. Chem.*, **36:**1555 (1958).

In accord with this expectation is the observation that 2-methoxycyclohexyl-mercuric bromide is recovered unchanged from bromine in warm pyridine solution, whereas cyclohexylmercuric bromide can essentially be titrated with the same reagent. Although steric factors may operate to some extent, this substantially different reactivity is more likely the result of the inductive effect of the 2-methoxyl group decreasing the electron density on the 1-carbon atom.

4-6   Other Radical Cleavages of Mercurials

The free-radical cleavage of organomercurials appears to be a very general reaction. Although often alluded to in the literature, it is one of the most poorly documented reactions of organometallics. The material presented here is limited in scope and selected to contrast with the polar cleavages. Reasonable mechanisms can be written for cleavage of mercurials by most radical sources.

Nesmeyanov and coworkers[41] have examined the benzoyl peroxide-catalyzed cleavage of organomercurials by carbon tetrachloride. The mechanism in Figure 4-24 has been postulated for this free-radical reaction.

$$(C_6H_5CO_2)_2 \rightarrow C_6H_5CO_2\cdot + C_6H_5\cdot + CO_2$$
$$C_6H_5\cdot + CCl_4 \rightarrow C_6H_5Cl + \cdot CCl_3$$
$$R - Hg - R' + \cdot CCl_3 \rightarrow RHg\cdot + RCCl_3$$
$$RHg\cdot + CCl_4 \rightarrow RHgCl + CCl_3\cdot$$

Figure 4-24   Peroxide-catalyzed cleavage
of mercurials by carbon tetrachloride

This reaction is a likely candidate of an example of a stereospecific cleavage by free radicals as discussed in Sec. 4-2.*

The reaction shows considerable selectivity when applied to unsymmetrical organomercurials (Table 4-10), and it is interesting to note similarity of this selectivity series to that found by Kharasch and coworkers for the protic acid cleavage reaction (Chap. 3). This observation, coupled with the racemization of starting material found in the acid cleavage of di-L-(—)-*sec*-butylmercury, stresses the importance of demonstrating the nature (electrophilic or radical) of any reaction involving the scission of a carbon-metal bond.

---

[41] a. A. N. Nesmeyanov, A. E. Borisov, A. I. Kovredov, and E. I. Golubeva, *Bull. Acad. Sci. USSR, Div. Chem. Sci.*, 141 (1960).

   b. *Ibid.*, 1477 (1961); c. *Ibid.*, *Tetrahedron*, **18**:683 (1962).

   * However, recent work has shown that tetrachlorides rather than trichlorides are the principal products of this reaction. Unpublished results by F. R. Jensen and H. E. Guard.

Table 4-10

$$R—Hg—R' \xrightarrow[(C_6H_5CO_2)_2]{CCl_4} R—HgCl + R'CCl_3$$

R	R'	RHgCl, %	R'CCl_3, %
C_2H_5—	C_6H_5	87	—
n-C_4H_9—	C_6H_5	76	72
$C_6H_5CH_2$—	n-C_4H_9—	73	58
n-C_4H_9—	C_2H_5—	71	20
$C_6H_5CH_2$—	C_6H_5—	73	33
cyclo-C_6H_{11}	C_6H_5—	81	43
cyclo-C_6H_{11}	n-C_4H_9—	85	61
cyclo-C_6H_{11}	$C_6H_5CH_2$—	60	42
C_6H_5—	$(CH_3)_3C_6H_5$—	94	31
α-$C_{10}H_7$—	$(CH_3)_3C_6H_5$—	73	36
C_6H_5—	α-$C_{10}H_7$	85	73
C_6H_5—	p-$CH_3C_6H_4$—	89	82

$$[(CH_3)_2CH]_2Hg \xrightarrow{O_2} [(CH_3)_2CH]_2Hg·O_2 \longrightarrow Hg$$
$$+ CH_3CHOHCH_3$$
$$+ (CH_3)_2CO$$

Figure 4-25   Oxygen scission of di-isopropylmercury

Table 4-11   The reaction of di-isopropylmercury with oxygen in chlorinated solvent

Solvent	Products, %				
	Hg	iso-C_3H_7HgCl	$(CH_3)_2CO$	$(CH_3)_2CHOH$	$(CH_3)_2CHCl$
CCl_4, 17-20°	14	71	54	11	11
CCl_4, 44°	0	86	33	0	44
$CHCl_3$	29	71	60	29	—

Dialkylmercurials also react readily with oxygen; a few isolated examples have been studied, e.g., di-isopropylmercury by Razuvaev and his coworkers.[42]

When this reaction is carried out in halogenated solvent, a variety of products are formed. Table 4-11 illustrates the complexity of the reaction in carbon tetrachloride and chloroform, and also the high degree of temperature dependence in the fully chlorinated solvent.

Alkylmercurials serve as a convenient alkyl radical source when heated with benzoyl peroxide (reference 11). This reaction is also believed to occur

$$(C_6H_5CO)_2O_2 \xrightarrow{\Delta} 2C_6H_5 \cdot + 2CO_2$$
$$C_6H_5 \cdot + RHgX \rightarrow [X(R)HgC_6H_5] \cdot$$
$$[X(R)HgC_6H_5] \cdot \rightleftharpoons R \cdot + C_6H_5HgX$$

Figure 4-26 Aryl radical displacement of alkyl radicals

through an electron deficient species of the type mentioned previously. Aryl-mercury and halogen-mercury bonds are much stronger than alkyl-mercury bonds; therefore alkyl radicals are readily displaced in this process.

[42] G. A. Razuvaev, G. G. Petukhov, S. F. Zhiltsov, and L. F. Kudryavtsev, *Proc. Acad. Sci. USSR, Chem. Sect.*, **141**:1097 (1961).

5

THE CLEAVAGE OF ORGANOMER-
CURIALS BY MERCURIC SALTS

5-1 Scope

We may envision a lengthy series of reactions involving the transfer of an organic group from one atom of mercury to another. The occurrence of some of these has been demonstrated experimentally; others are still in the realm of conjecture. A few of the many possibilities are shown in Figure 5-1.

$$(1) \qquad R_2Hg + HgX_2 \rightleftharpoons 2\,RHgX$$
$$(2) \qquad R_2Hg + R'HgX \rightleftharpoons RHgX + RHgR'$$
$$(3) \qquad R_2Hg + Hg^* \rightleftharpoons R_2Hg^* + Hg$$
$$(4) \qquad R_2Hg + RHg^*X \rightleftharpoons R_2Hg^* + RHgX$$
$$(5) \qquad RHgX + Hg^*X_2 \rightleftharpoons RHg^*X + HgX_2$$
$$(6) \qquad R_2Hg + R_2'Hg^* \rightleftharpoons R_2Hg^* + R_2'Hg$$

Figure 5-1 Alkyl group transfer reactions of mercurials

It is clear that any attempt to classify or subdivide these reactions into categories for the purpose of discussion must be arbitrary. Mechanistic similarities have not in most cases been well enough established to allow categorization on this basis, although it might be expected that reaction (3) of Figure 5-1, involving metallic mercury, would differ considerably from a reaction involving mercuric halide, e.g., Eq. (1).

The historical development of this area of chemistry suggests the divisions that will be used here; reaction (1), in its forward direction, is the classical example of cleavage by mercuric salts, and has received to date the most experimental attention. The discussion in this section will be limited to this reaction.

This same reaction in its reverse direction, which by the principle of microscopic reversibility has the same transition state, has acquired the name

100

"symmetrization." Because the equilibrium shown for (1) usually lies far to the right, special experimental conditions are required for the study of symmetrization, allowing it to be considered as a separate and distinct reaction.

The remaining examples, again on this more or less arbitrary and historical basis, will be termed "alkyl group exchange" reactions and will be discussed separately.

5-2   Product Distribution

The earliest information relating to the product distribution in the mercuric halide cleavage of an unsymmetrical dialkylmercurial is found in the work of Winstein, Traylor, and Garner.[1] Radioactive mercuric chloride was used in ether solution for the scission of *cis*-2-methoxycyclohexylneophylmercury (Figure 5-2).

Based on the distribution of radioactive mercury in the products, it was

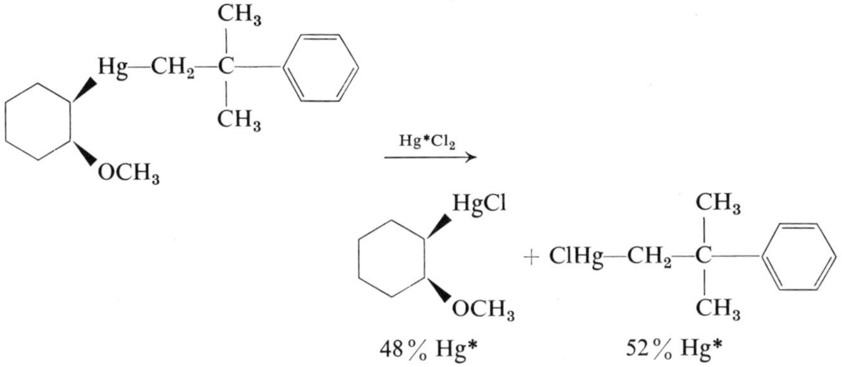

Figure 5-2   Product distribution and stereochemistry of cleavage by $^{203}HgCl_2$

concluded that 48% of the cleavage had occurred at the cyclohexyl-mercury bond and the remaining 52% at the neophyl-mercury bond.

The original report that cleavage of phenylethylmercury by radioactive mercuric chloride leads to statistical distribution of mercury[2] is apparently incorrect. Nesmeyanov and Reutov[3] found that phenylethylmercury was cleaved by mercuric (^{203}Hg) chloride or bromide in both hot and cold methanol; in all instances, the cleavage was found to occur 92 to 98% at the phenyl-mercury bond.

[1] S. Winstein, T. G. Traylor, and C. S. Garner, *J. Am. Chem. Soc.*, **77**:3741 (1955).

[2] R. E. Dessy, Y. K. Lee, and J. Kim, *J. Am. Chem. Soc.*, **83**:1163 (1961).

[3] a. A. N. Nesmeyanov and O. A. Reutov, *Proc. Acad. Sci., USSR, Chem. Sec.*, **144**:405 (1962).

   b. *Ibid.*, *Tetrahedron*, **20**:2803 (1964).

$$C_6H_5HgCH_2CH_3 + Hg^*X_2 \xrightarrow{CH_3OH} C_6H_5HgX + CH_3CH_2HgX$$

$$\sim 95\% \ Hg^* \quad \sim 5\% \ Hg^*$$

Figure 5-3   Distribution in cleavage by $^{203}HgX_2$

Comparable results were obtained with other arylalkylmercurials (reference 3b). A dissimilar, and surprising, series of results has been reported by Brodersen and Schlenker,[4] who cleaved a number of unsymmetrical organomercurials with $^{203}HgBr_2$ at $-20°$ in ether solution (Table 5-1). The cleavage

Table 5-1   (reference 4)

$$R\text{—}Hg\text{—}R' \xrightarrow[\text{ether, }-20°]{Hg^*Br_2} RHgBr + R'HgBr$$

R	R'	% RHg*Br
CH_3—	CH_3CH_2—	71
CH_3CH_2—	$CH_3CH_2CH_2$—	68
CH_3—	$CH_3CH_2CH_2$—	69
$CH_3(CH_2)_3$—	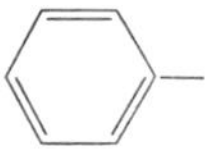 ⬡—	99
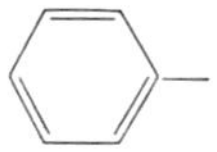 ⬡—	CH_3O—⬡— 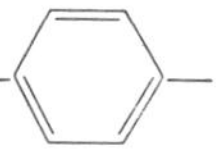	69
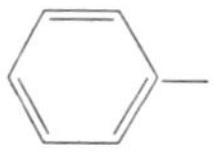 ⬡—	Br—⬡— 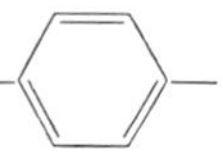	75

of phenylbutylmercury ($-20°$, ether) was found to occur 99% at the butylmercury bond, whereas Nesmeyanov and Reutov reported that the cleavage of phenylethylmercury (methanol) occurs about 95% at the phenyl-mercury bond (Figure 5-3). In general, the results given in Table 5-1 show the opposite trend to that followed in the protic acid cleavage of these compounds (Chap. 3). It may be as difficult to predict the effect of substituents on rate in electrophilic reactions as has often been the case for nucleophilic reactions. In the absence of evidence to the contrary, however, it is reasonable to expect that electrophiles will attack the carbon attached to the system which more readily supports a positive charge. Thus, cleavage of (4-methoxyphenyl)phenylmercury is expected to occur more rapidly at the methoxyphenylmercury bond if the transition state resembles that for electrophilic aromatic substitution, since the positive charge can be stabilized by conjugation with the methoxyl

[4] K. Brodersen and U. Schlenker, *Chem. Ber.*, **94**:3304 (1961).

group. However, destabilization by methoxyl could result if attack occurs on the carbon-mercury bond, and the data in Table 5-1 support this mode of reaction.

Strengthening of the C—Hg bond by resonance of the methoxyphenyl group was suggested by Brodersen and Schlenker to account for the slower

$$CH_3O\!-\!\!\!\bigcirc\!\!\!-\!Hg\!-\!C_6H_5 \;\longleftrightarrow\; CH_3\overset{+}{O}\!=\!\!\!\bigcirc\!\!\!=\!\overset{-}{Hg}\!-\!C_6H_5$$

Figure 5-4 Postulated resonance interaction (reference 4)

cleavage of this group. The available evidence from dipole moment and uv studies does not support this theory. Curran[5] demonstrated that the dipole moments of arylmercuric halides could be calculated from the moments of the individual groups, indicating that the phenyl carbon-mercury bond has practically no double bond character. Gowenlock and Trotman[6] suggested from uv data that some electronic interaction of phenyl and mercury occurs, but the effect is weak and it is unlikely that this small coupling could lead to appreciable bond strengthening.

In summary, no definite conclusions can be drawn concerning the polarization in the transition state from the product distribution studies. However, the accumulated evidence from rate studies and general experience for electrophilic substitution appears to indicate that the results of Brodersen and Schlenker (reference 4) are anomalous.

5-3 Kinetic Studies

Rate constants have been obtained for the cleavage of symmetrical and unsymmetrical disubstituted mercurials. The similarity in rates of cleavage of diethyl- and diisopropylmercury (reference 2) (Table 5-2) agrees with the lack

Table 5-2 Rate constants and activation parameters for cleavage of organomercurials by HgI_2 in dioxane at 25° (reference 2)

	k_2, liter/mole-sec	E_{act}, kcal/mole	$\Delta S^{\ddagger}$, eu
$Hg(CH_2CH_3)_2$	0.016	12.3	−28
$Hg(CH_2CH_2CH_3)_2$	0.019	12.2	−28
$Hg[CH(CH_3)_2]_2$	0.016	12.0	−29
$Hg(C_6H_5)_2$	2.0	12.8	−16
C_6H_5—Hg—C_2H_5	58.0	12.5	−11

[5] B. C. Curran, *J. Am. Chem. Soc.*, **64**:832 (1942).

[6] B. G. Gowenlock and J. Trotman, *J. Chem. Soc.*, 1454 (1955).

of selectivity between these two alkyl groups found by Brodersen and Schlenker (Table 5-1). Diphenylmercury reacts 125 times faster than diethylmercury, a result which supports the generalization that electrophilic substitution occurs more rapidly at aryl-carbon than at saturated carbon.[7] Phenylethylmercury reacts still faster, probably indicating that the electron donating power of the ethyl group accelerates cleavage at the phenyl-mercury bond.[8] The relative rates of mercuric iodide cleavage (solvent, dioxane or benzene) more or less parallel those for the hydrogen chloride cleavage[9] (solvent, dioxane-dimethylsulfoxide) of the same mercurials.

The similar relative rate sequence found for both electrophilic cleavage reactions does not necessarily provide a good criterion for similarity of mechanism. The parallelism may result from both reactions being electrophilic in character and not necessarily because of closely related transition states.[10]

Rate data (Table 5-3) for the cleavage of symmetrical mercurials by mercuric

Table 5-3   Rate constants and activation parameters (reference 11)

$$\left(Z-\!\!\left\langle \bigcirc \right\rangle\!\!- \right)_2 Hg \xrightarrow[\text{dioxane}]{HgI_2} 2\ Z-\!\!\left\langle \bigcirc \right\rangle\!\!-HgI$$

Z	k, (liters/mole-sec) 25°	E_{act}, kcal/mole	$\Delta S^{\ddagger}$, eu
CH$_3$O—	71.5	—	—
CH$_3$—	13.1	10.6	−20
C$_6$H$_5$	2.3	12.0	−19
H—	2.0	12.8	−16
F—	0.42	12.9	−19
Cl—	0.092	14.5	−17

[7] Although actual rate constants were not obtained, Kharasch's work (Sec. 3-3) on the protic acid cleavage of unsymmetrical organomercurials indicates that reaction invariably occurs more rapidly at aryl- than at alkyl-carbon, that is,

$$\text{aryl-Hg-alkyl} \xrightarrow{HCl} \text{aryl-H} + \text{alkyl-HgCl}$$

[8] Since the direction of cleavage is anomalous or controversial (Sec. 5-2), the possibility exists that the electron withdrawing effect of phenyl greatly increases the rate of cleavage of the alkyl-mercury bond.

[9] R. E. Dessy and J. Kim, *J. Am. Chem. Soc.*, **83**:1167 (1961).

[10] The data in Table 5-2 indicate that the rate increase found for aryl- over alkylmercurials is due to the activation entropy rather than energy, the latter quantity being apparently independent of structure. While it is difficult to predict the effect of structure on $\Delta S^{\ddagger}$, it seems reasonable that if the enhancement in rate were due to the greater ability of the aromatic ring to support charge, this should be reflected in the energy term for a given mechanism.

halides have been reported by Dessy and Lee.[11] Electron releasing substituents facilitate the reaction, indicating an increase in the positive character of the seat of reaction in going to the transition state. Unlike the protic acid cleavage, a simple Hammett $\rho\sigma$ behavior was followed, with $\rho = -5.9$.[12]

Rate constants for the cleavage of dialkylmercurials by HgI_2 in dioxane are found in Table 5-4. Although dimethylmercury was reported to be cleaved too

Table 5-4   Rate constants and activation parameters for cleavage of some symmetrical organomercurials (reference 11)

$$R_2Hg \xrightarrow[\text{dioxane}]{HgI_2} 2RHgI$$

R	10^2k, (liters/mole-sec) 25°	E_{act}, kcal/mole	$\Delta S^{\ddagger}$, eu
CH_3-	Too slow	—	—
CH_3CH_2-	1.63	12.3	-28
$CH_3CH_2CH_2-$	1.86	12.2	-28
$(CH_3)_2CH-$	1.60	12.0	-29
cyclo-C_3H_5-	7.67	12.8	-22
C_6H_5-	197	12.8	-16

slowly at 25° for convenient measurement, the similarity in rate constants for the other dialkylmercurials indicates that steric effects are not strongly felt in the mercuric halide cleavage under these reaction conditions. More facile cleavage of the cyclopropyl compound is reminiscent of the protic acid scission (Sec. 3-4), although in that instance reaction was faster by a factor of 8200 for dicyclopropylmercury relative to diethylmercury (HCl in 10:1 DMSO-dioxane at 25°). Diphenylmercury reacts 1200 times faster than diethylmercury with HCl in the mixed solvent. Variations in solvent and other reaction conditions make an extensive correlation of the protic acid cleavage and the mercuric halide cleavage reactions inadvisable. However, the available data support the idea that the scission by mercuric salts is less sensitive to electronic effects than the protic acid reaction, particularly with regard to the ability of the carbon seat of reaction to bear charge.

Dessy, Lee, and Kim (reference 2) have reported data for the cleavage of diphenylmercury in four solvents with mercuric iodide (Table 5-5). Apparently, rates and activation parameters vary in no systematic manner in

[11] R. E. Dessy and Y. K. Lee, *J. Am. Chem. Soc.*, **82**:689 (1960).

[12] Dessy and coworkers (references 9, 11) stress the fact that the Hammett plot is linear and that a four-center mechanism "would be best expressed by $\log k/k_0 = \sigma\rho + \sigma\rho'$. Such behavior is not noticed." It is clear that ρ can be the sum of any number of constants for symmetrical compounds and still be indistinguishable from ρ as a single constant. The arguments advanced by the above authors to rule out the four-center mechanism on this basis must be discounted.

Table 5-5 Kinetic data and activation parameters for cleavage of diphenylmercury by mercuric iodide in various solvents (reference 11)

Solvent	k_2, (liters/mole-sec) $25°$	E_{act}, kcal/mole	$\Delta S^{\ddagger}$, eu
Dioxane	2.0	12.8	−16
Dioxane 5% H_2O	3.5	—	—
Dioxane 10% H_2O	6.8	—	—
Cyclohexane	15.9	7.6	−31
Benzene	29.2	7.6	−28
Ethanol	62.8	11.7	−13

these solvents. A more extensive study would be welcome for correlation of this data with that of other scission reactions. Dessy and Lee (reference 11) found that adding water to dioxane as solvent caused a small increase in rate, as shown in Table 5-5.

Charman, Hughes, and Ingold[13] in 1959 published their observations on the kinetics and stereochemistry (to be discussed later) of the mercuric salt cleavage of di-*sec*-butylmercury. Particularly instructive results were obtained regarding the nature of the attacking electrophile. It was found that the more ionic the mercuric salt, the faster the reaction. Thus, for the reaction

$$R_2Hg + HgX_2 \rightarrow 2RHgX$$

the rate of reaction varies

$$Hg(NO_3)_2 > Hg(OAc)_2 > HgBr_2$$

Second-order kinetics were obeyed by each of the above salts. Reactivities varied sufficiently between the electrophiles that it was necessary to follow the faster reactions at reduced temperatures. The experimentally determined rate constants and the temperatures at which they were obtained are recorded in Table 5-6. Activation parameters were not determined for the cleavage by

Table 5-6 Rates of cleavage of di-*sec*-butylmercury with various mercuric salts (reference 13)

Salt	Solvent	Temp. °C	k_2, liters/mole-sec
$HgBr_2$	acetone	25	2.4
$HgBr_2$	ethanol	25	0.4
$Hg(OAc)_2$	ethanol	0	5.3
$Hg(NO_3)_2$	ethanol	−46.6	7.6

[13] H. B. Charman, E. D. Hughes and C. K. Ingold, *J. Chem. Soc.*, 2530 (1959).

the various mercuric salts; hence, it is not possible to make a direct comparison of relative reactivity at constant temperature. Calculating on the basis of an approximate rate increase of 2 to 3 per 10°, mercuric nitrate is 10^3 to 10^4 more reactive than mercuric bromide.

Dessy and Lee, (reference 11) in attempting to determine the reactivities of mercuric iodide, bromide, and chloride in the cleavage of diphenylmercury in dioxane solvent, used mixtures of two of the salts and followed the competitive disappearance spectrophotometrically. They established that a very rapidly attained equilibrium exists between the salts

$$HgI_2 + HgX_2 \rightleftharpoons 2HgXI$$

Spectral results indicated that the equilibrium constant for this reaction is unity; hence, a rather complex mixture is under examination using this method of relative rate determination. However, it was clearly established that a mixture of mercuric iodide and mercuric chloride reacted faster than a mixture of mercuric iodide and mercuric bromide, which in turn was more reactive than mercuric iodide alone:

$$HgI_2 + HgCl_2 > HgI_2 + HgBr_2 > HgI_2$$

While the results were interpreted as indicating that the order of reactivity for the mercuric halides is chloride > bromide > iodide, the mixed halide could conceivably be the more reactive species,[14] that is

$$Cl—Hg—I > Br—Hg—I > I—Hg—I$$

Dessy and Lee (reference 11) have also published preliminary data indicating the following order of reactivity in the cleavage reaction:

$$Hg(SCN)_2 > HgI_2 > Hg(CN)_2$$

More recently Rausch and Van Wazer[15] have determined the rate sequences for the cleavage of dimethylmercury by mercuric chloride, bromide, and iodide in the solvents methanol and dioxane. These results are shown in Table 5-7. Although the generalization that the more ionic mercuric salt reacts

[14] The spectrophotometric procedure described by Dessy and Lee has the added disadvantage that it does not consider halide exchange between the mercuric salt and the cleavage product:

$$HgX_2 + RHgY \rightleftharpoons HgXY + RHgX$$

In view of the reported rapid halide exchange between the simple mercuric salts, comparable exchange with the organomercuric halide is not unexpected. While Dessy's results indicate that the mixed salts react more rapidly than mercuric iodide alone, the observed optical density (absorption due to mercuric iodide) could be simply a reflection of an equilibrium constant favoring organomercuric bromide (or chloride) and mercuric iodide.

[15] M. D. Rausch and J. R. Van Wazer, *Inorg. Chem.*, **3**:761 (1964).

Table 5-7   Rate constants (liters/mole-sec) at 36°
for the reaction:
$$(CH_3)_2Hg + HgX_2 \longrightarrow 2CH_3HgX$$

Solvent	$HgCl_2$	$HgBr_2$	HgI_2
methanol	1.05	0.30	0.05
dioxane	0.0026	0.0035	0.0015

faster holds, an interesting inversion in the relative rates of cleavage by mercuric bromide and chloride was observed in dioxane.

The equilibrium constants for the reaction of the three mercuric halides with dimethylmercury have been calculated,[16] and are shown in Table 5-8. These values agree with the anticipated and generally observed rate sequences, i.e., the faster reaction occurs with the more ionic mercuric salt. The relatively low value for the equilibrium constant with mercuric iodide is also in agreement (although other factors are involved) with the observation that the reverse symmetrization reaction of certain organomercuric salts can be effected with iodide but not with other halide ions.

In connection with their kinetic study using nuclear magnetic resonance, Rausch and Van Wazer (reference 15) found that in general alkylmercuric salts and dialkylmercurials exhibit spin-spin coupling between ^{199}Hg (16.9 % natural abundance) and protons on adjacent carbons. Notable exceptions were the alkylmercuric iodides. These workers offered as a possible explanation of this phenomenon the rapid exchange of alkyl groups on mercury, as shown in Figure 5-5, mechanism (1). This explanation is untenable, however, in view of the known position of equilibrium and the measurably slow rate of cleavage of dialkylmercury by mercuric iodide. A possible alternative, mechanism (2) of Figure 5-5, may also be discounted, since this type of exchange (discussed in Chap. 7) is known to occur at too slow a rate to establish rapid equilibrium.

Table 5-8   Calculated equilibrium constants for the reaction (reference 16):
$$(CH_3)_2Hg + HgX_2 \overset{K}{\rightleftharpoons} 2CH_3HgX$$

X	K
Cl	3.5×10^{11}
Br	2.5×10^9
I	3.4×10^5

[16] K. Hartley, H. O. Pritchard, and H. A. Skinner, *Trans. Faraday Soc.*, **46**:1019 (1950).

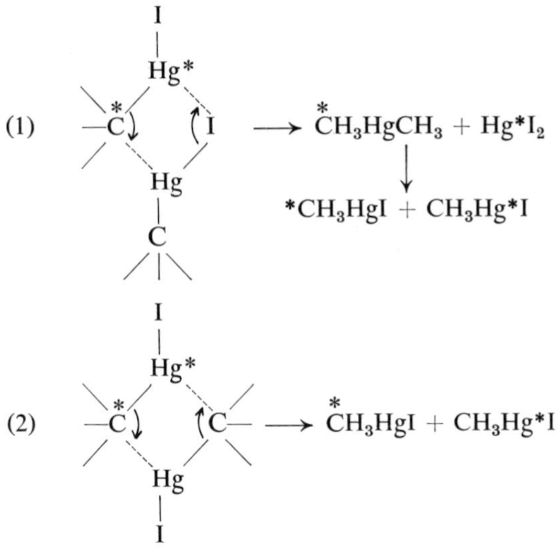

$$
(1) \qquad \longrightarrow \quad \overset{*}{C}H_3HgCH_3 + Hg^*I_2
$$

$$
\downarrow
$$

$$
^*CH_3HgI + CH_3Hg^*I
$$

$$
(2) \qquad \longrightarrow \quad \overset{*}{C}H_3HgI + CH_3Hg^*I
$$

Figure 5-5 Possible alkyl exchange mechanisms, which however should not occur rapidly enough to effect equilibration on the nmr time scale

The addition of iodide ion to a solution of methylmercuric chloride resulted in the collapse of the proton-mercury doublet (reference 15). Regardless of the reason for noncoupling in alkylmercuric iodides, this is the expected result if rapid exchange of halide ligand occurs on the organomercurial. In agreement with this suggestion, Rausch and Van Wazer found that mixtures of methylmercuric chloride, bromide, and iodide led to a sharp singlet nmr absorption, different in chemical shift from the individual alkylmercuric salts. It thus seems reasonable that halide exchange is very rapid in either methanol or dioxane solution with both inorganic and organic mercuric salts (footnote 14).

Additional information concerning the nature of the attacking species in the cleavage of dialkylmercurials by mercuric salts is found in the work of Charman, Hughes and Ingold (reference 13). The reaction of di-*sec*-butylmercury in acetone solvent followed normal second-order kinetics when mercuric bromide was used as the electrophile [Figure 5-6, Eq. (1)].

Added lithium bromide caused a decrease in reaction rate. When the concentration of lithium bromide was initially below that of the mercuric bromide, the kinetic expression shown in Fig. 5-6, Eq. (2), was followed. In other words, the simple rate constant k_2 could be retained by assuming that each mole of added LiBr effectively removed a mole of mercuric bromide. This presumably is due to formation of mercuric trihalide ion. Apparently

$$
HgBr_2 + Br^- \rightleftharpoons HgBr_3^-
$$

(1)   Rate $= k_2[R_2Hg][HgBr_2]$

(2)   Rate $= k_2[R_2Hg][(HgBr_2) - (LiBr)]$

Figure 5-6   Kinetic expressions for the cleavage of dialkylmercury in the absence (1) and in the presence (2) of lithium bromide

the trihalide anion is much less reactive than free mercuric bromide. If a four-center mechanism such as that pictured in Figure 5-7 is operative, the converse effect might be anticipated. Unlike many other cleavage reactions of mercurials (particularly of organomercuric salts, cf. Chap. 7), nucleophilic assistance appears to be relatively unimportant in scission of dialkylmercury

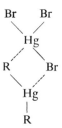

Figure 5-7   Improbable four-center transition state

compounds by mercuric halides. This observation is in agreement with the diminished tendency of dialkylmercurials to form higher complex anions.

The mole-to-mole correspondence of lithium bromide to mercuric bromide also indicates that under these conditions the mercuric tetrahalide dianion is less stable than the trihalide ion, i.e., mercuric tribromide does not disproportionate appreciably:

$$2HgBr_3^- \rightleftharpoons HgBr_4^{--} + HgBr_2$$

To the extent that it is possible to determine deviations from the kinetic expression, it may also be concluded that complex ion formation with the product is not appreciable.[17]

$$RHgBr + Br^- \rightleftharpoons RHgBr_2^-$$

[17] In fact the evidence indicates that the alkylmercuric halide cannot compete effectively with mercuric halide for halide ion. If this were the case, i.e., if the equilibrium fell far to the right,

$$RHgX + HgX_3^- \rightleftharpoons RHgX_2^- + HgX_2$$

the kinetic form would be rather unusual; each mole of mercuric halide consumed by reaction with dialkylmercury would create two more moles of mercuric halide by the above equation. This condition would hold until the excess halide ion was completely removed by complex ion formation, after which normal second-order kinetics would be restored.

In apparent contradiction to the results just discussed, Dessy and Lee (reference 11) reported that added lithium iodide, "to the extent of 5 mole %," had no effect on the rate of cleavage of diphenylmercury in dioxane solution.[18] It is conceivable that this low molar ratio of lithium to mercuric iodide (which, according to the work of Charman, Hughes, and Ingold (reference 13) should have caused approximately a 5% rate decrease) was too small to cause a detectable effect in the method used in this study. Another explanation may lie in the different behaviors of lithium bromide and lithium iodide in acetone and dioxane, respectively. In any event, it is clear that a number of points regarding the nature of the electrophile remain open to question, and an exploration in depth of this area should prove fruitful.

5-4   Stereochemistry

As stated at the outset of this section, the reason for considering the mercuric salt cleavage of organomercurials separately from other (often similar) cleavage reactions is largely historical. The earliest stereochemical studies of organomercurials made use of this reaction.[19] Wright cleaved bis-*cis*-2-methoxycyclohexylmercury and found only *cis*-2-methoxycyclohexylmercuric chloride as product. This important result has largely been ignored by subsequent workers.

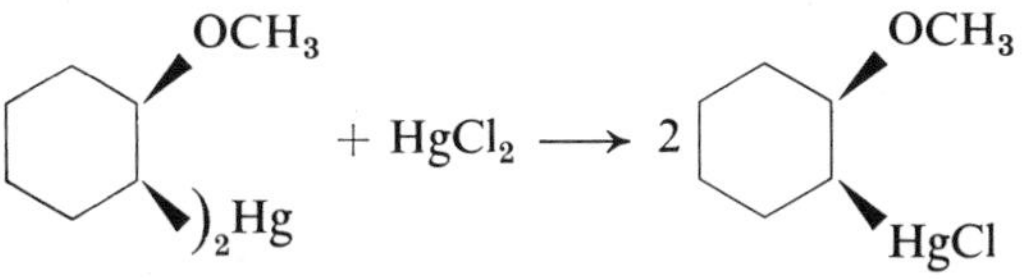

Figure 5-8   Stereochemistry of cleavage by mercuric chloride

Soon thereafter, Nesmeyanov, Reutov and Poddubnaya[20] reported that mercuric bromide cleavage of di-((−)-menthyl α-phenylacetate)-mercury gave products with racemization of the α-carbon. Fortunately, this report did not deter other studies of the stereochemistry of this reaction, as every subsequent report has indicated complete retention of configuration at the carbon seat of reaction. The observation implying racemization has subsequently been corrected.[21]

---

[18] The reagents and conditions were not explicitly stated by Dessy and Lee, but are assumed from the context.

[19] G. F. Wright, *Can. J. Chem.*, **30**:268 (1952).

[20] A.N. Nesmeyanov, O. A. Reutov, and S. S. Poddubnaya, *Bull. Acad. Sci. USSR, Div. Chem. Sci.*, 753 (1953).

[21] a. O. A. Reutov and E. V. Uglova, *Izv. Akad. Nauk SSSR, Otdel. Khim. Nauk*, 757 (1959).

b. An excellent review of this and other Russian work is O. A. Reutov, *Record Chem. Progr. (Kresge-Hooker Sci. Lib.)*, **22**:1 (1961).

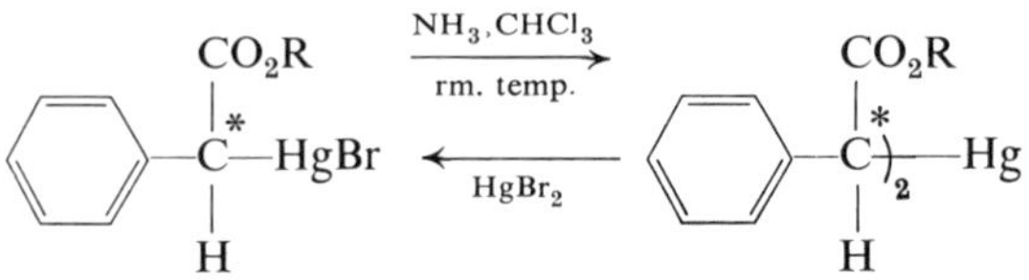

R = (−)-menthyl

Diastereomer I $[\alpha]_D^{18} - 86° \rightleftharpoons [\alpha]_D^{18} - 2°$

Diastereomer II $[\alpha]_D^{18} - 49° \rightleftharpoons [\alpha]_D^{18} - 8°$

Figure 5-9   Stereospecific symmetrization and cleavage

The forward reaction of Figure 5-9 is an example of symmetrization, to be covered in the next chapter. Stereospecificity for both forward and reverse (cleavage) reactions was shown by the fact that recovered alkylmercuric bromide which has been through the reaction cycle had the same rotation as the starting material.

In 1955, Winstein, Traylor and Garner (reference 1) reported the results of an investigation similar to but more involved than Wright's work (reference 19) and included a theoretical discussion of the results (Figure 5-10).

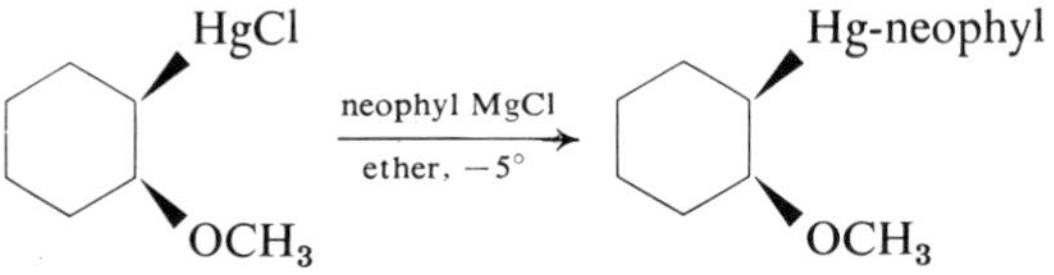

Figure 5-10   Preparation of (*cis*-2-methoxycyclohexyl)neophylmercury

The starting material was prepared by treatment of neophylmagnesium chloride with *cis*-2-methoxycyclohexylmercuric chloride; the product dialkylmercurial was then allowed to react directly (without isolation) with radioactive mercuric chloride.[22] The neophyl group was chosen because of its relatively low reactivity compared with other alkyl groups in the protic acid cleavage reaction. As noted previously, the results indicated approximately equal attack of the substituted cyclohexyl-mercury bond and the neophyl-mercury bond (footnote 22). In terms of the stereochemistry of the reaction, the important result was the demonstration

---

[22] Concern about isolation of the starting material is occasioned by potential alkyl group exchange, for example, $2R—Hg—R' \rightleftharpoons R_2Hg + R_2'Hg$. Note that this equilibrium would not affect the stereochemical arguments for retention in the present case (provided that both forward and reverse steps proceeded stereospecifically with retention); the difference would lie only in the nature of the substrate. However, attainment of such an equilibrium would clearly affect the distribution of radiomercury between the alkyl groups, depending on the position of equilibrium and relative reactivities of the various compounds involved.

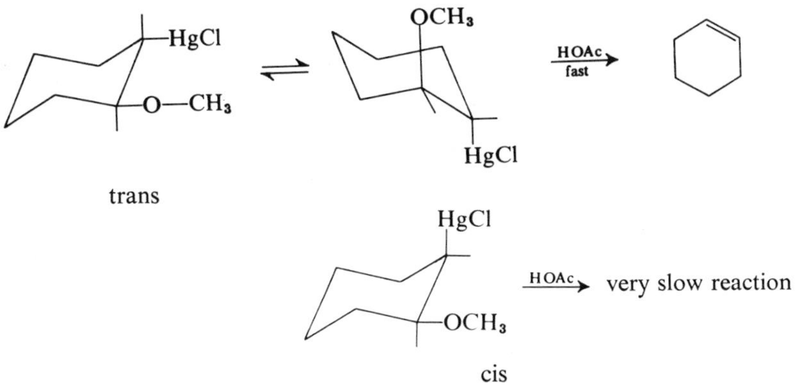

Figure 5-11 Relative rates of decomposition

that the substituted cyclohexyl product contained radioactive mercury, and that this material was entirely *cis*-2-methoxycyclohexylmercuric chloride. A negligible upper limit on the amount of trans isomer present was established by application of the demethoxymercuration reaction to the reaction products and residues, using essentially the method of Wright (reference 19) for analysis. Coupled with the value for incorporation of radiomercury in the cis product, this allowed the establishment of a stereospecificity limit of >99% retention for the mercuric chloride cleavage reaction.

The systems chosen for study by both Winstein and Reutov have the disadvantage of containing an additional asymmetric carbon, making them subject to possible asymmetric induction effects. Objections on these grounds are particularly serious when only one isomer is used. It is possible, for example, that in the studies by Winstein and coworkers the identical products would be obtained starting with either the cis or trans compounds.

This difficulty was circumvented almost simultaneously by workers in the United States, Great Britain, and Russia. Jensen, Whipple, Wedegaertner, and Langrebe[23] used di-*sec*-butyl-mercury in which only one of the alkyl groups had been resolved. The reaction, mercuric bromide cleavage in ethanol solvent, gave reproducible results with the product *sec*-butylmercuric bromide having essentially half the rotation of the starting material[24] (reference 23). The ratio of rotations (last column in Table 5-9) was, in fact, 0.50 to within the limits of reproducibility of the experimental data.

It is worthwhile considering in detail the rotational ratios that would be expected depending on the stereochemical course of the reaction. The interpretation is based on the fact that one of the mercurial bonds involves an

[23] F. R. Jensen, L. D. Whipple, D. K. Wedegaertner, and J. A. Landgrebe, *J. Am. Chem. Soc.*, **81**:1262 (1959).

[24] F. R. Jensen, *J. Am. Chem. Soc.*, **82**:2469 (1960).

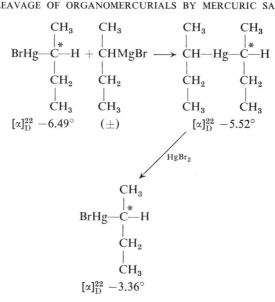

Figure 5-12 Relationship between starting and final rotations
in the cleavage of di-*sec*-butylmercury

optically active carbon center and the other a racemic carbon center.[25]
Assuming no preference (asymmetric induction) in the cleavage reaction
for one of these bonds over the other, it is possible to calculate the ratio of
rotations of product and starting material expected for the three extremes of
stereochemistry (Figure 5-13). The results, shown in Table 5-9, indicate a
very high degree of retention for the mercuric halide cleavage.

Table 5-9 Optical rotations of *sec*-butylmercury derivatives
in the mercuric bromide cleavage (reference 24)

$[\alpha]_D^{25}$, initial L($-$)-*sec*-butyl-mercuric bromide	$[\alpha]_D^{25}$, di-*sec*-butyl-mercury ($-$), ($\pm$)	$[\alpha]_D^{25}$, product L($-$)-*sec*-butyl-mercuric bromide	$\dfrac{\text{Final ratio}}{\text{Initial ratio}}$
-16.14	-11.50	-7.49	0.47
-6.49	-5.52	-3.36	0.52
-4.94	-3.95	-2.33	0.47
-19.28	-15.54	-9.37	0.49
-19.28	-15.54	-9.46	0.49
			Av. 0.49 $\pm$ 0.03

[25] More precisely, the di-*sec*-butylmercury is a mixture of ($-$). ($-$)(active) and
($-$)($+$)(meso) materials; in the absence of asymmetric induction, however, the argument
presented here will hold.

$$
\begin{array}{l}
\text{Racemization}\quad
\begin{array}{c}
(\pm) \\
| \\
\text{Hg} \\
| \\
(-)
\end{array}
\begin{array}{l}
\xrightarrow{\text{HgBr}_2} (-) + (\pm) \\[4pt]
\xrightarrow{\text{HgBr}_2} (\pm) + (\pm)
\end{array}
\end{array}
$$

Final/Initial
0.25

$$
\begin{array}{l}
\text{Retention}\quad
\begin{array}{c}
(\pm) \\
| \\
\text{Hg} \\
| \\
(-)
\end{array}
\begin{array}{l}
\xrightarrow{\text{HgBr}_2} (-) + (\pm) \\[4pt]
\xrightarrow{\text{HgBr}_2} (-) + (\pm)
\end{array}
\end{array}
$$

0.50

$$
\begin{array}{l}
\text{Inversion}\quad
\begin{array}{c}
(\pm) \\
| \\
\text{Hg} \\
| \\
(-)
\end{array}
\begin{array}{l}
\xrightarrow{\text{HgBr}_2} (-) + (\pm) \\[4pt]
\xrightarrow{\text{HgBr}_2} (+) + (\pm)
\end{array}
\end{array}
$$

0.0

Figure 5-13   Three possible stereochemical results

Charman, Hughes, and Ingold (reference 13) used optically active di-*sec*-butylmercury, prepared in a manner analogous to that just described (i.e., such that center is racemic), in a study of the stereochemistry of cleavage by various mercuric salts. Working at 0°, all of the reagents examined gave products with rotation essentially half that of the starting material, again indicating high retention of configuration at the carbon seat of reaction (Table 5-10). Hydrobromic acid cleavage of the same starting dialkylmercury also gave *sec*-butylmercuric bromide with a rotation half that of the initial alkylmercuric bromide. This result very strongly implies that little or no asymmetric induction occurs in the reaction of the initial *sec*-butylmercuric bromide with Grignard reagent to form dialkylmercury.[26]

Reutov and Uglova,[27] using a somewhat different alkyl substituent, also

Table 5-10   Stereochemistry of the cleavage of $(-), (\pm)$di-*sec*-butylmercury with various mercuric salts, 0° (reference 13)

Solvent	Reagent	RHgBr $[\alpha]_D^{20}$, prod.	$\dfrac{[\alpha]_{\text{final}}}{[\alpha]_{\text{initial}}}$
Ethanol	$HgBr_2$	$-7.6°$	0.50
Ethanol	$HgBr_2/LiBr = \tfrac{1}{3}$	-7.8	0.51
Ethanol	$Hg(OAc)_2$	-7.5	0.49
Ethanol	$Hg(NO_3)_2$	-7.8	0.51
50% aqueous ethanol	$Hg(NO_3)_2 = HNO_3$	-7.2	0.47

[26] Facile interconversion of the enantiomeric forms of the Grignard reagent is assumed.
[27] O. A. Reutov and E. V. Uglova, *Bull. Acad. Sci. USSR, Chem. Div. Sci.*, 1628 (1959).

found retention of configuration for the mercuric bromide cleavage reaction. Treating 5-methyl-2-bromomercurihexane, $[\alpha]_D^{18}$ $-36 \pm 1.1°$, with the corresponding Grignard reagent gave a dialkylmercury compound which, when cleaved with mercuric bromide, gave product with rotation $[\alpha]_D^{18}$ -18 ± 1.10. This is again one-half the rotation of the starting material. Cleavage of the dialkylmercury compound with hydrogen bromide in this system also gave product with one-half of the intial rotation. This result again provides evidence that no asymmetric induction occurs in the Grignard reaction.

Jensen and Landgrebe[28] have discovered a novel oxidation-reduction that allows the formation of dialkylmercurials in which both of the alkyl substituents are optically active.[29] This reaction, which will be discussed in detail in a later section, has been used for the preparation of di-L-(−)-sec-butylmercury.

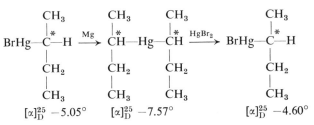

Figure 5-14 Stereospecific formation and cleavage of a dialkylmercury compound

Mercuric bromide cleavage of the dialkylmercurial prepared in this manner gives product with rotation diminished approximately 9%. Racemization could have occurred in either step, but the bulk of evidence suggests greater specificity associated with the cleavage reaction than with the magnesium symmetrization reaction. The rotation of the dialkylmercury produced by this symmetrization should be exactly twice that of material prepared by the Grignard procedure from the same starting alkylmercuric bromide if both reactions are stereospecific. That is, product from L-sec-butylmercuric bromide

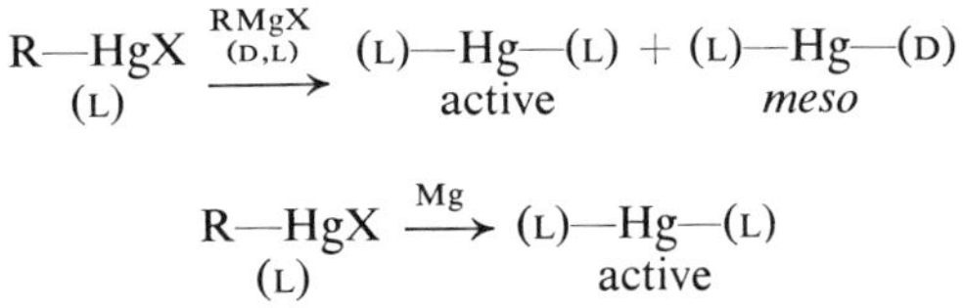

$$R-HgX \xrightarrow[(L)]{\overset{RMgX}{(D,L)}} (L)-Hg-(L) + (L)-Hg-(D)$$
$$\text{active} \qquad meso$$

$$R-HgX \xrightarrow[(L)]{Mg} (L)-Hg-(L)$$
$$\text{active}$$

Figure 5-15 Comparison of active dialkylmercurials

[28] F. R. Jensen and J. A. Landgrebe, *J. Am. Chem. Soc.*, **82**:1004 (1960).

[29] Other methods of symmetrization of organomercuric halides (e.g., iodide ion complexation) do not give satisfactory results with simple alkylmercuric halides.

and *sec*-butylmagnesium bromide will be an equal mixture of L,L-di-alkyl-mercury and D,L (racemic) material. The product of magnesium symmetriza-tion has rotation less than two times the rotation of the Gignard produced material (compare Figures 5-12 and 5-14). This implies that some racemiza-tion had occurred in the preparation of the dialkylmercury by the magnesium metal reaction. In this instance, the mercuric halide cleavage serves as a device for measuring the specificity of this symmetrization reaction.

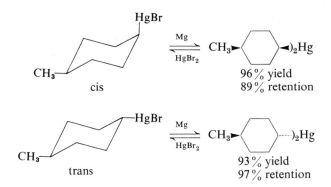

Figure 5-16   Stereospecific conversions with geometrical isomers

The magnesium symmetrization procedure has also been applied to *cis*- and *trans*-4-methylcyclohexylmercuric bromide, and the products obtained have been cleaved by mercuric bromide.[30] The trans,trans product is a solid which can be recrystallized to a high state of purity. Cleavage of the purified material yields within experimentally detectable limits only *trans*-4-methyl-cyclohexylmercuric bromide. Since the structures of the isomeric dialkyl-mercury compounds can be assigned with confidence, these results provide unequivocal evidence for the stereochemical course of each reaction.

5-5 Mechanism

Kinetics and stereochemistry are the two important implements of a mechanistic study. Although considerable kinetic information (including rate constants, solvent and salt effects, product distributions, etc.) is available for the mercuric salt cleavage of diorganomercurials, serious anomalies and many unsolved problems still exist. An attempt has been made in this chapter to point out one basic problem, namely, the inability to compare directly the data from any two laboratories. Too often there is insufficient information to allow a judgement concerning validity of experimental work or theoretical conclusions.

[30] F. R. Jensen, unpublished work.

The stereochemical studies represent the one great consistency of the mercuric salt scission reaction; retention has been observed with every substrate and every set of reaction conditions studied to date. Such a result is required by all of the cyclic transition states suggested for the cleavage but does not conversely prove the existence of such a mechanism. Oddly enough, reports in the literature indicate more ready acceptance of a cyclic transition state for the protic acid cleavage than for the mercuric salt cleavage, in spite of the fact that the only stereochemical study of the former reaction has indicated that the detection of retention requires very specific conditions.[31] There is a tendency to view the various electrophilic cleavage reactions as similar in nature. However, the more-ionized acids (those involving anions of low nucleophilicity) give slower reaction with dialkylmercury than do less-ionized acids (for example, $H_2SO_4 < HCl$), while the converse is observed with mercuric salts (for example, $Hg(NO_3)_2 > HgCl_2$). This implies a fundamental difference in mechanism for the two reactions. In the acid cleavage, this effect has been ascribed by some authors to coordination of the anion with substrate mercury. The low reactivity of mercuric tribromide ion as described by Charman, Hughes, and Ingold (reference 13) has been used as evidence that such coordination is unimportant in the transition state for mercuric halide cleavage. The relative weight to be placed on nucleophilicity toward mercury (mercurophilicity) and electrophilicity toward carbon in the attacking reagent can be accommodated, however, for either reaction using a four-center cyclic transition state which is not a regular parallelogram.

Several orbital pictures of four-center transition states are possible;

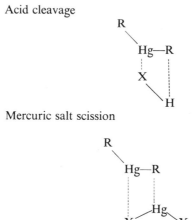

Acid cleavage

Mercuric salt scission

Figure 5-17 Possible four-center transition states showing differing extents of nucleophilic assistance

[31] L. H. Gale, F. R. Jensen, and J. A. Landgrebe, *Chem. & Ind.*, 118 (1960).

generalizations regarding these have been given in Chap. 1. The only example included here does not involve rehybridization of carbon, but has the electrophile attack the carbon-substrate mercury bond. In this depiction, both mercury bonds to carbon are through one sp^3 orbital of carbon. Only orbitals which participate in the reaction are shown; therefore one of the p orbitals on halogen is omitted.

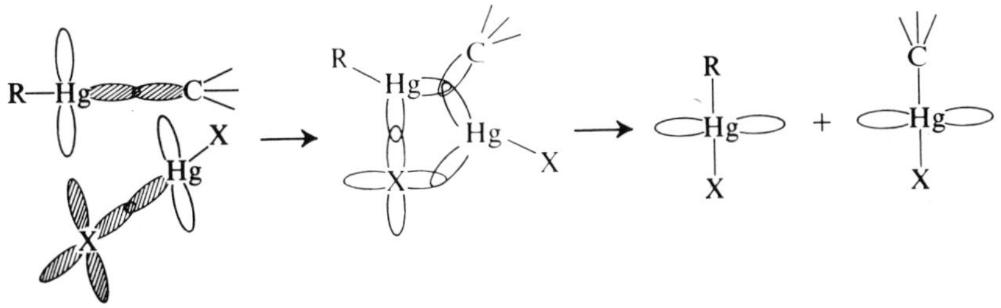

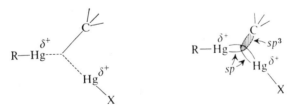

Figure 5-18 Simplified orbital representation of a four-center mechanism for mercuric halide cleavage

The results of Ingold and coworkers (reference 13) provide evidence for the view that this reaction depends primarily on the electrophilicity of the attacking mercury and that coordination of a nucleophile with substrate mercury is not very important. In the limiting mechanism, i.e., one in which no nucleophile participation occurs, the reaction would be classified as "pure" S_E2. Considering XHg^+ as the attacking species leads to a plausible

Figure 5-19 Partial bond and orbital pictures for the transition state of a S_E2 cleavage by XHg^+

transition state that involves no change in hybridization of mercury or carbon. Again, as shown in Figure 5-19, the electrophile seeks out the carbon-mercury bond rather than the carbon atom. The positive charge in the transition state may be formally divided between the mercury atoms or the three central atoms. For either charge distribution, it is reasonable to expect that the presence of electron donating substituents on carbon would result in a rate increase.

6

SYMMETRIZATION AND REDUCTION OF ORGANOMERCURIALS

6-1 Scope and Definition

Many aspects of electrophilic substitution are as old as organic chemistry; others are in such a state of infancy that proper classification with regard to reaction type is formally impossible. Much of the chemistry explored in this chapter falls into this latter category. It is included because it may later be classified as electrophilic substitution, and also because it represents interesting examples of the chemistry of organometallics. We are predisposed to think of the scission of a carbon-metal bond as involving polarization of the electron pair toward the more electronegative carbon.

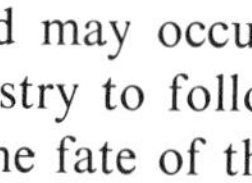

$$\underset{/}{\overset{\backslash}{>}}\!\!C \overset{\delta^-}{\underset{}{}} \!\!-\!\! M \overset{\delta^+}{\underset{}{}}$$

Figure 6-1   Carbon-metal
bond polarization

Under certain conditions, with some metals and organic substituents, homolytic cleavage of this bond may occur more readily than heterolytic cleavage. In much of the chemistry to follow this mechanistic controversy exists, that is, the question of the fate of the two electrons involved in the carbon-metal bond.

It should be noted that just as electrophilic cleavage or substitution does not necessarily involve the formation of a free carbanion, homolytic cleavage or substitution does not require the intermediacy of a free radical. Classification by reaction type will depend solely on the fate of the electron pair which comprised the bond destroyed during the reaction.

The two topics to be covered in this chapter are related most strongly by the fact that the product of reduction of an organomercurial is often (but not always) the same as the product of symmetrization, that is, the dialkyl- or diarylmercury. Mechanistically the two reactions are often dissimilar, although certain aspects of both may possess common features.

"Symmetrization" is a word referring to a process in which an alkylmercuric salt is converted to the corresponding dialkylmercury. Usually the reaction is regarded as the reverse of the previously described (Chap. 5) cleavage by mercuric halide.

$$R_2Hg + HgX_2 \underset{\text{symmetrization}}{\overset{\text{cleavage}}{\rightleftharpoons}} 2RHgX$$

Figure 6-2   Cleavage and symmetrization
of mercurials

The equilibrium in most cases lies far to the right; hence, the true equilibrium must be displaced to cause symmetrization. This is usually accomplished by removing the mercuric halide reactant, often by complex formation. One of the questions concerning the symmetrization reaction is its generality, since certain types of compounds are symmetrized with great ease (α-carbonylmercurials) while others (many alkylmercurials) are resistent to reaction. This distinction must be borne in mind in the discussion to follow.

6-2   Symmetrization by Removal of the Mercuric Salt

a. Iodide as the complexing agent.   Whitmore and Sobatzki were the first investigators to examine the symmetrization reaction in some detail.[1] Their studies were prompted by the very different behavior of *p*-tolyl- and phenylmercuric iodide on treatment with sodium iodide in ethanol. The *p*-tolyl compound was converted in high yield to the diarylmercury, while phenylmercuric iodide was unaffected. This apparent anomaly was explained by the much lower solubility of phenylmercuric iodide than of diphenylmercury, a pattern which was not followed by the other materials examined in the study.

In most of these other cases, when a mixture of arylmercuric halide and sodium iodide was refluxed in ethanol and the solution subsequently cooled, diarylmercury precipitated. If, on the other hand, the hot solution was poured into ice water (effectively freezing the equilibrium), and the precipitate analyzed, only very small percentages of the symmetrized products were obtained. It was thus demonstrated that the organomercuric halide predominates at equilibrium by large factors over the diorganomercurial. The results are shown in Table 6-1.

The two important observations from this work are (1) the definite existence of an equilibrium which is attained rapidly, and (2) the product obtained on slow cooling is that favored by reason of its lower solubility. Note that

[1] F. C. Whitmore and R. J. Sobatzki, *J. Am. Chem. Soc.,* **55:**1128 (1933).

Table 6-1 Organomercuric iodide—Diorganomercurial
equilibria with sodium iodide in ethanol

R	[NaI]/[RHgI]	$(RHgI/R_2Hg)_{equil.}$
benzyl	34	10
p-tolyl	4	40
p-tolyl	12	20
p-ethylphenyl	12	150
phenyl	16	50

only a single aliphatic mercurial is represented in the table, and this one happens to be benzyl; hence extending these results, which appear to be general for aromatic systems, to simple alkylmercurials is not warranted by this study.

This early work illustrates one method of symmetrization by complex ion formation, in this case the mercuric tetraiodide dianion.

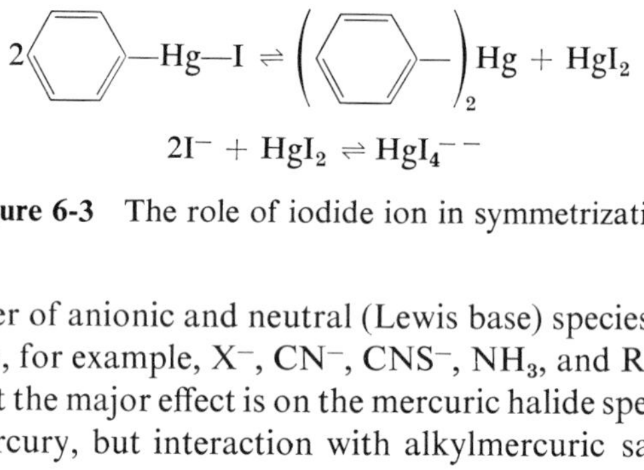

$$2 \langle \rangle -Hg-I \rightleftharpoons \left(\langle \rangle - \right)_2 Hg + HgI_2$$

$$2I^- + HgI_2 \rightleftharpoons HgI_4^{--}$$

Figure 6-3 The role of iodide ion in symmetrization

A large number of anionic and neutral (Lewis base) species may be used as complex formers, for example, X^-, CN^-, CNS^-, NH_3, and RNH_2. It appears fairly certain that the major effect is on the mercuric halide species, rather than on the diarylmercury, but interaction with alkylmercuric salt may provide catalysis.[2]

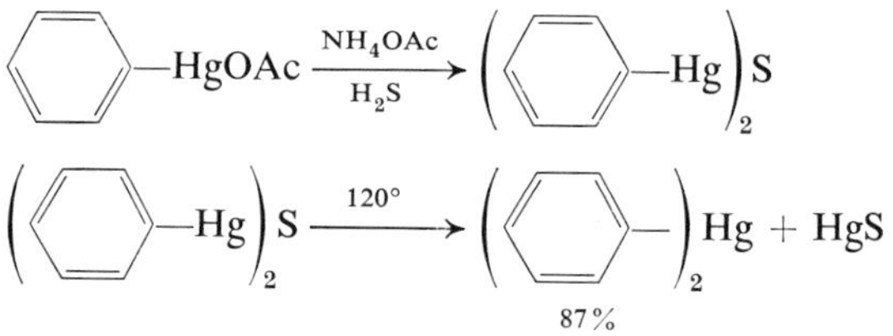

$$\langle \rangle -HgOAc \xrightarrow[H_2S]{NH_4OAc} \left(\langle \rangle -Hg \right)_2 S$$

$$\left(\langle \rangle -Hg \right)_2 S \xrightarrow{120°} \left(\langle \rangle - \right)_2 Hg + HgS$$

87%

Figure 6-4 Preparation of diphenylmercury
via bis-phenylmercuric sulfide

[2] This point has been covered in some detail in the discussion of cleavage of mercurials (Chap. 5).

b. Thermal decomposition of organomercuric sulfides.   Other more complex methods of symmetrization have been evolved, as shown by the work of McCutchan and Kobe (Figure 6-4).[3] This particular procedure gives excellent yields of diphenylmercury on heating the sulfide either with or without hydrocarbon solvent. According to Nesmeyanov and Kritskaia[4] this method alone is capable of symmetrizing the very unreactive α-chloromercuricamphenilone system.[5]

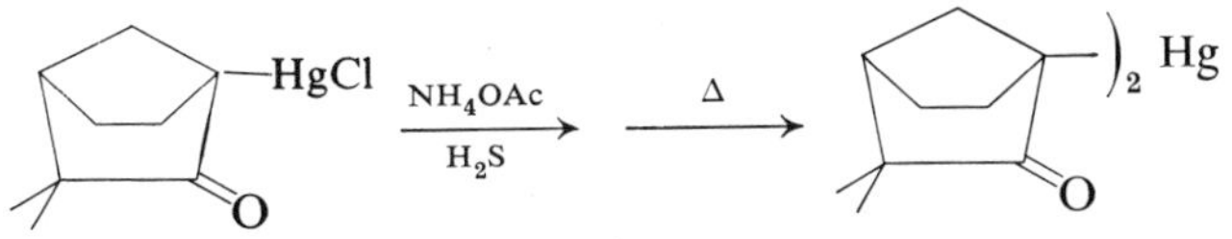

Figure 6-5   Symmetrization of α-chloromercuricamphenilone

c. Symmetrization by an alkyl-transfer reaction.   The very low solubility of phenylmercuric halide has also been utilized in a novel symmetrization

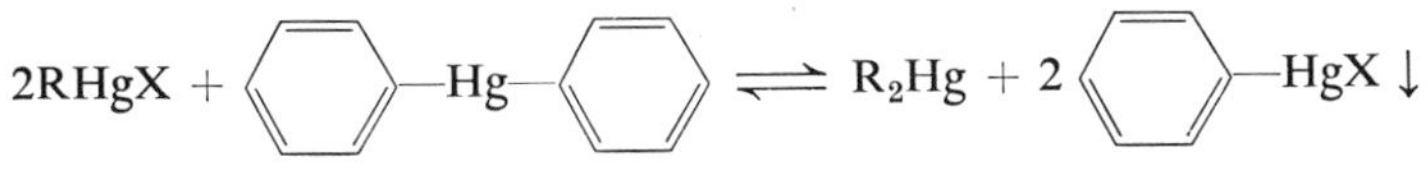

Figure 6-6   Symmetrization by precipitation of phenylmercuric halide

procedure.[6] In this instance the successful application of the reaction depends on the precipitation of phenylmercuric halide from solution. The reaction is limited to highly activated alkyl groups. This particular symmetrization reaction is discussed in the succeeding chapter on R-group exchange, where its mechanism is also covered.

d. Ammonia as a complexing agent.   Just as halide ion can displace the cleavage-symmetrization equilibrium to favor the latter process, ammonia may effectively remove mercuric halide by complex formation. The ammonia symmetrization method has been used extensively by the Russian school, and one of the earliest studies of the stereochemistry of

$$HgX_2 + 2NH_3 \rightarrow HgX_2(NH_3)_2 \downarrow$$

Figure 6-7   Ammonia-mercuric halide complex

[3] R. T. McCutchan and K. A. Kobe, *Ind. Eng. Chem.*, **46**:675 (1954).

[4] A. N. Nesmeyanov and I. I. Kritskaia, *Proc. Acad. Sci. USSR, Chem. Sect.*, **121**:569 (1958).

[5] The behavior of this material toward other reagents is discussed more fully in Chap. 3. According to these authors, "the usual symmetrizing agents, including KI" failed to cause reaction. Information on other reagents, especially those such as hydrazine and sodium stannite which act as reducing agents, would be instructive in this case.

[6] O. A. Reutov, I. P. Beletskaya and L. R. Filippenko, *Nauchn. Dokl. Vysshei. Shkoly, Khim. i Khim. Tekhnol.*, **4**:754 (1958).

symmetrization made use of the ammonia procedure.[7] This work gave spurious stereochemical results (apparently caused by the isomerization of the alkylmercuric halide in acid solution) which have been subsequently corrected.[8] In the later work it was shown that treatment of either of the diastereomeric (—)-menthyl α-bromomercuriphenylacetates with ammonia in chloroform solution gave rise to a single different product in each case. Subsequent cleavage with hydrobromic acid yielded starting material with no loss of rotation (Figure 6-8). Comparable results were obtained when the

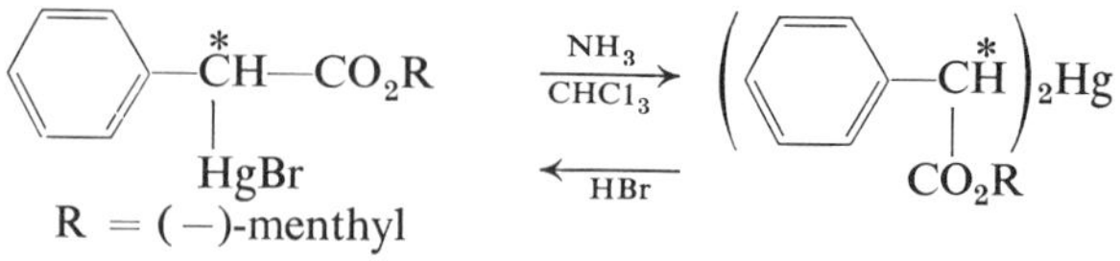

$$R = (-)\text{-menthyl}$$

Diasteriomer I: $[\alpha]_D^{18} - 86° \rightleftharpoons [\alpha]_D^{18} - 2°$

Diasteriomer II: $[\alpha]_D^{18} - 49° \rightleftharpoons [\alpha]_D^{18} - 8°$

Figure 6-8 Ammonia symmetrization with retention of configuration

dialkylmercury compounds were cleaved with mercuric bromide (reference 8). The overall stereochemical result including the protic acid cleavage could be explained by inversion during symmetrization followed by highly specific asymmetric induction in the scission of the original carbon-mercury bond. However the results with both diastereomers appear to rule out this interpretation. The retention of configuration demonstrated for the mercuric halide cleavage reaction constitutes added proof that the ammonia symmetrization involves retention of configuration of the newly formed carbon-mercury bond.

Kinetic data for the ammonia-induced symmetrization reaction have been obtained with the ethyl and *t*-butyl esters of this α-carbonyl system. Reutov, Beletskaya, and Mardaleishvili[9,10,11] found the ammonia-complexed mercuric bromide to be highly insoluble in the solvent chloroform and followed the course of the reaction nephelometrically, or in a few cases, by titration of the unreacted ammonia. It was necessary to conduct the study at high dilution of the mercurial to prevent aggregation of the precipitate, which was

[7] A. N. Nesmeyanov, O. A. Reutov, and S. S. Poddubnaya, *Bull. Acad. Sci. USSR, Div. Chem. Sci.*, 753 (1953).

[8] A. N. Nesmeyanov, O. A. Reutov, W. Yang-Chieh and L. Ching-Chu, *Bull. Acad. Sci. USSR, Div. Chem. Sci.*, 1280 (1958).

[9] O. A. Reutov, I. P. Beletskaya, and R. E. Mardaleishvili, *Proc. Acad. Sci. USSR, Chem. Sect.*, **116**:901 (1957).

[10] O. A. Reutov, I. P. Beletskaya and R. E. Mardaleishvili, *Zh. Fiz. Khim.*, (*SSSR*), **33**:152 (1959).

[11] O. A. Reutov, I. P. Beletskaya, and R. E. Mardaleishvili, *Russ. J. Phys. Chem.*, (*Eng. Transl.*), **33**:240 (1959).

$$2RHgBr \xrightarrow[\text{CHCl}_3]{2NH_3} R_2Hg + HgBr_2(NH_3)_2\downarrow$$

Figure 6-9 Removal of mercuric halide by complex precipitation. The stoichiometry shown has been demonstrated by Reutov et al., reference 9

subsequently shown to be free of both starting material and dialkylmercury product. The reaction was reported to have certain characteristics: (1) to be second-order in alkylmercuric halide; (2) to be second-order in ammonia; (3) to be subject to inhibition (first-order) by *added* product (Reutov and his coworkers failed to recognize that formed product would also be expected to cause inhibition if the report regarding inhibition by added product proved to be true); (4) to be reversible overall; (5) not to occur at low ammonia concentration; and (6) to proceed to completion only with a very large excess (fifteenfold) of ammonia. These reports obviously are partly in contradiction[12] and have clouded the understanding of this reaction.[13]

However, a detailed reinvestigation of the kinetics has been reported, establishing that the reaction proceeds to completion according to the equation of 6-9, even at low ammonia concentration.[14,15] The report of inhibition by added products (references 9, 10, 11) has been shown to be in error[16,17] (reference 14), and thus the reaction satisfactorily follows fourth-order kinetics (Figure 6-10).

[12] The experimental (references 9, 10, 11) data were not reported fully and the reported data were frequently presented in a very confusing manner. For example, the original data are given in most instances in concentration per volume of solvent, not total volume of solution, which leads to some error in the rate constants.

For the tenacious reader who attempts to interpret the results in reference 10, note that the quantities plotted $(C_0 - C)/6.8 \times 10^{-5}$ rather than $C_0 - C$. The quantities plotted in the calibration curve (fig. 1 of reference 10) appear to be the infinity values obtained in the kinetic runs of table 1 (reference 10). The quantity plotted on the y-axis of fig. 3 appears to be $6.8 \times 10^{-5}(C_0 - C)/C_0C$.

[13] F. R. Jensen and B. Rickborn, *J. Am. Chem. Soc.*, **86**:3784 (1964).

[14] F. R. Jensen, B. Rickborn, and J. Miller, *J. Am. Chem. Soc.*, **88**:340 (1966).

[15] At least part of the difficulties in the earlier kinetic determinations (references 9, 10, and 11) probably arose from failure to recognize that nephelometry as an analytical method is expected to fail for this reaction when the rate is very slow, because the colloid precipitates from solution. Note that the rate of a fourth-order reaction such as the ammonia symmetrization greatly decreases as the reaction proceeds.

[16] O. A. Reutov, *Proc. Acad. Sci. USSR, Chem. Sect.*, **163**:744 (1965).

[17] After the present authors transmitted a preprint of their results (reference 13) and their criticisms regarding his experimental data and interpretation to Professor Reutov in January, 1964, he replied that these objections must have resulted from our use of incorrect translations of the Russian articles. Nevertheless, he subsequently made partial (but still unsatisfactory) revisions of his interpretations [reference 16 and O. A. Reutov, I. P. Beletskaya, and G. A. Artamkina, *J. Gen. Chem. USSR*, (*Eng. Transl.*), **34**:2850 (1964)]. Aware of the existence of this prior correspondence, the reader may find many of the remarks in reference 16 amusing.

$$\text{Rate} = k_4[\text{RHgBr}]^2[\text{NH}_3]^2$$

$$\text{where R} = \text{Ar}—\overset{\displaystyle |}{\underset{\displaystyle |}{\text{C}}}—\text{CO}_2\text{R}'$$
$$\text{H}$$

Figure 6-10 Complete kinetic expression
for symmetrization (Figure 6-9) by
ammonia in chloroform solution

The second-order dependence in each reagent was found to hold satis-factorily on changing the initial concentrations of reactants. With tenfold variation of the initial mercurial concentration (0.399 to 0.0396 M, [NH_3] ~ 1 M) the rate constant showed a small downward trend (16.6 $\times$ 10^{-4} to 11.4 $\times$ 10^{-4} liter^3/mole^3-sec). At constant alkylmercuric bromide concen-tration ($\sim$0.4 M) a somewhat larger decrease (but amounting only to a fraction of an order) was observed with variation of ammonia concentration; thus with ammonia 1.05 M to 0.0987 M, a change in rate constant from 16.6 $\times$ 10^{-4} to 8.4 $\times$ 10^{-4} liters^3/mole^3-sec was observed (reference 14). These variations of the rate constant are sufficiently small that they do not cast doubt on the reported orders. They are probably a reflection of the change in polarity of the reaction medium or possibly a complication due to complex formation. The extent of complex formation between ammonia and the mercurial in solution is unknown. However, mercurials, especially when negatively substituted, are known to complex strongly with ammonia and amines.[18] At *high* ammonia concentrations a complex may be fully formed between the mercurial and ammonia. Since the extent of complex formation is unknown, the kinetic dependence on ammonia of two represents a minimum number under these pseudo second-order conditions.

Reutov and coworkers have proposed the mechanism shown in Figure 6-11 to account for their results. In subsequent papers,[19] this scheme has been

[18] G. Spengler and A. Weber, *Brennstoff-Chem.*, **43**:234 (1962). Also see Sec. 2-2.

[19] a. O. A. Reutov and I. P. Beletskaya, *Proc. Acad. Sci. USSR, Chem. Sect.*, **131**:333 (1960).

   b. O. A. Reutov, I. P. Beletskaya, and G. A. Artamkina, *J. Gen. Chem. USSR (Eng. Transl.)*, **30**:3190 (1960).

   c. O. A. Reutov, *Record Chem. Progr. (Kresge-Hooker Sci. Lib.)*, **22**:1 (1961).

   d. I. P. Beletskaya, G. A. Artamkina, and O. A. Reutov, *Bull. Acad. Sci. USSR, Div. Chem. Sci.*, 691 (1963).

   e. I. P. Beletskaya, G. A. Artamkina, and O. A. Reutov, *Proc. Acad. Sci. USSR, Chem. Sect.*, **149**:181 (1963).

   f. O. A. Reutov, I. P. Beletskaya, and G. A. Artamkina, *Russ. J. Phys. Chem. (Eng. Transl.)*, **36**:1407 (1962).

   g. I. P. Beletskaya, G. A. Artamkina, and O. A. Reutov, *Bull. Acad. Sci. USSR, Div. Chem. Sci.*, 1651 (1963).

   h. G. A. Artamkina, I. P. Beletskaya, and O. A. Reutov, *Proc. Acad. Sci. USSR, Chem. Sect.*, **153**:939 (1963).

$$(1) \quad 2RHgBr \underset{k_{-1}}{\overset{k_1}{\rightleftharpoons}} \left[\begin{array}{c} Br \\ | \\ Hg \\ R \diagup \quad \diagdown Br \\ \diagdown \quad \diagup \\ Hg \\ | \\ R \end{array} \right]^{\ddagger} \rightleftharpoons R_2Hg + HgBr_2$$

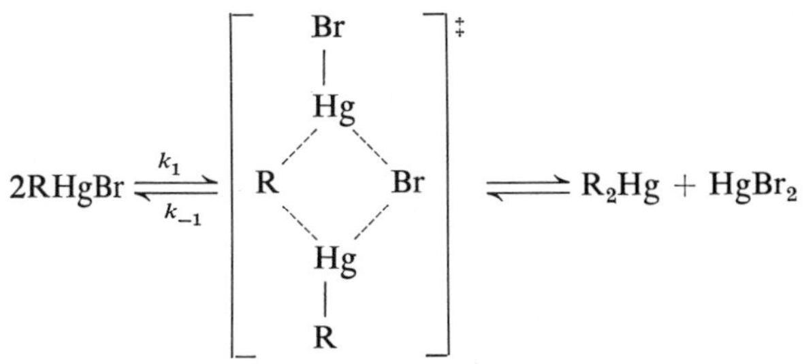

$$(2) \quad HgBr_2 + 2NH_3 \xrightarrow{k_2} HgBr_2 \cdot 2NH_3 \downarrow$$

Figure 6-11   Mechanism proposed by Reutov and his coworkers to account for the kinetics in Figure 6-10

used to interpret various factors affecting rates. However, this reaction scheme does not follow the observed kinetics (Figure 6-10) but rather the kinetics shown in Figure 6-12. Obviously, the data in this group of papers,

$$Rate = \frac{k_1 k_2 [RHgBr]^2 [NH_3]^2}{k_{-1}[RHgR] + k_2[NH_3]^2}$$

For $k_{-1}[RHgR] > k_2[NH_3]^2$ and $\dfrac{k_1}{k_{-1}} = K_1$

$$Rate = \frac{k_2 K_1 [RHgBr]^2 [NH_3]^2}{[RHgR]}$$

For high $[NH_3]$ $K[NH_3]^2 = k'$

$$Rate = \frac{k'K[RHgBr]^2}{[RHgR]} = \frac{k''(a-x)^2}{x}$$

$$kt = \frac{x}{a-x} + \log_\epsilon \frac{a-x}{a}$$

Figure 6-12   Correct kinetic expressions for the mechanism shown in Figure 6-11

(reference 19) are in need of reassessment. The need for reevaluation is especially vital since the results were discussed *in terms of the transition state* for equilibrium (1) of Figure 6-11.[20] Quite clearly the rates would be in

---

[20] This position was clearly taken by Reutov and his coworkers. For example in reference 9, bottom of p. 903, (the same material appears in the original Russian, p. 620) it is specifically stated that reaction (1) of Figure 6-11 (present text) is reversible and that in the second reaction ammonia complexes with the mercuric bromide, shifting equilibrium (1) to the right. In reference 11 it is again specifically stated that the role of ammonia is to bind the mercuric bromide in the insoluble complex $HgX_2 \cdot 2NH_3$, thereby displacing equilibrium (1) to the right. Since no counter statements had been made there can be no doubt that Reutov et al. (references 9, 10, 11, 19) interpreted their rate constants in terms of the *transition state for this proposed preequilibrium.*

no way related to the transition state for reaction (1), since it was thought to be fast and reversible. Because reaction (2) as postulated must be the same for all reactions, the difference in rate would merely reflect variations in the position of equilibrium for reaction (1). To discuss the rate in terms of the transition state for reaction (1), this must be the slow step; but as already noted, the rate is proportional to $[NH_3]^2$. Therefore, the conclusions drawn by Reutov and his coworkers (references 9, 10, 11, 16, 19) are not valid.[21]

In support of their mechanism (Figure 6-11) Reutov et al. have offered the observation that ethyl α-bromomercuriphenylacetate is symmetrized by diphenlymercury. The assumption was made that this reaction must occur by the scheme shown in Figure 6-13.[22] However, it has been demonstrated that

(1) $2RHgBr \rightleftharpoons R_2Hg + HgBr_2$

(2) $HgBr_2 + (C_6H_5)_2Hg \rightarrow 2C_6H_5HgBr \downarrow$

Figure 6-13 Proposed symmetrization mechanism (reference 22)

this reaction proceeds in two stages according to the reactions of Figure 6-14.[23] Therefore the observed symmetrization by diphenylmercury cannot be used as an argument favoring a rapid preequilibrium, as suggested by Reutov.

The ammonia symmetrization very likely occurs through complex formation between reactants prior to the rate determining step, and two equally plausible pathways are possible (Figure 6-15).[24] These are indistinguishable on the basis of available kinetic data. Mechanism I has actually been considered by Reutov, but rejected because of erroneous conclusions regarding the role of diphenylmercury in symmetrization (Figures 6-13 and 6-14). An argument favoring the second mechanism of Figure 6-15 may be given. One would

---

[21] Reutov and his coworkers have more recently claimed that Mechanism I of Figure 6-15 and that shown in Figure 6-11 are essentially the same. They say the differences are minor and involve solvation rather than complex formation by ammonia prior to symmetrization. The mechanism of Figure 6-11 is regarded as a "pure" form of Mechanism I. This, of course, is scientifically incorrect, for the two are readily distinguished in several ways, the most logical and definitive being that they follow different kinetic orders.

[22] O. A. Reutov, I. P. Beletskaya, and L. R. Filippenko, *Nauchn. Dokl. Vysshei Shkoly, Khim. i Khim. Tekhnol.*, **4**:754 (1958).

[23] F. R. Jensen and J. Miller, *J. Am. Chem. Soc.*, **86**:4735 (1964).

[24] Many other variations are possible. In addition to those shown in Figure 6-15 the slow step may reasonably involve any of the following species:

a. $[RHg—NH_3]^+ + [RHgBr_2NH_3]^-$

b. $[RHg(NH_3)_2]^+ + [RHgBr_2]^-$

c. $[RHgNH_3]^+Br^- + RHgBrNH_3$

d. $RHg^+Br^- + RHgBr \cdot 2NH_3$

    et cetera

(1) $RHgBr + (C_6H_5)_2Hg \xrightarrow{\text{fast}} RHgC_6H_5 + C_6H_5HgBr \downarrow$

(2) $RHgBr + RHgC_6H_5 \xrightarrow{\text{slow}} R_2Hg + C_6H_5HgBr \downarrow$

Figure 6-14 Correct reaction sequence for symmetrization
by diphenylmercury (reference 23)

anticipate step (2) of Mechanism I (cleavage of the monoammonia complex by the monoammonia complex) to be slower than the cleavage of the monoammonia complex by alkylmercuric halides, since the uncomplexed material should be much more electrophilic. If this latter process were operative, the overall reaction would be first-order rather than second-order in ammonia. Consequently, Mechanism II, involving the reaction of readily cleaved diammonia complex with alkylmercuric halide, appears to be the more reasonable pathway for ammonia symmetrization.

The effect of alkyl group variation (alcohol part of the ester) on the rate of symmetrization by ammonia in chloroform when using alkyl α-bromo-mercuriphenylacetates as substrates has been examined by Reutov and Beletskaya (reference 19a,b). Their observations, recorded in Table 6-2, indicate a substantial steric effect for this reaction. These rate data were obtained using very high concentrations of ammonia; the ammonia concentration (squared) is included in the listed rate constants.

Ring-substituted materials were examined in an effort to clarify the electronic demands of the symmetrization transition state. Electron-withdrawing substituents enhanced the rate and the reactions proceeded more slowly with electron donating groups (Table 6-3, reference 19g,h). Unfortunately, no

Mechanism I

(1) $RHgBr + NH_3 \underset{\text{fast}}{\overset{K}{\rightleftharpoons}} RHgBr{\cdot}NH_3$

(2) $2RHgBr{\cdot}NH_3 \xrightarrow[\text{slow}]{k} R_2Hg + HgBr_2{\cdot}2NH_3$

Mechanism II

(1) $RHgBr + 2NH_3 \underset{\text{fast}}{\overset{K}{\rightleftharpoons}} RHgBr{\cdot}2NH_3$

$$+$$
$$NH_3$$
$$|$$
(2) $RHgBr^{--} + RHgBr \xrightarrow[\text{slow}]{k} R_2Hg + HgBr_2{\cdot}2NH_3$
$$|$$
$$NH_3$$
$$+$$

Figure 6-15 Mechanisms for symmetrization consistent with
the kinetic data and all other available information

Table 6-2 Effect of structure variation on rate of symmetrization (reference 19a,b)

R	k_2(liters/mole-sec)
CH_3	0.18
CH_3CH_2	0.11
$(CH_3)_2CH$	0.026
$CH_3(CH_2)_7CH_2$	0.01
$(-)$-menthyl	0.007
$(CH_3)_3C$	Immeasurably small[a]

[a] This result is incorrect. In fact this compound has been utilized in a detailed kinetic study of the ammonia symmetrization reaction (reference 14).

Table 6-3 Effect of substituents on rate of symmetrization

Z	k_2(liters/mole-sec)
p-I	0.67
p-Br	0.53
p-Cl	0.47
p-F	0.13
H	0.11
p-$(CH_3)_3C$	0.03
p-CH_3	0.03
m-Br	1.42
o-Br	0.42
m-CH_3	0.07
o-CH_3	0.03

experimental data exist which would allow a direct comparison of these results with other electrophilic substitution reactions at a benzylic carbon. It is worth pointing out, however, that the electronic demands of this symmetrization reaction appear to be the opposite of those found[25] for the mercuric halide cleavage of ring-substituted diarylmercurials.

Reutov and his coworkers have assumed a priori that the effect of substituents on rate in an electrophilic substitution process should be the reverse of that obtained for nucleophilic substitution. However, the effect on rate cannot be predicted for concerted reactions and both orders have been realized (reference 19g,h[26]). These workers now apparently prefer (references 16, 17) the mechanisms shown in Figure 6-15, but regard these as essentially the same as those shown in Figure 6-11 (reference 21). But just as they incorrectly attempted to evaluate rate constants on the basis of the transition state for a preequilibrium, they now wish to evaluate rate constants which include a preequilibrium solely on the basis of the transition state for the slow step. This is not valid. Since the observed rate constant is the product of an equilibrium constant and a rate constant ($k' = Kk_s$), the effect of substituents on the slow step (k_s) cannot be evaluated until the nature of the preequilibrium (Figure 6-15) is known and the necessary equilibrium constants (K) are evaluated.

Thus, a reaction constant ($\rho_{k'}$) is obtained for the observed rate constants (k'), but the desired value (ρ_{k_s}) is for the slow step. This value may be either

$$\rho_{k'} = \rho_K + \rho_{k_s} = 2.85$$

$$\rho_{k_s} = 2.85 - \rho_K$$

positive or negative, depending on the value for the preequilibrium (ρ_K). One can assign with confidence a positive value to ρ_K. Reutov et al. have repeatedly indicated their belief that ρ should be negative for an S_E2 reaction, but they have failed to recognize that the observed reaction constant is the sum of two ρ's. In fact the value (ρ_{k_s}) for the rate determining electrophilic substitution (Figure 6-15) may be negative if ρ_K is sufficiently large. Our view is that $\rho_K < 2.85$ and therefore that ρ_{k_s} is also positive.

Limited data are available for the "cosymmetrization" or symmetrization of a mixture of two organomercuric halides. Reutov and his coworkers (reference 19), using the mixed reagents shown in Table 6-4 and ammonia in chloroform, reported that the initial rate in each case is faster than the sum of the individual rates of the components. This method could give rise to three dialkylmercurials, two symmetrical and one unsymmetrical.

The values of the cosymmetrization initial rates are given in the right-hand

[25] R. E. Dessy and Y. K. Lee, *J. Am. Chem. Soc.*, **82:**689 (1960); cf. Table 5-3.

[26] H. Minato, J. C. Ware, and T. G. Traylor, *J. Am. Chem. Soc.*, **85:**3042 (1963), and the references cited therein.

$$2RHgBr \xrightarrow{k} R_2Hg$$

$$2R'HgBr \xrightarrow{k_1} R_2'Hg$$

$$RHgBr + R'HgBr \xrightarrow{k_2} RHgR'$$

Rate $= k[RHgBr]^2 + k_1[R'HgBr]^2 + k_2[RHgBr][R'HgBr]$

Rate (initial) $= [k + k_1 + k_2][RHgBr]^2$ ($[RHgBr] = [R'HgBr]$)

Figure 6-16 Symmetrization and cosymmetrization of
a mixture of alkylmercuric salts by excess ammonia

column of Table 6-4. Beletskaya, Artamkina, and Reutov viewed these values as appreciable, indicating a highly polarized transition state. In fact, they are surprisingly small, since in no instance is the rate of formation of the cross product significantly larger than the greater of the component rates. For the unsubstituted and *p*-bromo substituted compounds, the cosymmetrization rate is about one-half that of faster compounds alone.

Table 6-4 Cosymmetrization of organomercuric halides

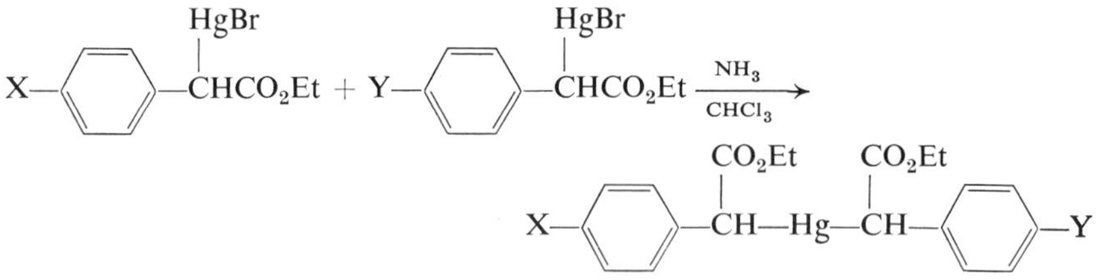

| | | Initial rates | |
X	Y	Observed[a]	Cosymmetrization[b]
H	H	0.055	—
CH$_3$	CH$_3$	0.025	—
Br	Br	0.17	—
H	CH$_3$	0.145	0.065
H	Br	0.32	0.095
CH$_3$	Br	0.37	0.175

[a] These values were taken from reference 19e and were reported in "relative units". However, no simple relationship holds between these values and the pseudo second-order rate constants listed in this reference.

[b] Although not explicitly stated in reference 19e, apparently all reactions were carried out with the initial concentration of each mercuric salt at 6.8×10^{-2} mole/liter. The initial rate for cosymmetrization was then obtained by subtracting the corresponding values for each pure component from the observed initial rate. The variations in rates of cosymmetrization probably reflect differences in ammonia-complex equilibria; consequently it is not possible to ascribe these variations to specific effects of ring substituents on the rate-determining step of symmetrization.

The degree of selectivity of cosymmetrization over symmetrization has also been investigated through the use of isotopically labeled organomercuric halide. In theory, using a combination of the known rates of symmetrization and cosymmetrization, it should be possible to further break down the two types of cosymmetrization according to the scheme of Figure 6-17. It is

(1) $$2RHg^*Br \xrightarrow{k_1} RHg^*R + HgBr_2{\cdot}2NH_3 \downarrow$$

(2) $$2R'HgBr \xrightarrow{k_2} R'HgR' + HgBr_2{\cdot}2NH_3 \downarrow$$

(3) $$RHg^*Br + R'HgBr \xrightarrow{k_3} RHg^*R' + HgBr_2{\cdot}2NH_3 \downarrow$$

(4) $$R^*HgBr + R'HgBr \xrightarrow{k_4} RHgR' + Hg^*Br_2{\cdot}2NH_3 \downarrow$$

Figure 6-17 Combinations of symmetrical and unsymmetrical reactions

interesting to note that in a mixture the ratio of rates of symmetrization [Eqs. (1) and (2)] changes constantly, since the ratio of concentrations changes, but the rate ratio for cosymmetrization [Eqs. (3) and (4)] remains constant.

Using the procedure outlined above with a mixture of p-bromo (labeled with ^{203}Hg) and p-methyl compounds, it was found that 18.8% of the activity remained in solution, the remainder being present in the precipitate. Therefore cosymmetrization must be occurring to a substantial extent, selectively, and with the substitution occurring predominately on the carbon of the p-bromo compound. These results indicate that at least 63% of the product is formed by cosymmetrization. With a mixture of p-bromo and p-isopropyl (labeled with ^{203}Hg) compounds 70.5% of the activity remained in solution, indicating again that the substitution occurred primarily on the carbon of the p-bromo compound.

Although benzylmercuric bromide does not undergo symmetrization in the presence of ammonia, cosymmetrization does occur with ethyl α-bromo-mercuriphenylacetate and with the corresponding p-bromo derivative of this ester (reference 19d). From the weight of precipitate formed, it was concluded that about 60% of the benzylmercuric bromide enters the co-symmetrization reaction. Using ^{203}Hg-labeled benzylmercuric bromide, about 17% of the activity was found in the precipitate. Since benzylmercuric bromide does not symmetrize under these conditions, this corresponds to at least 72% cosymmetrization by reaction of mercury on the α-carbon of the ester. Reutov and his coworkers suggested that the reverse type of cosym-metrization is unlikely under these conditions and assumed that the activity in the precipitate was due to exchange. However, the present results only imply that mercury attack on the hydrocarbon benzylic carbon occurs to a maximum of 28%.

Reutov and Beletskaya (reference 19a) found that the reaction occurs much more readily in chloroform than in benzene, and that nitromethane, nitrobenzene, or methanol in chloroform also enhance the rate. These results are consistent with the finding that the overall reaction ρ is not zero,

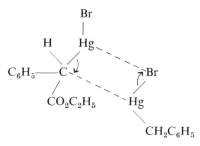

Figure 6-18 Direction of principal bond changes for a possible four-center mechanism (ammonia molecules have been omitted from this figure)

i.e., that appreciable charge separation may occur in the transition state. However, these solvent effects may again be interpreted as due to variations in ammonia-complex preequilibria.

Considering the mechanism of the symmetrization reaction, Reutov and his coworkers have consistently proposed a four-center process. Although they have repeatedly stated that the four-center reaction has been proven, in fact there is almost no evidence bearing on this point and many equally plausible mechanisms are possible. The transition state may be open or closed (four-center), and various possibilities exist for bridging.

The experimental evidence that bears on the mechanism of symmetrization may be summarized as follows: (1) the reaction proceeds stereospecifically with retention of configuration; (2) the kinetic expression, Rate = $k_4[NH_3]^2[RHgBr]^2$, is obeyed; (3) a positive ρ (2.85) is observed for the overall reaction; (4) the reaction is not reversible. Clearly, these results *do not require a four-center transition state*. The only requirements (other than retention) are that two ammonia atoms be attached to mercury and that the halide ions not be present as separated ionic species (reference 24). One may write numerous transition states for the reaction that are consistent with all the available data; only a few of these are the four-center type. An equal number of structures analogous to those shown in Figure 6-19 may be written for the di-ammonia complex alkylmercuric halide reaction (Figure 6-15 and reference 24).

Numerous examples exist in the literature of mercurials which apparently cannot be symmetrized by ammonia. One of these is trichloromethylmercuric chloride, which is reported to give only infusible precipitate under these

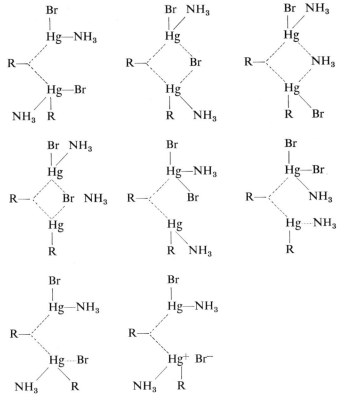

Figure 6-19 Some of the possible transition states (simplified structures) for the ammonia-symmetrization reaction using *only* various forms of the mono-ammonia complexes

conditions.[27] Similar behavior had been noted for trifluoromethylmercuric halides by Emeleus and Haszeldine;[28] these materials are saltlike in properties, i.e., they are soluble in water and their solutions are conductive. A variety of symmetrizing agents ($Na_2S_2O_3$, KI, Na·Hg) caused decomposition with formation of fluoroform.

Other ammonialike complexing agents have been used in the symmetrization reaction. For instance, EDTA (ethylenediaminetetraacetic acid) has

$$CCl_3HgCl \xrightarrow{NH_3} NH_2{-}HgCl + CHCl_3$$

Figure 6-20 Failure of attempted symmetrization

[27] A. N. Nesmeyanov, R. K. Friedlina, and F. K. Velichko, *Bull. Acad. Sci. USSR, Div Chem. Sci.*, 36 (1958).

[28] J. J. Emeleus and R. N. Haszeldine, *J. Chem. Soc.*, 2953 (1949).

been reported to give diphenylmercury in 90% yield.[29] The use of other chelating agents represents a relatively unexplored area in the chemistry of organometallics.

e. Thiosulfate as the complexing agent. Aside from the α-halomercuriphenylacetate systems, the materials most extensively studied to date by Reutov and his coworkers[30] are the 3-halomercuricamphors (D and L). Treatment of a single diastereomer of 3-bromomercuri-*l*-camphor with sodium thiosulfate leads to a single symmetrized product, contaminated with only a small amount of isomeric material. Further work has demonstrated that only sodium thiosulfate or hydrazine is suitable as the symmetrizing agent.[31] No reaction occurred with ammonia, while other reagents caused complete scission of all carbon-mercury bonds.[32]

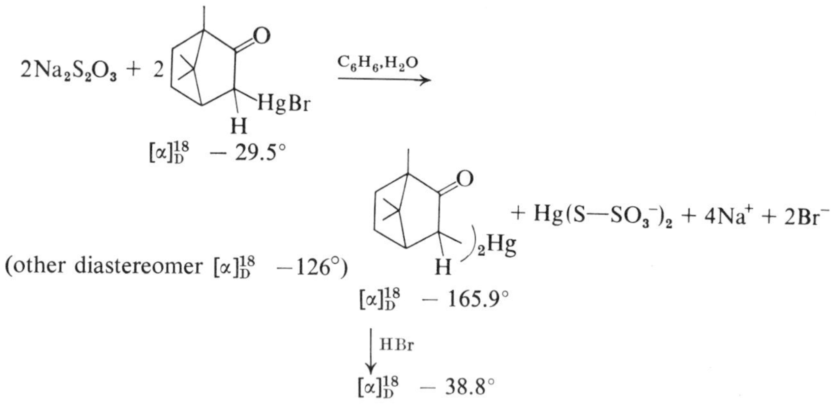

Figure 6-21 Thiosulfate symmetrization with retention of configuration (stoichiometry is assumed)

The α-mercuricamphor system appears to be more readily epimerized than most of the previously mentioned mercurials. The increased rotation of hydrobromic acid cleavage product over that of the starting material indicates some racemization in one of the two reaction steps. Mercuric bromide cleavage causes extensive epimerization, the product having a rotation of $[\alpha]_D^{18} -68°$ (reference 8).[33] The dialkylmercury product was also isomerized

---

[29] Z. E. Jolles and E. V. Caldwell, Brit. Pat. 901,562 (1962).

[30] O. A. Reutov and L. Tszin-Chzhu, *Proc. Acad. Sci. USSR, Chem. Sect.*, **110**:593 (1956).

[31] O. A. Reutov and L. Chin-chu, *J. Gen. Chem. USSR (Eng. Transl.)*, **29**:184 (1959).

[32] Specifically mentioned reagents in this latter category were potassium iodide, potassium hydroxide, potassium thiocyanate, sodium sulfide, and sodium stannite.

[33] This result is somewhat surprising, since mercuric halide cleavage generally gives high stereospecificity, which in turn is difficult to achieve with protic acid scission.

by heating in dioxane; subsequent hydrobromic acid cleavage gave mercuribromide with $[\alpha]_D^{18}$ $-54.9°$. It appears likely that racemization occurs after symmetrization and hence that thiosulfate is a stereospecific reagent. The very high rotation of the alternate diastereomer coupled with the value for the cleavage product shown in Figure 6-21 shows that little epimerization has occurred in this sequence.

6-3 Symmetrization by Reduction

a. One- and two-electron reactions. Reduction of alkylmercuric salts can occur by one-electron or two-electron transfers. The source of the electrons may be a cathode, a metal, or another reducing agent.

$$RHgX + e^- \rightarrow RHg\cdot + X^-$$
$$RHgX + 2e^- \rightarrow RHg^- + X^-$$

Figure 6-22 One- and two-electron reductions

The bond dissociation energy for RHg· is very small, probably varying from 0 to 6 kcal/mole. Therefore the decomposition of RHg· in the gas phase can be expected to be a very fast process. As discussed more fully below, the compound RHg· exists in a stable polymeric form at low temperature, decomposition becoming rapid at room temperature and above. There is also evidence that RHg· has a finite existence on the surface of metallic mercury.[34] Although there are no experimental data bearing on this point, it is not unreasonable that solvation, or complex formation with nucleophiles can greatly stabilize RHg·.

Figure 6-23 shows the known stabilization by mercury and the postulated stabilization by nucleophiles of RHg·. It is also probable that RHg· is stabilized at the surface of other metals.

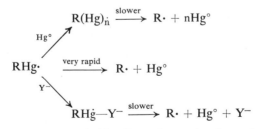

Figure 6-23 Probable effect of complex formation on stability of alkylmercury groups

---

[34] a. R. Benesch and R. E. Benesch, *J. Am. Chem. Soc.*, **73**:3391 (1951).
  b. *Ibid.*, *J. Phys. Chem.*, **57**:648 (1952).

Our view therefore will be that in a one-electron transfer reaction both RHg· (stabilization assumed) and R· are present. Free radicals unfortunately racemize optically active mercury compounds and their presence renders the determination of the stereochemistry of dialkylmercury formation impossible.[35,36,37] Racemization occurs much more rapidly in concentrated than in dilute solutions.

$$sec\text{-BuHgBr} \xrightarrow[\substack{95°, 30 \text{ min.}}]{\substack{\text{benzoyl peroxide} \\ 5 \text{ mol.} \%}} sec\text{-BuHgBr}$$

$0.24M$ in C_6H_5 70 % recovery
$[\alpha]_D$ $-4.94°$ $[\alpha]_D$ $-2.65°$
                    42 % racemized

Figure 6-24 Racemization of L-(−)-2-bromomercuributane by free radicals (reference 35)

Dimerization and disproportionation of alkylmercury groups to yield dialkylmercurials can readily be envisioned: $2\text{RHg·} \rightarrow \text{RHgR} + \text{Hg}°$. Similarly, coupling of radicals and alkylmercuric groups should be expected: $\text{R·} + \text{RHg·} \rightarrow \text{RHgR}$. However, the reaction of radicals with alkylmercuric salts will probably take varied courses depending upon the anion. For example, adding alkyl radicals to alkylmercuric bromides to form dialkylmercury compounds with ejection of a bromide radical will probably not occur because the strength of the C—HgR(Me_2Hg) bond is about 50 kcal/mole and of the RHg—Br bond is about 70 kcal/mole.[38] It is possible that alkyl halides or alkanes are formed in these reactions, although there is little evidence available in this regard. Dialkylmercurials may be obtained by reduction of the hypothetical adduct formed between radicals and alkylmercuric halides, as shown in Figure 6-25 (also, see footnote 46, Sec. 3-5).

Direct formation of dialkylmercurials may occur by the reaction of radicals and mercuric carboxylates. The decomposition of peroxides in the

$$\text{R·} + \text{RHgBr} \rightleftharpoons [\text{R}_2\text{HgBr}]· \xrightleftharpoons{e^-} \text{R}_2\text{Hg} + \text{Br}^-$$

Figure 6-25 Proposed addition and reduction reactions

[35] F. R. Jensen, unpublished results.

[36] F. R. Jensen and L. H. Gale, *J. Am. Chem. Soc.*, **81**:6337 (1959).

[37] Possible mechanisms for the racemization are given in Sec. 3-5. Radicals may also be generated by the sequence:

$$\text{R}^- + \text{R'HgBr} \longrightarrow \text{R·} + [\text{R'HgBr}]^-$$
$$[\text{R'HgBr}]^- \longrightarrow \text{R'Hg·} + \text{Br}^-$$

[38] T. L. Cottrell, "The Strengths of Chemical Bonds," Butterworth Scientific Publications, London, 1958.

presence of mercury carboxylates to form organomercury compounds has been studied by Russian workers in recent years.[39] These latter reactions probably occur by pathways similar to the chain reaction proposed in Figure 6-26 for reduction-initiated chain decomposition of an alkylmercuric carboxylate to form a dialkylmercury compound. It may be concluded that

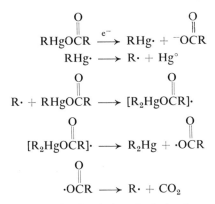

Figure 6-26   Reduction-induced chain decomposition to form dialkylmercury compounds

reasonable pathways exist for reactions of $R\cdot$, $RHg\cdot$, and $RHgX$ to yield dialkylmercurials.

The product from a two-electron transfer (RHg^-) has been postulated as a reactive intermediate in the reduction of alkylmercuric bromides by magnesium; it is discussed more fully below. It is also a reasonable intermediate in certain electrolytic reactions.

In symmetrization by complex formation, the evidence points to the reagent acting by catalysis through complex formation with halide. Evidence for direct reduction of the organomercuric salt rests largely on the observation that reduction reactions occur in instances where complex formation fails and, more importantly, the reductions occur exceedingly rapidly. Although no kinetic data for reductive symmetrization are available, mercury can often be seen falling from solution.

b. Reduction by electrolysis.   Kraus[40] demonstrated in 1913 that many alkylmercuric halides can be reduced electrolytically. Methylmercuric chloride in liquid ammonia, for instance, gives a dark, spongy precipitate at the cathode. The exact nature of this precipitate, which is a good electrical conductor, remains in question today. It is perhaps best described as

[39] For example, see G. A. Razuvaev, Yu. A. Oldekop, and N. A. Maier, *J. Gen. Chem. USSR* (*Eng. Transl.*), **25**:666 (1955).

[40] C. A. Kraus, *J. Am. Chem. Soc.*, **35**:1732 (1913).

$(CH_3Hg\cdot)_n$. Warmed to about room temperature, this material gives mercury and dimethylmercury in an exothermic reaction.

$$(CH_3Hg\cdot)_n \to n/2\ CH_3HgCH_3 + n/2\ Hg°$$

Figure 6-27   Thermal decomposition
of methylmercury

In a recent investigation of the structure of the Kraus product, Billinge and Gowenlock[41] electrolyzed optically active *sec*-butylmercuric bromide. The *sec*-butylmercury compound obtained in this manner was decomposed to di-*sec*-butylmercury, which in turn was cleaved with mercuric bromide. The final product obtained in this manner was optically inactive.

The observed total racemization could have occurred in either the first step (electrolysis) or in the thermal decomposition of the initial product to give di-*sec*-butylmercury. The optical instability of dialkylmercury compounds in the presence of free radicals has been noted previously (Secs. 3-5 and 6-3a).

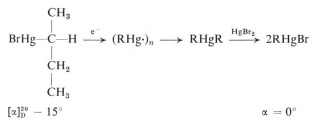

Figure 6-28   Racemization in the electrolytic
formation of di-*sec*-butylmercury

Related polarographic studies have been carried out by Benesch and Benesch (reference 34) on a number of alkylmercuric salts. This work established that the reduction can either be a one-electron or a two-electron transfer, depending upon potential. The first step is analogous to Kraus's electrolysis. The evidence supports the reactions shown in Figure 6-29,

$$RHgX + e^- \to RHg\cdot + X^-$$
$$2RHg\cdot \to RHgR + Hg°$$
$$RHg\cdot + H^+ + e^- \to RH + Hg°$$

Figure 6-29   Suggested polarographic
reductions (reference 34)

where the path taken by $RHg\cdot$ depends upon its concentration, the applied potential and the acid concentration. The $RHg\cdot$ formed in the reduction is adsorbed at the dropping mercury electrode, and therefore may have the structure $R(Hg)_n$.

[41] B. H. M. Billinge and B. G. Gowenlock, *J. Chem. Soc.*, 1201 (1962).

c. Symmetrization with magnesium. Electropositive metals in general react with organomercurials by an oxidation-reduction process. The reduction usually proceeds to the dialkylmercury compound and then more slowly to give the metal alkyl and more free mercury. Depending on the quantities of reagents used and the reaction conditions, excellent yields of either type of product can often be obtained. The latter reaction, i.e., replacement of mercury by another metal, has been widely used for the preparation of organometallic compounds because of the ready availability of the mercurials.

The reduction of alkylmercuric salts to dialkylmercurials by electropositive metals may follow two general pathways: (1) coupling of reduced forms of the mercurial, or (2) through formation of the organometallic alkylmercuric salt (Figure 6-30).

$$
\text{(1)} \qquad \text{RHgX} \xrightarrow{\text{M}}
\begin{array}{c} \text{R}\cdot \\ \text{or RHg}\cdot \\ \text{or RHg}^- \\ + \text{MX} \end{array}
\xrightarrow{\text{RHgX}} \text{RHgR}
$$

$$
\text{(2)} \qquad \text{RHgX} \xrightarrow{\text{M}}
\begin{array}{c} \text{RM} \\ + \text{Hg}^\circ \\ + \text{MX} \end{array}
\xrightarrow{\text{RHgX}} \text{RHgR} + \text{MX}
$$

Figure 6-30 Possible reaction sequences for reduction and coupling

Among the various electropositive metals, only magnesium has been used in a study of the stereochemistry of symmetrization.[42] The most important aspect of this reaction is that it gives a stereospecific reaction, and retention of configuration in both groups is obtained. Magnesium symmetrization is the only general method[43] which allows this stereochemical result.[44] Thus, L-2-bromomercuributane, $[\alpha]_D^{25}$ $-5.05°$ undergoes symmetrization by magmesium followed by cleavage with mercuric bromide to yield L-2-bromomercuributane, $[\alpha]_D^{25}$ $-4.60°$ (Figure 5-14). The small extent of racemization ($\sim 10\%$) almost certainly occurred in the symmetrization step; whether this partial specificity is inherent in the reaction of magnesium with alkylmercuric halides or is due to a side reaction which causes racemization is not known at present.

cis-4-Methylcyclohexylmercuric bromide gives results comparable (89% retention) to those obtained with the open-chain system. The trans

[42] F. R. Jensen and J. A. Landgrebe, *J. Am. Chem. Soc.*, **82**:1004 (1960).

[43] Symmetrization with complexing agents, e.g., iodide, ammonia, thiosulfate, would presumably fall into this category. However, these reagents fail to cause symmetrization of simple alkylmercuric halides, and hence cannot be considered general methods.

[44] Treatment of optically active alkylmercuric halide with the corresponding (necessarily inactive) Grignard reagent has been widely used in the preparation of "symmetrized" products in which the metal is bonded to only one asymmetric carbon.

analog appears to react with somewhat higher specificity (97% retention) (Figure 5-16).

Evidence bearing on the mechanism of the reaction has been obtained. When carried out in the presence of 1-butanol or carbon dioxide, no hydrocarbon or carboxylic acid is observed. A carbanion intermediate (R^-, or RMgBr) appears to be ruled out by these results, since reaction with alcohol or carbon dioxide is expected to be more rapid than with RHgBr.

Similarly, the intervention of radicals (except perhaps as minor side reactions) also appears to be ruled out, since the reaction may be carried out in the presence of styrene and the styrene recovered unchanged from the reaction mixture. This result also tends to discount the formation of RHg· in the free form as a principal intermediate because of its expected instability.

Since magnesium is divalent, it is reasonable to expect reaction by a two-electron transfer with formation of RHg^-. The observation that *cis*- or *trans*-2-methoxycyclohexylmercuric bromide yields only cyclohexene and no dialkylmercury compound (Figure 6-31) may be considered as evidence in

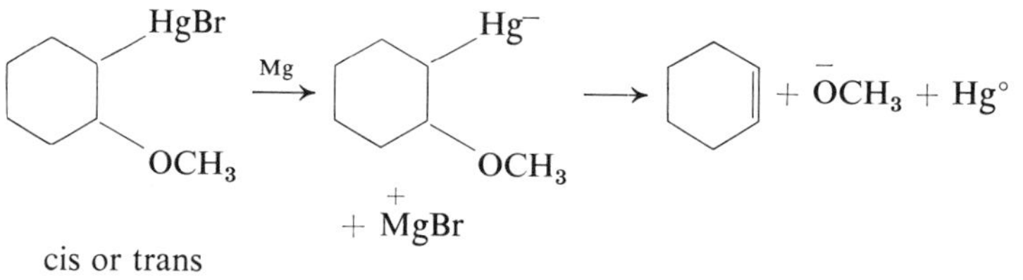

Figure 6-31 Proposed mechanism of reduction and elimination (reference 42)

support of this intermediate. In contrast, other reducing agents considered later gave some dialkylmercurial with these compounds, and arguments are presented which indicate that these are one-electron reductions. Although its generality has not yet been tested, reduction of *cis*- and *trans*-2-methoxycyclohexylmercuric bromide could constitute a valuable test in determining whether reduction reactions involve one- or two-electron transfers.

A reasonable mechanism to account for the above results is given in Figure 6-32. Equation (2) could reasonably be a one- or two-step reaction, the one-step process consisting of nucleophilic substitution on mercury. Equation

(1) $RHgBr + Mg \longrightarrow RHgBrMg \longrightarrow RHg^- + BrMg^+$

(2) $RHg^- + RHgBr \longrightarrow R-Hg-\overset{|}{\underset{Br}{Hg}}-R \longrightarrow RHgHgR + Br^-$

(3) $RHgHgR \longrightarrow R-\overset{|}{\underset{Hg^+}{Hg}}-R \longrightarrow RHgR + Hg°$

Figure 6-32 Mechanism of reduction by magnesium (reference 42)

(3) is treated as a simple 1,2-alkyl shift with its pair of electrons and can be properly regarded as an electrophilic substitution reaction on carbon. The reverse of Eq. (3) represents an attractive mechanism for the exchange of ^{203}Hg with organomercurials, which is known to proceed with retention of configuration (Sec. 7-4).[45]

As noted above, a small amount of racemization accompanies the overall retention of configuration. This could readily be accounted for in terms of RHg$^-$ losing mercury to form the carbanion R$^-$ which racemizes and then couples with RHgBr. However, the amount of racemization tends not to be highly reproducible and may result from the intervention of radicals. The presence of a small amount of impurity in the magnesium could result in one-electron reduction to form RHg· and radicals. Since radicals efficiently racemize mercurials, the amount produced may have been insufficient to polymerize the styrene.

d. Sodium stannite.   Sodium stannite has been widely used as a reducing agent for mercurials and it gives excellent yields of product. The dialkyl compounds are generally stable to further reduction or they are reduced slowly.

According to Sand,[46] the reduction with alkaline sodium stannite occurs in two stages. Oxymercuration products are rapidly reduced to insoluble reddish-violet mercurous compounds, which usually decompose rapidly to give the corresponding dialkyl compounds. Mercurous compounds derived from *bis*-mercury compounds sometimes have unusual stabilities. Sand tentatively assigned monomeric cyclic structures for these mercurous compounds. However, since they are highly insoluble in all solvents, it appears more likely that they are polymeric in nature and owe their stability to being in a solid insoluble form. Sand assigned tentative monomeric structures to II and III of Figure 6-33. The dimer structure III has been shown to be correct by Grdenic.[47]

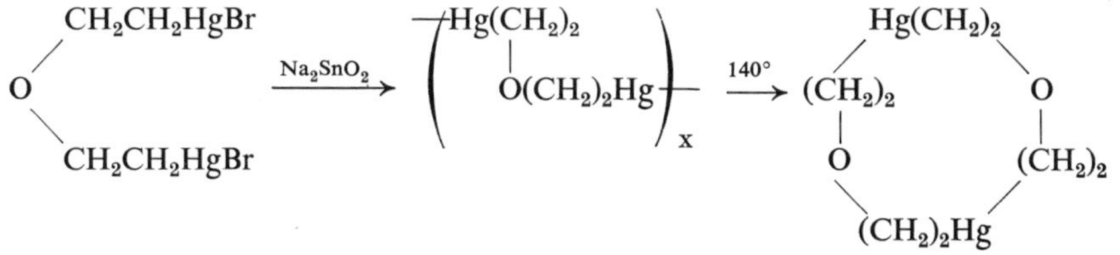

Figure 6-33   Formation and decomposition of a mercurous compound

[45] a. O. A. Reutov, P. Knoll, and Yan-Tsei U, *Dokl. Akad. Nauk SSSR*, **120**:1052 (1958).

    b. O. A. Reutov, *Izv. Acad. Nauk SSSR, Otd. Khim. Nauk* 684 (1959).

[46] J. Sand, *Chem. Ber.*, **34**:2906, 2910 (1901).

[47] D. Grdenic, *Acta Cryst.*, **5**:367 (1952).

3,6-Bis(bromomercurimethyl)dioxane is similarly reduced. The mercurous derivative is quite stable, although it is decomposed by strong sunlight (reference 46). Summerbell and Stephens[48] have reinvestigated this work and have shown that the substituent groups on the dioxane ring are trans and therefore the dialkylmercury compound must be polymeric. It then follows that the mercurous compound in this instance is also polymeric. These experiments in

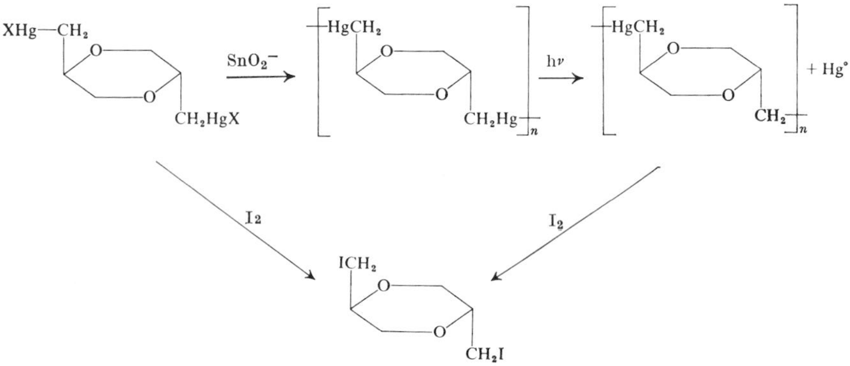

Figure 6-34 A stable mercurous compound and conversions

which stable (highly insoluble polymeric) mercurous compounds are formed provide compelling evidence that stannite directly reduces the alkylmercuric salt.[49]

Stereochemical evidence bearing on sodium stannite reduction is available from several sources. Reutov and Lu[50] prepared two epimeric 2-chloromercuricamphanes by the sequence shown in Figure 6-35. Both isomers

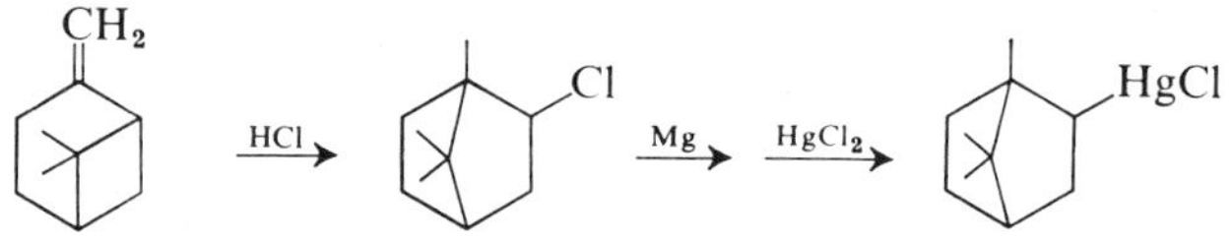

β-pinene

Diastereomer I mp 165–166°
  $[\alpha]_D^{18}$ −10.1° ± 1°
Diastereomer II mp 169–170°
  $[\alpha]_D^{18}$ +15.4° ± 1.2°

Figure 6-35 Synthesis of epimeric 2-chloromercuricamphanes

[48] R. K. Summerbell and J. R. Stephens, *J. Am. Chem. Soc.*, **77**: 6080 (1955).

[49] The mercurous structures shown in Figures 6-33 and 6-34 are assumed. More work is necessary to determine whether these are alkylmercury groups, mercurous compounds or have other structures.

[50] O. A. Reutov and Tsin-Chzhn Lu, *J. Gen. Chem. USSR (Eng. Transl.)*, **29**:1592 (1959).

proved to be relatively stable, their rotations being unaffected by refluxing in ethanol or xylene. In accord with the general behavior for aliphatic-mercuric salts, neither diasteromer could be symmetrized by ammonia or sodium thiosulfate, but both responded to reduction by hydrazine or sodium stannite.

Regardless of which diastereomeric 2-chloromercuricamphane was used, treatment with sodium stannite (or hydrazine) led to a single identical di-2-camphylmercury. On cleavage with hydrogen chloride or mercuric chloride this material gave only diastereomer I, $[\alpha]_D^{18}$ $-10°$. Treatment of the thermodynamically less stable diastereomer II with a small amount of hydrazine in refluxing ethanol caused it to be very largely converted into isomer I.[51] Isomerization prior to reaction was also postulated with sodium stannite.

The 3-bromomercuricamphor system gives only camphor when treated with stannite (reference 30). This result is unusual; reduction to the hydrocarbon ordinarily cannot be accomplished with this reagent.

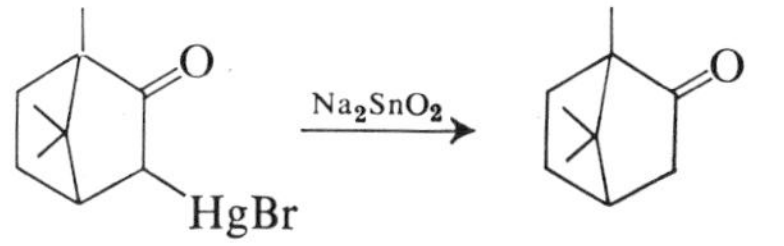

Figure 6-36   Complete scission of carbon-mercury bonds

Traylor and Winstein[52] have examined the stereochemical course of the sodium stannite symmetrization of *trans*-2-methoxycyclohexylmercuric iodide. The dialkylmercurial was formed in low yield (13 %) and not examined directly, but cleaved with mercuric chloride in ether. The resulting 2-methoxycyclohexylmercuric chloride was shown to be a mixture of approximately 85 %

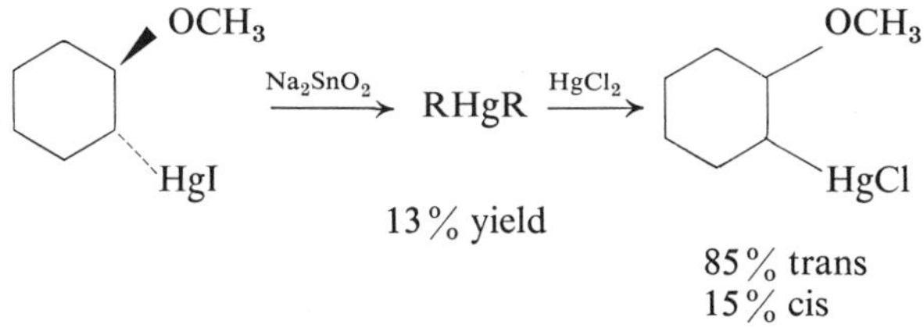

Figure 6-37   Stannite reduction of *trans*-2-methoxycyclohexylmercuric iodide

[51] The energetics of this situation are of particular interest because of the small conformational preference of the halomercuri group in cyclohexane [F. R. Jensen and L. H. Gale, *J. Am. Chem. Soc.*, **81**:6337 (1959)] which is mainly ascribed to the long carbon-mercury bond. The identity of the more stable isomer in the bicyclic camphane system is open to question.

[52] T. G. Traylor and S. Winstein, *J. Org. Chem.*, **23**:1796 (1958).

trans and 15% cis material. Since the yield was low and only one isomer was used in the study, no mechanistic inferences should be drawn from this data.

Jensen (reference 35) has investigated the reduction by sodium stannite of an open chain, optically active mercurial salt. Using the conventional procedure; D-(+)-bromomercuributane was reduced in 87% yield to D-(+)-di-*sec*-butylmercury with 4% net retention of configuration. This corresponds to 100% racemization of one group and 92% of the other, or an average of

$$\text{D-(+)-}sec\text{-butylmercuric bromide} \xrightarrow{\text{SnO}_2^{--}} \text{D-(+)-di-}sec\text{-butylmercury}$$

4% retention

Figure 6-38 Reduction with predominate loss of configuration in both groups

96% for both groups. A reaction was then carried out to about 30% completion, and the unreacted *sec*-butylmercuric bromide examined. Racemization had occurred to the extent of about 8%. However, this result has doubtful mechanistic significance and represents only a minimum value for racemization; in the conventional method of carrying out the reaction, the solid alkylmercuric bromide is present as a separate phase. Racemization is expected to occur much more rapidly with the dissolved material. Partial substitution of ethanol for water as the solvent still gave a heterogeneous mixture, but this time the recovered *sec*-butylmercuric bromide was racemized to the extent of 38%. Thus, as Reutov and Lu (reference 50) had reported for the camphane system with hydrazine, racemization of starting material also occurs with stannite.

Racemization of starting material precludes the determination of stereochemistry of the reduction by Sn(II), but the various observations that have been made do permit a discussion of the mechanism. Racemization suggests the presence of radicals, since these are the only reagents which are definitely known to racemize mercurials (Secs. 3-5 and 7-2). Occurrence of a one-electron transfer is also strongly suggested, since reduction of *trans*-2-methoxycyclohexylmercuric halide by stannite yields some dialkylmercurial (Figure 6-32), but reduction by magnesium, which is believed to be a two-electron transfer, yields only olefin. Color changes, possibly suggesting the presence of Sn(III), also occur during the reaction (reference 36). The exact colors are obscured and influenced by the appearance of colloidal mercury. Initially a reddish-brown color develops in what appears to be a colloidal precipitate. This is reminiscent of the reddish-violet color reported by Sand for mercurous compounds (reference 46). The solution itself appears to become green or greenish-blue, but then in seconds becomes darker blue from decomposition of metallic mercury. Since Sn(II) and Sn(IV) are ordinarily colorless, Sn(III) is a possible source of the green-blue color. The mechanisms of reduction by stannite in Figure 6-39 could be accompanied by a substantial amount of a two-electron transfer reaction, Sn(II) + RHgBr → RHg⁻ + Sn(IV), and still show the

(1) $RHgBr + SnO_2^{--} \rightarrow RHgBr:SnO_2^{--} \rightarrow RHg\cdot + BrSnO_2^{--}$

(2) $RHg\cdot \rightarrow R\cdot + Hg°$

(3) $R\cdot + RHgBr \rightleftharpoons [R_2HgBr]\cdot$

(4) $R_2HgBr + SnO_2^{--} \rightarrow R_2Hg + BrSnO_2^{--}$

$$\overset{\displaystyle Hg^+}{\underset{\displaystyle |}{}}$$

(5) $2RHg\cdot \rightarrow RHgHgR \rightarrow R{-}Hg^{--}R \rightarrow RHgR + Hg°$

Figure 6-39   Reduction by stannite ion

observed effects.[53] Racemization could reasonably occur by reaction (3) and its reversal. The structure of the product of reaction (3) can best be considered as a resonance hybrid, $R\cdot Hg{-}R({-}Br) \leftrightarrow R{-}Hg{-}R(\cdot Br) \leftrightarrow R{-}Hg\cdot R({-}Br)$.

The reaction scheme presented for the stannite reduction does not show the fate of the Sn(III). This material could readily serve as a reducing agent, or undergo disproportionation, $2Sn(III) \rightarrow Sn(II) + Sn(IV)$. Variations of the scheme given in Figure 6-39 for the basic reactions are possible.

e. Hydrazine.   Gilman and Wright[54] were the first to note the formation of diorganomercurial on treatment of an organomercuric halide with hydrazine. The stoichiometry and other products of the reaction are unknown (postulates regarding these facets are given at the end of this section).

$$2RHgX \xrightarrow{\ N_2H_4\ } R_2Hg + Hg°$$

Figure 6-40   Reductive symmetrization
by hydrazine

Subsequently it has been established that prolonged treatment causes further reduction with concurrent formation of hydrocarbon and olefinic products.[55] This important work also established that treatment of a single diastereomer of 2-methoxycyclohexylmercuric chloride with hydrazine gives rise to a mixture of diastereomeric dialkylmercury products.

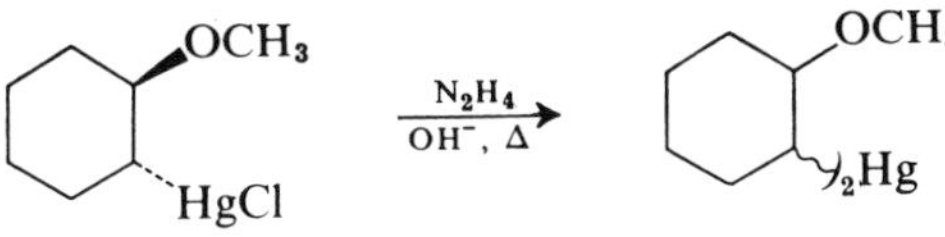

α or trans

$\xrightarrow[OH^-, \Delta]{N_2H_4}$

α, α
α, β
β, β

Figure 6-41   Nonstereospecific
symmetrization with hydrazine

[53] The tin ions are probably hydrated and the structures given here are simplified.

[54] H. Gilman and G. F. Wright, *J. Am. Chem. Soc.*, **55**:3302 (1933). Also, H. Gilman and M. M. Barnett, *Rec. Trav. Chim.*, **55**:563 (1936).

[55] G. F. Wright, *Can. J. Chem.*, **30**:268 (1952).

Most significantly, the isolation of the *cis,cis*-di-2-methoxycyclohexyl-mercury *(β,β* in Figure 6-41) establishes that the stereointegrity of both carbon-mercury bonds has been disrupted. Since only a single bond scission and reformation is needed to accommodate the symmetrization reaction, this result may well be due to subsequent racemization of the product. The hydro-carbon and olefin products obtained on prolonged heating of the dialkyl-mercury suggest a free-radical reaction, not necessarily involving hydrazine.

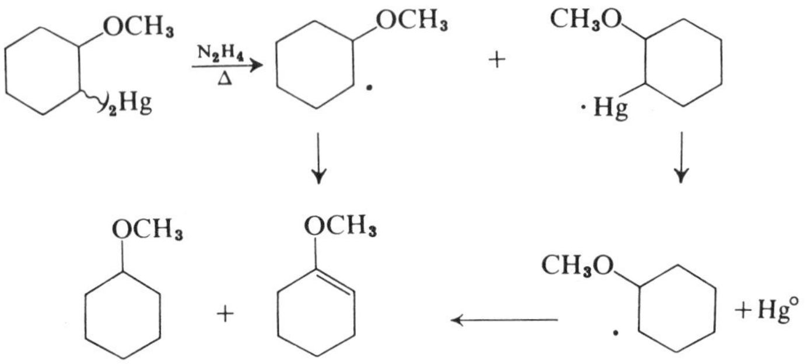

Figure 6-42   Free-radical pathway for decomposition

Similar results were obtained by Reutov and Tszin-Chzhu (reference 30) with the α-bromomercuricamphor system. Treatment of a single diastereomer ($[\alpha]_D^{18}$ $-29.5°$) with hydrazine followed by hydrobromic acid cleavage gave a mixture of diastereomeric α-bromomercuricamphors, $[a]_D^{18}$ $-58.8°$ (see Figure 6-21).[56] The same treatment of the alternate diastereomer ($[\alpha]_D^{18}$ $-126°$) gave a mixture with $[\alpha]_D^{18}$ $-73°$ (reference 56). Use of insufficient hydrazine gave recovered material for the first diastereomer with $[\alpha]_D^{18}$ $-39°$, indicating that epimerization of starting material is not extensive but does occur slowly. It was subsequently shown that the dialkylmercury is isomerized by hydra-zine.[57] Reutov and Ching-Chu have suggested that the facile isomerization of the dialkylmercurial is due to enolization in the α-mercuricamphor system.

To test their enolization postulate, Reutov and Ching-Chu prepared several 3-alkyl-3-bromomercuricamphors; these tertiary organometallics proved to be very unstable. The 3-methyl- and 3-ethyl-3-bromomercuricamphor could be obtained in one diastereomeric form only.

[56] Since the two products are diastereomers (actually exo-endo related), there is no basis for expecting complete "racemization" to give an equal mixture. This rotation is somewhat different from the value obtained after thermal (radical?) equilibration in dioxane ($[\alpha]_D^{18}$ $-68°$), (references 8) a result which could be interpreted as indicating partial retention of configuration for this reaction. However, no such comparison can be made without a knowledge of the solvent and temperature effects on the diastereomer equilibrium.

[57] O. A. Reutov and L. Ching-Chu, *J. Gen. Chem. USSR (Eng. Transl.)*, **29**:1177 (1959).

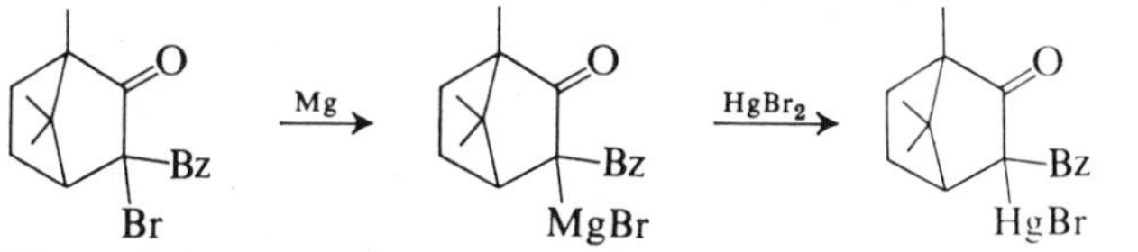

Figure 6-43 Synthesis of 3-benzyl-3-bromomercuricamphor

As noted in the discussion of stannite reduction, Reutov and Lu (reference 50) found that treatment of either epimeric 2-chloromercuricamphane with hydrazine gave the identical product, and also that hydrazine interconverts the starting materials.

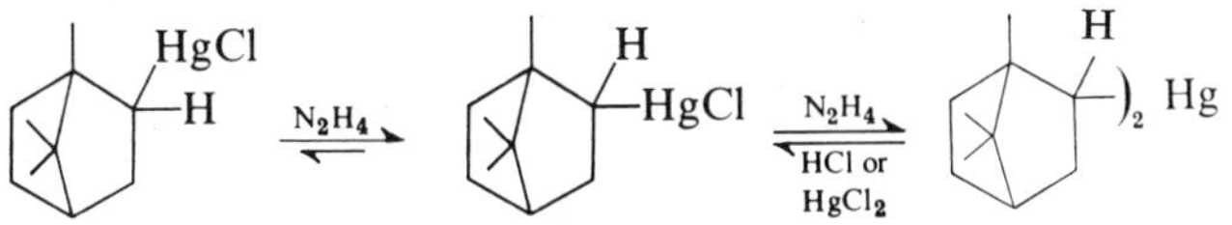

Figure 6-44 Effect of hydrazine on the diastereomeric 2-chloromercuricamphanes

Similar results are obtained in the reduction of D-(+)-2-bromomercuributane (reference 35). Reduction of this material with hydrazine and sodium hydroxide gives D-(+)-di-*sec*-butylmercury in poor yield with 19% retention of configuration (vs. 4% with stannite). Again, as in the case with stannite, racemization must have occurred in both alkyl groups. Partial reaction followed by isolation of starting material showed some racemization. Again the observed nonstereospecific reaction may be an artifact due to racemization of starting material and product.

Racemization and formation of diorganomercurial from 2-methoxycyclohexylmercuric halides are considered indications of a one-electron transfer reaction for stannite (Sec. 6-3d); similar arguments hold for hydrazine. However, hydrazine alone reduces alkylmercuric halides very slowly, whereas the reaction proceeds rapidly in the presence of alkali, suggesting an (at least partially) ionic mechanism. The stoichiometry of this reduction is unknown, and consequently a mechanistic discussion must be speculative. An overall reaction scheme is presented in Figure 6-45, in which a two-electron

(1) $RHgBr + H_2NNH_2 \rightleftharpoons \overset{-}{R}\overset{+}{Hg}-NH_2NH_2 \xrightarrow{\text{base}} RHgNHNH_2$
$\qquad\qquad\qquad\qquad\qquad\quad |$
$\qquad\qquad\qquad\qquad\qquad\; Br$

(2) $RHgNH-NH_2 \overset{\text{base}}{\rightleftharpoons} RHgN\overset{-}{H}N\overset{..}{H} \longrightarrow RHg^- + HN{=}NH$

(3) $RHg^- + RHgBr \longrightarrow RHgHgR \longrightarrow \overset{-}{R}HgR \longrightarrow RHgR + Hg^\circ$
$\qquad\qquad\qquad\qquad\qquad\qquad\qquad |$
$\qquad\qquad\qquad\qquad\qquad\qquad Hg^+$

Figure 6-45 Two-electron reduction and formation of diimide

reduction occurs with production of diimide, and in Figure 6-46, where subsequent reduction by diimide is postulated as a homolytic reaction.

$$H—N{=}N—H + 2RHgBr \rightarrow 2RHg\cdot + N_2 + 2HBr$$
$$2RHg\cdot \rightarrow RHgHgR \rightarrow RHgR + Hg^\circ$$
$$RHg\cdot \rightarrow R\cdot + Hg^\circ$$
$$R\cdot + RHgBr \rightleftharpoons [R_2HgBr]\cdot \xrightarrow{\text{reduction}} R_2Hg + Br^-$$

Figure 6-46 Scheme for reduction by diimide

The principal basis for proposing the heterolytic reaction of Figure 6-45 is the observation that the reaction rate is enormously accelerated by the addition of alkali. However, the function of base could be to form $RHgNHNH_2$ or $RHgNHNHHgR$, followed by homolytic cleavages to

$$RHgBr + H_2NNH_2 \xrightarrow{\text{base}} RHg—NHNH_2$$
$$RHgBr + RHgNHNH_2 \xrightarrow{\text{base}} RHg—NHNH—RHg$$
$$RHg—NHNH—HgR \longrightarrow 2RHg\cdot + HN{=}NH$$
$$2RHg\cdot \longrightarrow \text{as in Figure 6-46}$$
$$HN{=}NH \longrightarrow \text{as in Figure 6-46}$$

Figure 6-47 Alternate homolytic path for reduction by hydrazine

form $RHg\cdot$ and diimide. These alternate schemes appear to be subject to test. Thus, any diimide formed might be trapped by a high concentration of olefin,[58] conceivably leading to stereospecific formation of dialkylmercury.

The diimide postulated as an intermediate in these reactions could also partially reduce the mercurial to hydrocarbon. The diimide reduction of

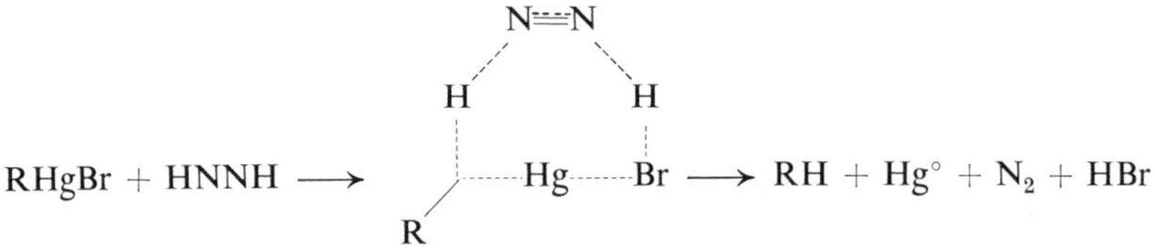

Figure 6-48 Possible formation of hydrocarbon

dialkylmercurials may be a highly stereospecific reaction; this interesting possibility has not yet been examined.

The products obtained by Wright (reference 55) (Figure 6-42) are readily explained by disproportionation of the radicals formed in Figure 6-46. It should be noted that the stannite reduction may give some of the other

[58] By *cis*-hydrogenation; E. J. Corey, D. J. Pasto and W. L. Mock, *J. Am. Chem. Soc.*, **83**:2957 (1961).

products found in the hydrazine reduction (Figure 6-42), but Traylor and Winstein (reference 52) reported only diorganomercurial (15% yield).

6-4   Hydride Reduction

Very few of the available reducing agents have been used on organometallics. Catalytic reduction and the many metal hydrides should furnish interesting new results in the future. Lithium aluminum hydride appears to be the only such reagent which has been actively investigated. Barton and Rosenfelder[59] found that diphenylmercury is converted to benzene with this reagent, and Winstein and Traylor[60] have subsequently demonstrated an analogous reduction of alkylmercuric halides to the hydrocarbon.

Traylor[61] found that the hydrocarbon is not formed directly in this reaction, but rather by hydrolysis (during isolation) of an intermediate organoaluminum compound. Thus, diphenylmercury and lithium aluminum hydride gave mercury, hydrogen, and lithium tetraphenylaluminate as the direct reaction products. Subsequent treatment of the aluminum compound (not

$$LiAlH_4 + 2(C_6H_5)_2Hg \rightarrow 2Hg° + 2H_2 + LiAl(C_6H_5)_4$$
$$100\% \quad 80\%$$
$$LiAl(C_6H_5)_4 + 4HgCl_2 \rightarrow 4C_6H_5HgCl + AlCl_3 + LiCl$$
$$60\%$$

Figure 6-49   Hydride reduction of diphenylmercury

isolated) with mercuric chloride gave a 60% yield of phenylmercuric chloride. The absence of highly nucleophilic (e.g., phenyllithium) organometallics in the hydride reduction product was demonstrated by the lack of reaction with carbon dioxide.

Similar treatment of phenylmercuric chloride with lithium aluminum hydride gave a product which, on hydrolysis, yielded benzene.

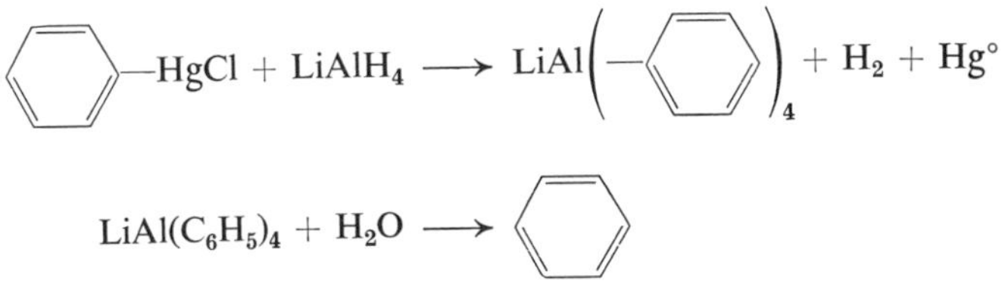

$$LiAl(C_6H_5)_4 + H_2O \longrightarrow$$

Figure 6-50   Hydrocarbon formation on hydrolysis
of organoaluminum intermediate

[59] D. H. R. Barton and W. J. Rosenfelder, *J. Chem. Soc.*, 2385 (1951).
[60] S. Winstein and T. G. Traylor, *J. Am. Chem. Soc.*, **78**:2597 (1956).
[61] T. G. Traylor, *Chem. & Ind.*, 1223 (1959).

Although no quantitative kinetic data exist which pertain to this reaction, Traylor (reference 61) has reported the rate sequence diphenylmercury $\gg$ di-*sec*-butylmercury $>$ di-*n*-butylmercury $>$ dineophylmercury or dicamphylmercury. This order is similar to that found by Winstein and Traylor for the acetic acid cleavage of these same materials.[62] Nesmeyanov and Kritskaia (reference 4) have also noted the extreme sluggishness of α-chloromercuricamphenilone in its reaction with lithium aluminum hydride (see Figure 6-5) (reference 5).

The work of Zakharkin and Khorlina[63] is also relevant to hydride reduction. In this instance, diethylaluminum hydride, when treated with diethylmercury, diethylcadmium, diethylzinc, or diethylmagnesium, gave the results shown in Figure 6-51. Note that at 90 to 100°, ethane is obtained from the mercurial directly, before hydrolysis of the intermediate aluminum product. No hydrogen is evolved in the magnesium case; rather, magnesium hydride is formed. This may well be a clue to the mechanism of hydride reductions of organometallics in general, i.e., initial formation of unstable metal hydrides which decompose further to give the metal and hydrogen gas.

$$(CH_3CH_2)_2AlH + (CH_3CH_2)_2Hg \xrightarrow{90 \text{ to } 100°} (CH_3CH_2)_3Al + H_2 + CH_3CH_3 + Hg°$$

$$(CH_3CH_2)_2AlH + (CH_3CH_2)_2Zn \xrightarrow{25 \text{ to } 30°} (CH_3CH_2)_3Al + Zn° + H_2$$
$$90\%$$

$$(CH_3CH_2)_2AlH + (CH_3CH_2)_2Cd \xrightarrow{40°} (CH_3CH_2)_3Al + Cd° + H_2$$
$$92\%$$

$$(CH_3CH_2)_2AlH + (CH_3CH_2)_2Mg \xrightarrow{60 \text{ to } 80°} (CH_3CH_2)_3Al + MgH_2$$
$$80\%$$

Figure 6-51 Reduction of various organometallics with diethylaluminum hydride

[62] S. Winstein and T. G. Traylor, *J. Am. Chem. Soc.*, **77**:3747 (1955).
[63] L. I. Zakharkin and I. M. Khorlina, *Zh. Obshch. Khim.*, **32**:2783 (1962).

7

ALKYL TRANSFERS ON MERCURY

7-1 Introduction

A partial list of the many plausible exchange reactions of organomercurials was given in Sec. 5-1. Of these, the cleavage of dialkyl- and diaryl-mercurials and the reverse symmetrization reaction were discussed separately, mainly because the bulk of the literature suggests such a division.

This chapter will include the remaining reactions of organomercurials that involve either the breaking or formation of a carbon-mercury bond. Some of these reactions probably do not involve electrophilic substitution at the carbon atom, although exact mechanistic criteria have in many cases not been applied. Awareness of these processes is important in the study of electrophilic substitution of mercurials because their appearance as side reactions may cause confusion. An example is the exchange reaction with metallic mercury, of obvious importance in radiomercury work in view of the facile formation of the free metal under a variety of conditions.

7-2 Alkylmercuric Halide Exchange with Mercuric Salts

Many of the reactions of organomercurials cannot be detected without the use of isotopic mercury. Falling into this category is the exchange of an alkylmercuric halide with an inorganic mercury salt, which was first observed by Nefedov, Sintova, and Frolov.[1] Mechanistically, there are a number of pathways by which this exchange might occur; some of these can be discounted by the kinetic data which have been obtained. Regardless of the mechanism, the operational process is shown in Figure 7-1. The radiolabel may reside in either reactant initially because the forward and reverse reactions are identical.

$$R—Hg—X + {}^{203}HgX_2 \rightleftharpoons R—{}^{203}Hg—X + HgX_2$$

Figure 7-1 The one-alkyl exchange reaction

[1] V. D. Nefedov, E. N. Sintova, and N. Ya. Frolov, *Zh. Fiz. Khim.*, **30**:2356 (1956).

Reutov, Knoll, and Ian-Tsei[2] used the diastereomeric *cis-* and *trans-*2-methoxycyclohexylmercuric chlorides to investigate the stereochemistry of exchange with radioactive mercuric chloride. The study was carried out in acetone, dioxane, and isobutyl alcohol as solvents at 120 to 135°, conditions which led to concurrent formation of mercurous precipitates. In spite of this decomposition,[3] these workers found complete retention of configuration for both diastereomers.[4]

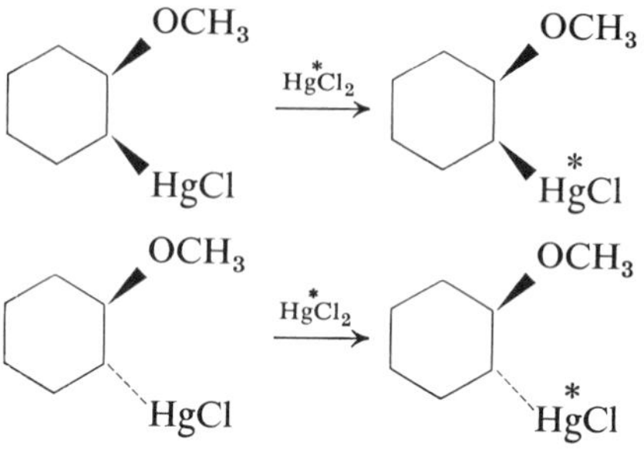

Figure 7-2 Retention of configuration with diastereomeric methoxycyclohexylmercuric chlorides

A systematic study of this reaction, termed the "one-alkyl-mercury exchange," has been carried out by Hughes, Ingold, Thorpe, and Volger.[5] Optically active *sec*-butylmercuric acetate, when treated with radiomercuric acetate in ethanol solution at 60°, underwent exchange with retention of configuration. When carried through as many as eight half-lives for exchange, the rotation of recovered mercuric compound remained essentially unaltered. Much longer treatment however led to extensive racemization. This was attributed to a secondary process which also involved the slow formation of a precipitate from solution.

In this connection, it was noted that precipitation was so extensive with *sec*-butylmercuric bromide and iodide and their respective inorganic mercuric salts that making kinetic and stereochemical studies with them is inadvisable (reference 5).

[2] O. A. Reutov, P. Knoll, and U. Ian-Tsei, *Proc. Acad. Sci. USSR, Chem. Sect.*, **120**:477 (1958).

[3] This and related decompositions are probably demercuration reactions, $RHg^+ \rightarrow R^+ + Hg^\circ$, in certain instances assisted by mercuric salts; J. H. Robson and G. F. Wright, *Can. J. Chem.*, **38**:21 (1960). See also F. R. Jensen and R. J. Ouellette, *J. Am. Chem. Soc.*, **83**:4477, 4478 (1961).

[4] The products were recrystallized before counting, but according to Reutov et al. (reference 2) the diastereomers are not separated by this procedure. Nonetheless it is difficult to completely rule out partial fractionation (especially if the products are close to purity initially); hence the high degree of specificity claimed by these authors is not necessarily warranted.

[5] E. D. Hughes, C. Ingold, F. G. Thorpe, and H. C. Volger, *J. Chem. Soc.*, 1133 (1961).

$$
\begin{array}{ccc}
\text{CH}_3 & & \text{CH}_3 \\
| & & | \\
\text{AcOHg}\!\blacktriangleright\!\text{C}\!\blacktriangleleft\!\text{H} & \xrightarrow{\overset{*}{\text{Hg}}(\text{OAc})_2} & \overset{*}{\text{AcOHg}}\!\blacktriangleright\!\text{C}\!\blacktriangleleft\!\text{H} \\
| & & | \\
\text{CH}_2 & & \text{CH}_2 \\
| & & | \\
\text{CH}_3 & & \text{CH}_3
\end{array}
$$

Figure 7-3   Retention in mercuric acetate exchange
with *sec*-butylmercuric acetate

The net stereochemical result for the alkylmercuric halide-mercuric salt reaction—retention of configuration at the carbon seat of reaction—does little to differentiate the two most plausible mechanistic pathways. One may consider direct interaction between the two species, in a manner comparable to the mercuric halide cleavage of dialkylmercury compounds (Sec. 5-5). Alternatively, symmetrization to dialkylmercury followed by cleavage with

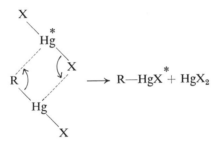

Figure 7-4   A possible mechanism
for one-alkyl exchange

mercuric halide would be expected to occur with retention. We may with confidence assign relative velocities to the reactions shown in Figure 7-5,

$$
2\text{RHgX} \xrightarrow{\text{slow}} \text{RHgR} + \text{HgX}_2
$$
$$
\text{R}\!-\!\text{Hg}\!-\!\text{R} + \overset{*}{\text{Hg}}\text{X}_2 \xrightarrow{\text{fast}} \text{R}\!-\!\overset{*}{\text{Hg}}\text{X} + \text{RHgX}
$$

Figure 7-5   Exchange via symmetrization
and cleavage of a dialkylmercurial

since the position of equilibrium in this case is known to greatly favor the alkylmercuric salt over the dialkylmercurial. Since the same stereochemistry is expected for both of the processes outlined above, a distinction must rest on kinetic arguments. Retention of configuration is a geometrical requirement of the process shown in Figure 7-4; both reactions in Figure 7-5 are known to proceed with retention of configuration (Secs. 6-2 and 5-4).

Although both of the mechanistic pathways outlined should follow second-order kinetics overall, the dependence on each substrate differs. The four-center mechanism will give rise to rates which are proportional to the mercuric halide concentration,

$$\text{Rate} = k_2[\text{RHgX}][\text{HgX}_2]$$

while the equilibrium mechanism (Figure 7-5) will give rates which are independent of the mercuric halide concentration,

$$\text{Rate} = k_2[\text{RHgX}]^2$$

The unimolecular dependence in each reagent was shown to hold for methylmercuric iodide, acetate, and nitrate as well as for sec-butylmercuric acetate with the corresponding mercuric salts in ethanol solvent (reference 5). The pertinent data are collected in Table 7-1. These data are compelling

Table 7-1 Kinetic data for the reaction:
$$\text{RHgX} + \overset{*}{\text{Hg}}\text{X}_2 \longrightarrow \text{R}\overset{*}{\text{Hg}}\text{X} + \text{HgX}_2$$

RHgX	Temp.	$10^4 k_2$(liters/mole-sec)	Rel. rate (60°)
CH_3HgNO_3	0.0°	16.9	2.4×10^5
CH_3HgOAc	59.8°	50	1.0×10^3
sec-ButylHgOAc	59.8°	3.05	61
CH_3HgI	100.2°	10.1	7.9
CH_3HgBr	59.8°	0.05	1

Solvent: ethanol in all cases except methylmercuric nitrate exchange, where ethanol with HNO_3 (0.32 M) and 0.8% H_2O was used.

evidence favoring a direct mechanism for the exchange process. Although it does not hold in this case, the mechanism shown in Figure 7-5, that is, symmetrization followed by cleavage of dialkylmercury, is a reasonable sequence. The fact that it is not observed in the work under discussion is a reflection of relative rates. Available information points to the velocity sequence shown in Figure 7-6, that is, cleavage of dialkylmercury by mercuric halide occurs more readily than the analogous cleavage or exchange of alkylmercuric halide, which in turn is faster than symmetrization of alkylmercuric halide. The last reaction may be viewed as the cleavage of alkylmercuric halide by alkylmercuric halide, which would be expected to occur less readily than cleavage by the more electrophilic inorganic mercuric salt.

$$R_2Hg + HgX_2 > RHgX + HgX_2 > 2RHgX \rightarrow R_2Hg$$

Figure 7-6 Predicted relative velocities
of three reactions of mercurials

The data in Table 7-1 point up several other interesting aspects of this reaction. The gross rate changes associated with changes in the methylmercuric salt anion suggest a polar transition state, since the rates decrease with decreasing ionic character. Further, it was shown that increasing the polarity of the solvent (from ethanol to 90% aqueous ethanol) caused the rate to increase by a factor of 1.83 with methylmercuric bromide as substrate. A comparable increase was found on the addition of lithium nitrate to this system; an enhancement factor of 2.5 was observed when the concentrations of mercuric bromide, methylmercuric bromide, and lithium nitrate were equal (0.1 M). This behavior, as well as the special salt effect associated with halide ion (covered in the next section), led the authors of this work (reference 5) to postulate that the reaction is not assisted by coordination between the anion of the substituting agent and the mercury atom being expelled, and that the transition state is open, not closed. Although a detailed picture was not shown, the mechanism of Figure 7-7 was inferred. This mechanism must

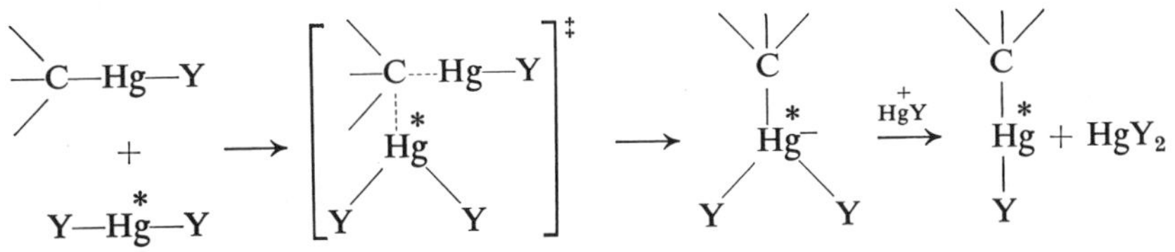

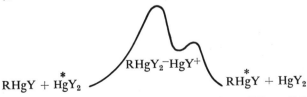

Figure 7-7 Open transition state, or S_E2, cleavage mechanism

have a parallel path wherein the transition state and the unstable intermediate exchange positions along the reaction coordinate; otherwise, it would violate the principle of microscopic reversibility.

The extensive studies of ^{203}Hg exchange in mercurials by Hughes, Ingold, and coworkers contain significant experimental findings. However, their interpretations of the experimental results in some instances require alterations to avoid violation of the principle of microscopic reversibility, which requires that the reverse reaction be exactly the same as the forward reaction. For a symmetrical reaction, i.e., one in which the starting materials and products are identical, the reaction pathway must be symmetrical. The energy profile for the mechanism proposed by Hughes, Ingold, and coworkers is not symmetrical (Figure 7-8), and the forward and reverse reactions are not identical. Clearly

$$RHgY_2^-HgY^+$$

$$RHgY + \overset{*}{Hg}Y_2 \qquad\qquad R\overset{*}{Hg}Y + HgY_2$$

Figure 7-8 Energy profile for the mechanism of Figure 7-7

the principle of microscopic reversibility refutes this pathway.[5a] However, this mechanism becomes acceptable and an overall symmetrical energy profile in effect is achieved by proposing two forward and two reverse pathways in each case, the parallel pathways being mirror images except for isotopic labeling.

Several other mechanisms, consistent with the observed results, can be proposed for the reaction. One of these, which is a variation of the mechanism of Hughes, Ingold, and coworkers, has a number of intermediates along the reaction path (Figure 7-9). This mechanism and the reaction-coordinate

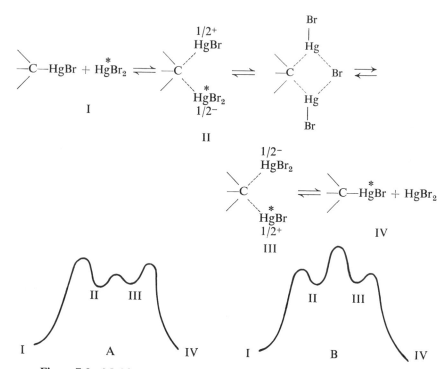

Figure 7-9　Multistep reaction and possible shapes of the energy profile

diagrams fulfill the reversibility and symmetry requirements. The bonding in the intermediates could be of several types, but the simplest involves overlap of a carbon sp^3 atomic orbital with mercury sp or p orbitals. Profile B is

[5a] The conclusions derived from the application of the principle of microscopic reversibility to the reactions discussed in this book were at the time of the writing different from those of common usage. The authors had originally intended to include a discussion of the applicability of their conclusions to chemical reactions in general, but an excellent paper on this subject has recently appeared, R. L. Burwell, Jr., and R. G. Pearson, *J. Phys. Chem.*, **70**:300 (1966).

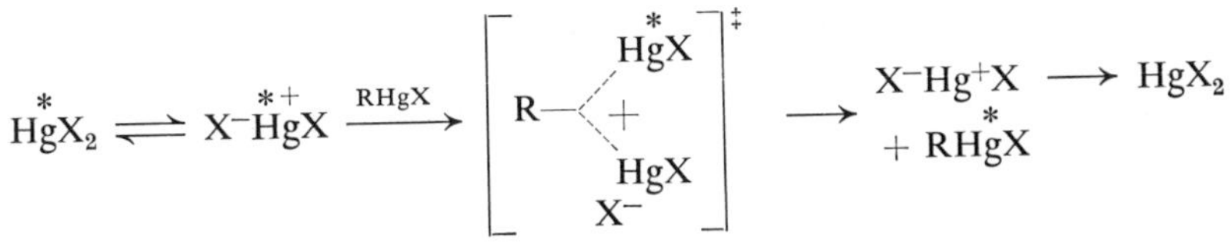

$$\overset{*}{\text{HgX}}_2 \rightleftharpoons X^-\overset{*}{\text{Hg}}^+ \xrightarrow{\text{RHgX}} \left[R \underset{X^-}{\overset{\overset{*}{\text{HgX}}}{\underset{\text{HgX}}{\diagdown} \diagup}} + \right]^{\ddagger} \longrightarrow \begin{array}{l} X^-\text{Hg}^+X \longrightarrow \text{HgX}_2 \\ + \overset{*}{\text{RHgX}} \end{array}$$

Figure 7-10   Exchange with mercuric salt-ion pairs

not consistent with the interpretation of Hughes, Ingold, Thorpe, and Volger (reference 5) that bridging is absent in the slow step.

No evidence is available which requires the intervention of these intermediates, nor are data available which refute their existence. However, in the absence of a suitable analogy it is desirable to look for other possibilities.

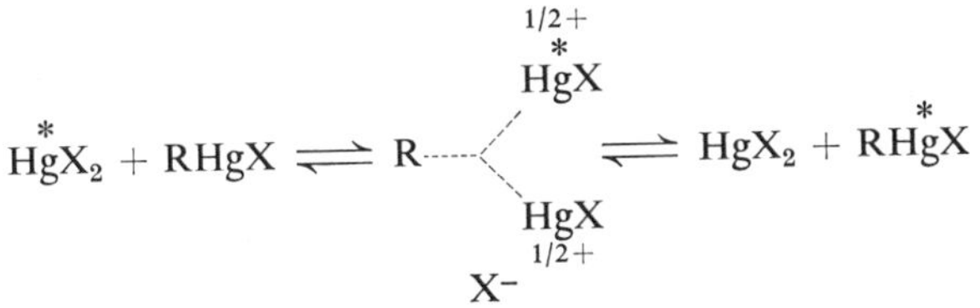

$$\overset{*}{\text{HgX}}_2 + \text{RHgX} \rightleftharpoons R \underset{\underset{X^-}{\text{HgX}}}{\overset{\overset{1/2+}{\overset{*}{\text{HgX}}}}{\diagdown}} \rightleftharpoons \text{HgX}_2 + \overset{*}{\text{RHgX}}$$

Figure 7-11   A possible one-alkyl exchange mechanism involving formation of an intermediate cation

An attractive possibility involves prior ionization of the inorganic mercuric salt (Figure 7-10), but the kinetic evidence appears to rule this out for mercuric halides unless the charged species are present as ion pairs. A closely related mechanism (Figure 7-11), in which a free anion is lost as the reaction proceeds, is allowed only if an intermediate is formed in the reaction.

Hughes, Ingold and coworkers stated that their results could not be explained on the basis of a closed transition state (Figure 7-12) largely because of the increase in rate noted with increasing ionic character of the

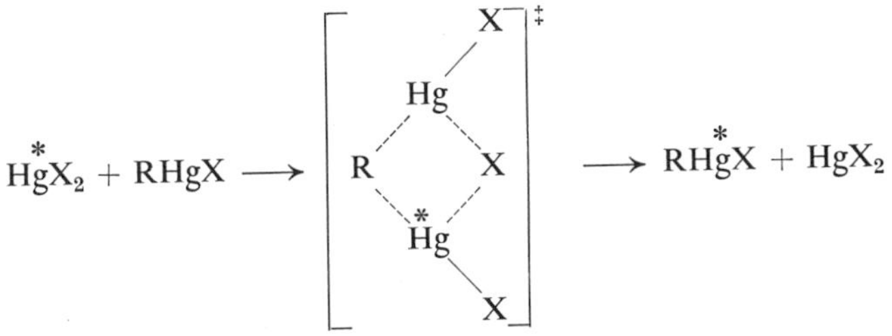

$$\overset{*}{\text{HgX}}_2 + \text{RHgX} \longrightarrow \left[R \underset{\overset{*}{\text{Hg}}}{\overset{\text{Hg}}{\diamond}} X \right]^{\ddagger} \longrightarrow \overset{*}{\text{RHgX}} + \text{HgX}_2$$

Figure 7-12   The closed transition state model for one-alkyl exchange

salts. Implicit in this hypothesis is the assumption that there is an inverse correspondence between ionic character of the mercury-anion bond and bridging ability. It is perhaps more reasonable to expect this relationship to hold for closely related groups such as substituted acetates, but not for comparisons between halides, acetates, and nitrates. In particular, because of geometric considerations, i.e., the formation of six-membered rings, acetates and nitrates may be excellent bridging groups. Furthermore, the electrophilicity of mercury should increase with the more ionized ligands, and this effect may well overshadow decreased bridging. Too many different effects are in operation to rule out any participation of anion in these systems. The increase in rate observed with increased ionic character could thus be explained by an open transition state of the type shown in Figure 7-10, or by the closed transition state model (Figure 7-12). The process involving intermediates (Figure 7-11) is less satisfactory in this regard. Our interpretation is that the results do not allow a choice to be made between the former two mechanisms.

The nature of the bonding in the closed transition state (Figure 7-12) is of interest. For carbon, the hybridization may be of various forms, but sp^3 seems most probable and only this possibility will be considered. On mercury the hybridization may be sp and p or sp^2 and p; in addition, bonding with (empty) d-orbitals may occur. The former could involve either π or σ bonding on mercury to the bridging X group. The general chemical experience is that π-bonding (p–p) is not important for higher than second-row elements. Thus the atomic orbital on mercury which contributes in the bonding to the bridging atom may be either p (σ-bonding) or sp^2. For X = halogen, the bridging orbitals on halogen may reasonably be either one or two p-orbitals (σ-bonding). (For further discussion see Chap. 1.)

The diminished rate of sec-butylmercuric acetate relative to methylmercuric acetate (Table 7-1) appears to be due to steric effects. Additional work by Hughes and Volger[6] has led to the relative rate sequence shown in Table 7-2. The neopentyl compound undergoes reaction at essentially the

Table 7-2 Steric effects in the alkylmercuric salt-mercuric salt exchange reaction:
$$RHgY + Hg^*Y_2 \longrightarrow RHg^*Y + HgY_2$$

R	Relative rate
sec-butyl	0.06
neopentyl	0.33
ethyl	0.42
methyl	1.00

[6] E. D. Hughes and H. C. Volger, *J. Chem. Soc.*, 2359 (1961).

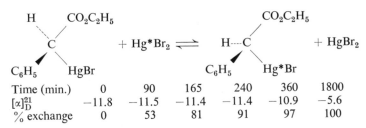

$$\text{Rate} = k_2[\text{RHgBr}][\text{Hg*Br}_2]$$

$$k_2 = 1.1 \times 10^{-3} \text{ liter/mole-sec (pyridine, } 60°)$$

$$E_{act} = 16.3 \text{ kcal/mole} \qquad \Delta S^{\ddagger} = -15.5 \text{ eu}$$

Figure 7-13   Exchange of an α-halomercuriacetate in pyridine

same rate as the ethylmercuric salt, demonstrating the insensitivity of this exchange to β-carbon substitution. Larger steric effects are evinced by α-substituents, as shown by the rate decrease in going from methyl to ethyl to *sec*-butylmercuric bromide. These effects are still small, as expected for reactions involving front-side attack of carbon.

Kinetic studies have also been carried out on the α-halomercuriphenyl-acetates by Reutov and coworkers[7a-g] and Ingold and coworkers[7h]. Second-order kinetics, first-order in each reactant, were established for ethyl α-bromomercuriphenylacetate and radiomercuric bromide in pyridine, 80% aq. ethanol (reference 7f) and 70% aq. dioxane (reference 7h). In other solvents, highly varied reactivities and in some instances changes in kinetic order were observed.

Hughes, Ingold, and Roberts (reference 7h) carried out stereochemical studies in 70% aq. dioxane and found the exchange to occur with retention of

Time (min.)	0	90	165	240	360	1800
$[\alpha]_D^{21}$	−11.8	−11.5	−11.4	−11.4	−10.9	−5.6
% exchange	0	53	81	91	97	100

Figure 7-14   Comparison of exchange and racemization in 70% aq. dioxane at 59.2°

[7] a. O. A. Reutov, V. I. Sokolov, and I. P. Beletskaya, *Proc. Acad. Sci. USSR, Chem. Sect.*, **136**:115 (1961)

b. *Ibid., Bull. Acad. Sci. USSR, Div. Chem. Sci.*, 1123 (1961).

c. *Ibid.*, p. 1328.

d. *Ibid.*, p. 1127.

e. *Ibid.*, p. 1458.

f. O. A. Reutov, V. I. Sokolov, I. P. Beletskaya, and Y. S. Ryabokobylko, *ibid.*, 879 (1963).

g. O. A. Reutov, B. Praisnar, I. P. Beletskaya, and V. I. Sokolov, *ibid.*, 884 (1963).

h. E. D. Hughes, C. K. Ingold, and R. M. G. Roberts, *J. Chem. Soc.*, 3900 (1964).

Table 7-3 Substituent effects in the one-alkyl exchange reaction
of *para*-substituted bromomercuri-ester

S_E2 Reaction (reference 7f) 65°, 80% aq. EtOH		S_E1 Reaction (reference 7g) 30°, DMSO	
para-substituent	k_{rel}	*para*-substituent	k_{rel}
NO$_2$	—	NO$_2$	4.0
Br	1.2	I	1.3
H	1.0	H	1.0
CH$_3$	0.93	CH$_3$	—
t-C$_4$H$_9$	0.41	*t*-C$_4$H$_9$	0.71

configuration. Little (essentially negligible) racemization accompanied the exchange.

The effect of *para*-substituents on the rate of this reaction has been determined by Reutov and coworkers (reference 7f). The relative second-order rate constants along with those obtained in a first-order process are listed in Table 7-3. The effect of substituents on the rate is actually very small and it is similar for both the S_E2 and S_E1 reactions. The results indicate that in going to the transition state, the central carbon atom becomes more negatively charged.

Reutov and coworkers have proposed that the reactions occur by a four-center process (S_Ei) while Hughes, Ingold, and Roberts tentatively assigned the mechanism as S_E2 (for the second-order process). However, the results are far from conclusive and either pathway might apply.

For the second-order reaction, Reutov postulated that the reactive species is the pyridine-mercuric halide complex, and that the transition state is Structure I of Figure 7-15. However, this mechanism also violates the principle of microscopic reversibility (unless multiple intermediates are invoked to give a symmetrical energy profile). This is also true of an alternate transition state with pyridine complexed to the alkylmercuric halide (Figure 7-15, Structure II). Allowable four-center or five-center transition states may involve complex formation with one or two moles of amine (Figure 7-16).

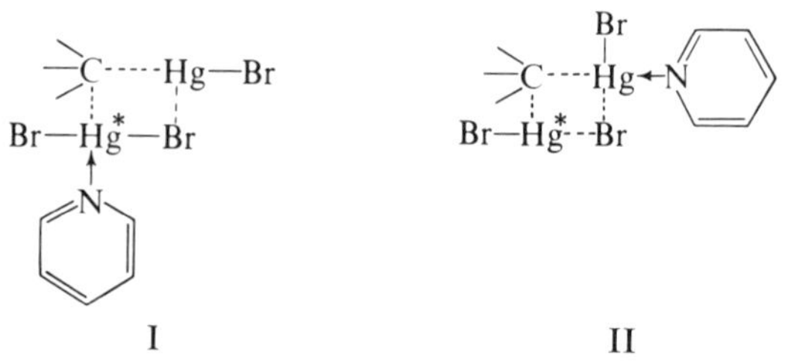

Figure 7-15 Pyridine-catalyzed four-center exchange mechanisms

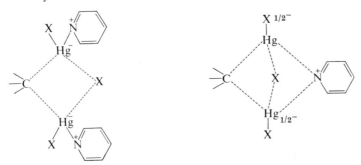

Figure 7-16 Allowable transition states which account for the catalytic effect of amines

The charge distributions shown are the expected formal values for the transition state, but the values may vary slightly and the central carbon atom may bear a partial charge. In both of these transition states, carbon and the two mercury atoms have tetrahedral type bonding. This particular feature is expected to give considerable stabilization for these processes. Bonding with nitrogen is by overlap with the sp^2 orbital; the bonding with the X group is expected to vary with anion. Any of the mechanisms proposed previously can account for the results providing the role of amine and the principle of microscopic reversibility are accommodated.

In the 70% aq. dioxane system, very interesting results were obtained upon adding bromide ion and mineral acid to the solution (reference 7h). The halide serves as a catalyst for the formation of hydrocarbon, while the acid acts to increase the rate of acid cleavage of the carbon-mercury bond. At 60°, in the presence of bromide ion, the one-alkyl exchange requires a few hours and the hydrolytic loss of mercury takes place at a comparable rate. However, if acid is added, the acid cleavage requires a few minutes. In the absence of free bromide ion, the exchange requires a few hours and no hydrolytic loss of mercury occurs. With added perchloric acid, no hydrolytic loss of mercury could be detected in a period of 24 hours. The absence of acid cleavage when catalytic anions are excluded provides additional evidence that under these conditions the mercury (II) exchange does not occur by an S_E1 process. Similarly, the results in the presence of bromide ion strongly suggest that a carbanion-forming reaction is occurring.

In DMSO as solvent both Reutov and his group (reference 7g) and Ingold and coworkers (reference 7h) observed first-order kinetics for the one-alkyl exchange of mercuric bromide and the bromomercuri-ester. These results are indicative of a carbanion type reaction, and experiments with the optically-active ester support this view. The first-order rate constants for racemization ($k_1 = 3.4 \times 10^{-4}$ sec^{-1}) and for exchange ($k_1 = 3.75 \times 10^{-4}$ sec^{-1}) are approximately equal at 59° (reference 7h). Furthermore, the rate of racemization is the same in the presence and in the absence of mercuric bromide.

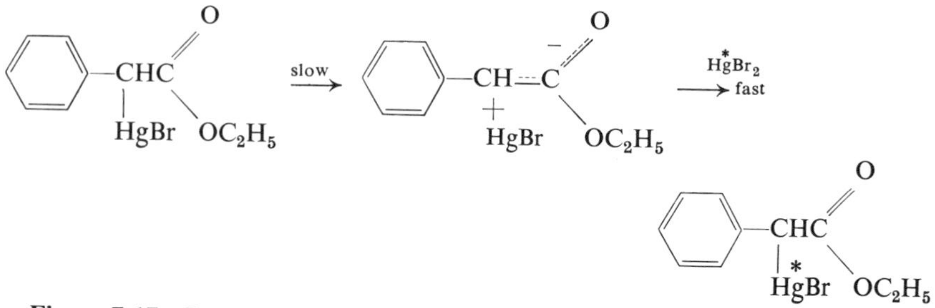

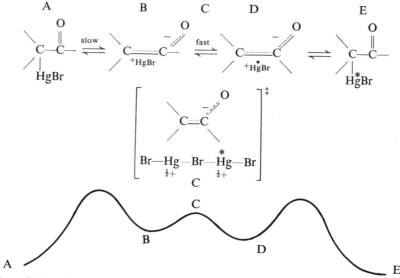

Figure 7-17   Rate-controlling ionization scheme proposed for unimolecular exchange

Both groups have proposed that the slow unimolecular reaction occurs by rate-controlling ionization followed by rapid exchange (Figure 7-17). Again, this mechanism violates the principle of microscopic reversibility, which requires that the mercury species that is lost and readded be identical, i.e. either $HgBr^+$ and $\overset{*}{H}gBr^+$, or $HgBr_2$ and $\overset{*}{H}gBr_2$. It is difficult to write a mechanism for this reaction which does not violate the microscopic reversibility requirements and yet yields $k_{rac} = k_{exchange}$, and which does not show a catalytic effect of mercuric bromide or the α-bromomercuri-ester. The devices used previously for the second-order processes do not work here. Halide exchange at the enolate ion-pair stage can account for these results, but the added transition state (C) must be of lower energy than the one preceding it to accommodate the observed kinetic order.

Figure 7-18   Mechanism and energy profile which satisfy microscopic reversibility requirements for the S_E1 reaction

Certain peculiarities in this system occur which suggest the need for a reinvestigation. Although both groups observed first order kinetics, their thermodynamic parameters show substantial disagreement. Thus, the reactions are not highly reproducible. In Table 7-3 the effect of *para*-substituents on rate are given for both the S_E2 type and S_E1 processes. Ignoring possible solvent effects the data indicate that the S_E2 process probably has more carbanionic character in the transition state. However, the effect of substituents on rate is remarkably small for the reactions in both solvents; in fact the change in rate for the S_E1 reaction is so insensitive to substituent that either this data or the assignment as S_E1 appears to be questionable. Table 7-4

Table 7-4 Exchange of $^{203}HgBr_2$ with ethyl α-bromomercuriphenylacetate in various solvents

Reference	Solvent	Mech.	Temp.	k
7a,b	Pyridine	S_E2	60°	1.1×10^{-3} liter/mole-sec
7f	80% aq. EtOH	S_E2	65°	1.87×10^{-3} liter/mole-sec
7h	70% aq. dioxane[a]	S_E2	57.8°	2.8×10^{-3} liter/mole-sec
7g,h	DMSO	S_E1	40°[7h]	$1.04^{b} \times 10^{-4}$ sec^{-1}
			40°[7g]	1.45×10^{-4} sec^{-1}
7h	DMF		60°	No exchange
7e	DMF			Exchange upon maturation of solutions
7h	Acetone	S_E2?		Rate too fast to measure but no racemization
7g	CH_3NO_2		0°	Instantaneous
7h	$CH_3C\equiv N$			Rate too fast to measure

[a] Reutov et al. had initially reported second-order kinetics (reference 7a,b) but later decided on first-order kinetics (reference 7c–f). The report of second-order kinetics in reference 7h is well documented.

[b] Interpolated from the data in reference 7h.

summarizes data for the one-alkyl exchange reaction in various solvents. The dependency of rate and mechanism on solvent is unexpected and not easily explained. It is possible that this is another example of a radical-catalyzed exchange and racemization reaction of mercurials.

Spurious results have been obtained in several studies. Reutov et al. (reference 7a–f) reported in 70% dioxane second-order and later first-order kinetics, but Ingold and coworkers (reference 7h) provided good evidence for second-order kinetics. Reutov and coworkers reported substituent effects for the reaction in this solvent but under their spurious "first-order" conditions; therefore these results are not included here.

In DMF as solvent, Reutov and coworkers (reference 7e) reported the reaction of ethyl α-bromomercuriphenylacetate with radiomercuric bromide to follow second-order kinetics ($k_2 = 2.3 \times 10^{-4}$ liter/mole-sec, 60°C), provided the DMF and mercuric halide were heated together prior to addition of organomercurial. Without this treatment, the reaction appeared to be auto-catalytic, i.e., the instantaneous rate constants increased with time. This effect was attributed to the formation of a complex between the solvent and the mercuric halide, analogous to that proposed with pyridine. It was suggested that formation of the complex with amide occurs at a rate comparable to that of the exchange reaction, and hence prior heating is needed to preform it. The complex must, of course, be of greater reactivity than the free form of the mercuric salt. Although this evidence is rather circumstantial, other work has definitely demonstrated the existence of acid-amide[8] and iodine-amide[9] complexes. Ingold and coworkers (reference 7h) also studied the reaction in DMF but did not observe the autocatalytic effect. However they confirmed the activating influence of preheating DMF and the mercuric halide.

The slow complex formation proposed by Reutov and coworkers seems unreasonable because of the general observation that complex formation occurs instantly between mercuric halides and donor compounds. A more probable explanation is that under the reaction conditions dimethylformamide undergoes decomposition to yield dimethylamine. Substantial evidence is presented in Chap. 6 and the present chapter that amines promote exchange reactions of mercury compounds. Of course peroxides, which catalyze the exchange, are also expected to be readily formed at this temperature under air atmosphere.

To circumvent the difficulties associated with the enolizable α-phenyl-acetate system, Reutov, Smolina, and Kalyavin[10] determined substituent effects with simple ring-substituted benzylmercuric halides. In this system the second-order rate constants for mercuric halide exchange follow the common behavior, i.e., increase with alkyl groups and decrease with halogen substituents. The data are shown in Table 7-5. This reaction was run in quinoline at 70°. Numerous other solvents[11] were tried but found to be un-suitable, either because the exchange reaction was too slow for measurement or because decomposition of starting material occurred too readily.

A quinoline-mercuric bromide complex, analogous to that proposed for the pyridine catalyzed reaction, was suggested. This proposal again can be discounted on the basis of microscopic reversibility. The catalytic effect of quinoline may arise from any of the possibilities noted previously for pyridine.

[8] G. Fraenkel and C. Franconi, *J. Am. Chem. Soc.*, **82:**4478 (1960).

[9] C. D. Schmulbach and R. S. Drago, *J. Am. Chem. Soc.*, **82:**4484 (1960).

[10] a. O. A. Reutov, T. A. Smolina, and V. A. Kalyavin, *Proc. Acad. Sci. USSR, Chem. Sect.*, **139:**697 (1961).

   b. *Ibid.*, *Russ. J. Phys. Chem. (English Transl.)*, **36:**59 (1962).

[11] Toluene, bromobenzene, alcohol, acetone, dioxane, acetonitrile, dimethylformamide, acetic acid, formic acid, isoamyl acetate, isoamyl ether, carbon tetrachloride, and pyridine were all noted as being unsatisfactory (reference 10).

Table 7-5   Substituent effects—the benzyl system

$$Y-\underset{}{\bigcirc}-CH_2\overset{*}{Hg}Br + HgBr_2 \longrightarrow Y-\underset{}{\bigcirc}-CH_2-\overset{*}{Hg}Br + HgBr_2$$

Y	$10^5 k_2$(liters/mole-sec)
—CH(CH$_3$)$_2$	6.6
—CH$_3$	5.7
—H	4.1
—Cl	3.6
—F	3.4

The substituent effect order shown in Table 7-5 is clearly opposite to that noted for the α-halomercuriphenylacetate system (Table 7-3); the explanation offered by Reutov and coworkers (reference 10) for this behavior was purely a ground-state argument, i.e., by virtue of its inductive effect the halogen causes a partial positive charge to develop at the benzyl carbon which diminishes its responsiveness to an electrophile. We must emphasize the more exact approach, namely, that the sign of any charge developed at the benzyl carbon during the course of the reaction is unknown; it must only become relatively more positive in going from ground state to transition state. The small rate effects which are observed indicate very little charge dispersal in progressing along the reaction coordinate.

Some additional work by this group is mentioned by Reutov in a brief review.[12] Although experimental data were not available at the time of this writing, and rate constants were not given, the relative velocities for alkylmercuric halide-mercuric halide exchange of a variety of substrates were shown; these are reproduced in Figure 7-19. It was further noted (reference 12) that simple alkylmercuric halides, not activated by an adjacent α-carbonyl or α-methoxyl group, failed to undergo exchange with the mild conditions (unspecified) employed in obtaining this rate sequence.

Closely related to the amine complex effects discussed previously are the effects of added anions on the mercuric halide exchange reaction. Research in this area has been very fruitful, and the results obtained have shed a good deal of light on the nature and reactivity of mercurials in solution. The causes of the interesting effects observed are not entirely known, and this is a promising area for further work.

A "normal" salt effect was noted in the work of Hughes, Ingold, Thorpe, and Volger (reference 5) on mercuric bromide exchange with methylmercuric bromide and mercuric acetate exchange with *sec*-butylmercuric acetate. Added lithium nitrate (concentration equal to that of both reagents, 0.1 M) caused a 250% rate increase in the former case and a 50% increase in the

[12] O. A. Reutov, *Record Chem. Progr.* (*Kresge-Hooker Sci. Lib.*), **22:**1 (1961).

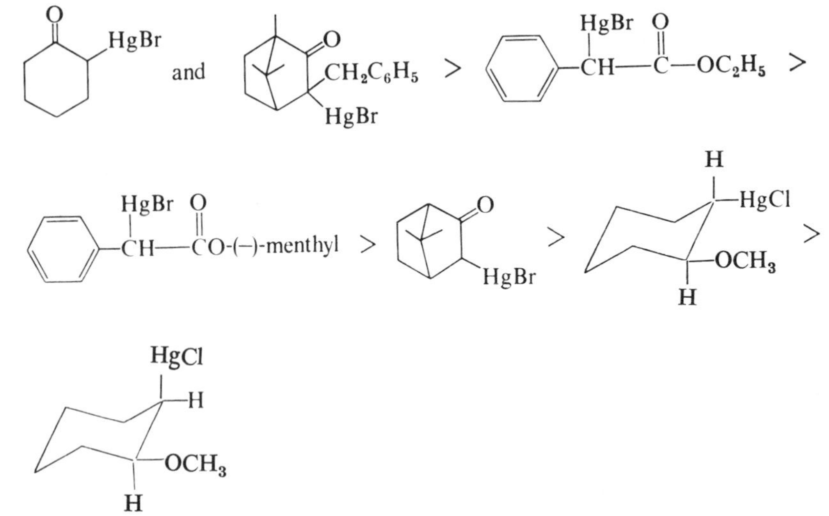

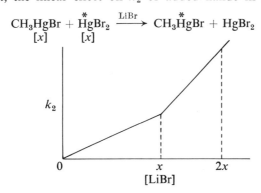

Figure 7-19 Reactivities of various mercurihalides toward exchange with radio-mercuric halide

latter. This behavior is expected for a reaction in which a polar transition state is developed. (It is also possible that the observed effect results from anion exchange.)

Added halide ion showed very different behavior, which was treated as "anion catalysis" involving true molecular interactions.[13] In fact, it was postulated that two mechanisms, differing from the one already proposed for the uncatalyzed exchange, become operative, depending on relative concentrations of the reactive species. Figure 7-20 illustrates the experimental observations. First, the linear effect on k_2 of added halide in the concentration

$$CH_3HgBr + \overset{*}{H}gBr_2 \xrightarrow{\text{LiBr}} CH_3\overset{*}{H}gBr + HgBr_2$$
$$[x] \qquad [x]$$

Figure 7-20 Effect of added lithium bromide on the second-order rate constant for methylmercuric halide exchange

[13] H. B. Charman, E. D. Hughes, C. Ingold, and H. C. Volger, *J. Chem. Soc.*, 1142 (1961).

range 0 to X was attributed to the formation of $HgBr_3^-$; this complex ion is of much greater reactivity in this exchange reaction than the uncomplexed mercuric halide. Thus, a rate increase factor of approximately 80 is involved at the point where $[LiBr] = [CH_3HgBr] = [HgBr_2] \sim 0.1\ M$.

When the concentration of alkali halide exceeds mercuric halide, another linear relationship between the second-order rate constant and lithium salt concentration becomes apparent. This effect was attributed to formation of the halide complex of the alkylmercuric bromide.

$$HgBr_2 + Br^- \xrightleftharpoons{K_1} HgBr_3^-$$

$$CH_3HgBr + Br^- \xrightleftharpoons{K_2} CH_3HgBr_2^-$$

$$K_1 > 1 > K_2\dagger$$

Figure 7-21   Complex ion formation

† It is not possible to distinguish this equilibrium from that for formation of mercuric tetrahalide dianion:

$$HgX_3^- + X^- \rightleftharpoons HgX_4^{--}$$

Indeed, as pointed out by Hughes and coworkers (reference 13), both equilibria may play a role.

The particular two-straight-line behavior demonstrated in Figure 7-20 leads to a number of conclusions. Under these reaction conditions (ethanol at 60°) K_1 (Figure 7-21) must be quite large. Otherwise no break in the line would be experienced when $[LiBr] = [HgBr_2]$. Furthermore, K_2 must be small, or an additional break would occur when $[LiBr] = ([HgBr_2] + [RHgBr])$; hence the inequality stated in Figure 7-21 must hold.

We may consider the expected behavior of a plot of alkali halide concentration vs. k_2 if other conditions were applicable. Some such predictions are shown in Figure 7-22. Others are feasible, particularly in view of the number of variables potentially involved in the exchange reaction. One important aspect is the slope of the line (Figure 7-20 and II of Figure 7-22) between $[LiBr] = x$ and $[LiBr] = 2x$; in both instances this slope is greater than that

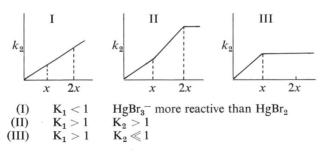

(I)	$K_1 < 1$	$HgBr_3^-$ more reactive than $HgBr_2$
(II)	$K_1 > 1$	$K_2 > 1$
(III)	$K_1 > 1$	$K_2 \ll 1$

Figure 7-22   Predicted effects of added halide depending on equilibria

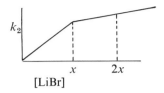

Figure 7-23 Effect of added halide
on the exchange rate constant of
neopentylmercuric bromide

between [LiBr] $= 0$ and x, but there is no reason why this must be the case. Hughes and Volger (reference 6) have indeed found a different behavior in the exchange between neopentylmercuric bromide and radiomercuric bromide in ethanol at 100.3°. In this system excess lithium bromide (beyond one mole per mole of mercuric bromide) does cause an increase in the rate constant, but the effect is less pronounced than that observed in the lower concentration range.

The anion effect was examined with a number of *sec*-butylmercuric salts with added alkali metal salts; in addition, acetic acid was shown not to alter the rate of reaction. Of particular interest is the observation that lithium

$$sec\text{-butyl-HgX} + \overset{*}{\text{Hg}}\text{X}_2 \xrightarrow{\text{MX}} sec\text{-butyl—}\overset{*}{\text{Hg}}\text{X} + \text{HgX}_2$$

$$\text{X} = \text{I}^-, \text{Br}^-, \text{Cl}^- \text{ in acetone at } 35°$$

$$\text{X} = \text{OAc}^- \text{ in ethanol at } 60°$$

Figure 7-24 Systems used in the study of anion effects

acetate shows catalytic behavior only up to the point where its concentration equals that of the mercuric salt. Beyond this concentration added lithium acetate has no effect (or a very slight effect) on k_2. This behavior is depicted in Figure 7-22 (III); it may be due to an extremely low degree of complex formation between acetate ion and alkylmercuric acetate, to steric interference of additional groups in the transition state or to other factors.

It is worth noting that a more highly complexed system might well react more slowly. Thus a decrease in rate with added salt beyond the [MX] = [HgX$_2$] range could also be envisioned, although this has not as yet been observed.

The data obtained with the *sec*-butyl system indicate that the order of catalytic effectiveness is $\text{I}^- > \text{Br}^- > \text{Cl}^- > \text{OAc}^-$; these are of course not direct comparisons, since the corresponding mercuric salts were used with each anion. Catalysis constants derived from the equation (Figure 7-25) give an indication of the relationships involved; these are shown in Table 7-6. With added anion, the contribution of the uncatalyzed reaction is often sufficiently small that it may be disregarded.

Where $[MX] < [HgX_2]$:

$$k \text{ (obs.)} = k_2 + k' \frac{[MX]}{[HgX_2]} \qquad k' = \text{rate increase when } [MX] = [HgX_2]$$

Where $[MX] > [HgX_2]$:

$$k \text{ (obs.)} = k_2 + k' + k''([MX] - [HgX_2])$$

Figure 7-25 Expressions used to determine catalysis constants—effects of added salts (reference 13)

Retention of configuration was demonstrated for *sec*-butylmercuric bromide under both sets of conditions, i.e., low and high concentrations of added lithium bromide.

The anion catalysis was attributed to the intervention of a four-center mechanism (labeled S_Ei), involving bridging halogen or acetate. The transition state for the one-anion catalyzed reaction (I of Figure 7-26) proposed by Hughes and Ingold again violates the principle of microscopic reversibility, although the two-anion mechanism (III) does not.[15] While another mechanism must be sought for the one anion-catalyzed reaction, the mechanism proposed for the two-anion-catalyzed reaction appears to be required, since no

Table 7-6 (reference 14)

R	X	Solvent	Temp.	RHgX + $\overset{*}{HgX_2}$ $\xrightarrow{MX}$ $\overset{*}{RHgX}$ + HgX₂	
				$10^5 k'$ (liter/mole-sec)[a]	$10^5 k''$ (liters²/mole²-sec)[b]
methyl	Br	ethanol	59.8°	35	500
sec-butyl	OAc	ethanol	59.8°	200	small
neopentyl	Br	ethanol	100°	26.4	122
sec-butyl	I	acetone	35°	5	400
sec-butyl	Br	acetone	35°	small	9
sec-butyl	Cl	acetone	35°	small	0.8

[a] One anion-catalyzed rate constant.
[b] Two anion-catalyzed rate constant.

[14] In general data were obtained where $[RHgX] = [HgX_2]$, where difficulties associated with lack of knowledge of the exact state of complexation are largely avoided (for a more complete discussion of this problem and the kinetic scheme, see the appendix in reference 13). In fact, varying these concentrations appears to be a suitable method to determine the degree of complexing of the various reactants, i.e., whether $(RHgX_2^- + HgX_3^-)$ or $(RHgX + HgX_4^{--})$ or $(RHgX_3^{--} + HgX_2)$ is the better representation of the actual situation. A systematic study of this sort is needed to solve this important problem.

[15] Structure I of Figure 7-26 may represent one of several intermediates along the reaction path without violating microscopic reversibility (for an analogous example, see Figure 7-9) or parallel paths may occur (see Figure 7-7).

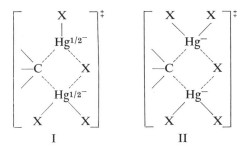

Figure 7-26 Transition states suggested for the exchange reaction catalyzed by one and two anions (reference 13)

other reasonable pathway is available. Another possibility for the latter process is a reaction between RHgX and HgX_4^{--}; however, if reaction occurs directly between these species, then during the course of the reaction at least three anions, singly (with multiple intermediates) or at once, must be involved in bridging, a most improbable situation.

A compelling argument for bridging in the one-anion-catalyzed reaction is the expectation that HgX_3^- should be a weaker electrophile than uncharged HgX_2 and hence should result in a slower reaction unless some additional effect intervenes (e.g., nucleophilic attack on substrate mercury). On the other hand $RHgX_2^-$ should be more susceptible to electrophilic attack than the uncomplexed organomercurial, and the observed one-anion effect could result from formation of this intermediate. Although indirect evidence, the discontinuity in the plot of halide concentration vs. rate constant (Figures 7-20 and 7-23), coupled with the fact that the inorganic salt should have a greater tendency to form complex anions (cf. Chap. 2), suggests that the former mechanism is operating. The transformation may be classified as S_E2 (Figure 7-27) or multi-centered (Figure 7-28). The hybridization in the latter transition state is particularly interesting. A reasonable electron configuration is sp^3 on carbon, sp^3 on mercury, with bonding on one or two p-orbitals of X (X = halogen). Tetrahedral bonding on mercury is clearly reasonable for two-anion bridging. Note that the transition state for Figure 7-28 could also

$$\overset{*}{R}HgX + HgX_3^- \rightleftharpoons \overset{*}{R}HgX_2^- + \overset{*}{H}gX_2$$

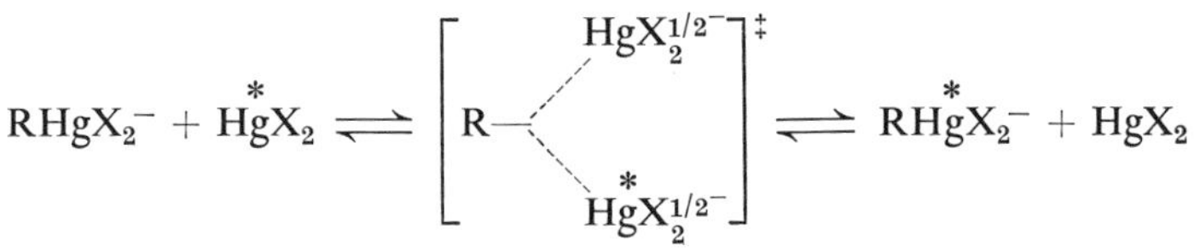

$$RHgX_2^- + \overset{*}{H}gX_2 \rightleftharpoons \left[R\!\!-\!\!\!\!\!\underset{\overset{*}{H}gX_2^{1/2-}}{\overset{HgX_2^{1/2-}}{\diagup}} \right]^{\ddagger} \rightleftharpoons \overset{*}{R}HgX_2^- + HgX_2$$

$$\overset{*}{R}HgX_2^- + HgX_2 \rightleftharpoons \overset{*}{R}HgX + HgX_3^-$$

Figure 7-27 Open transition state (S_E2) for one-anion-catalyzed exchange

$$\text{RHgX} + \overset{*}{\text{Hg}}\text{X}_3^- \;\rightleftharpoons\; \left[\begin{array}{c} \text{X} \\ | \\ \text{Hg}^{1/2-} \\ R{-}\!\!\diamond\!\!\begin{array}{cc} \text{X} & \text{X} \end{array} \\ \overset{*}{\text{Hg}}{}^{1/2-} \\ | \\ \text{X} \end{array} \right]^{\ddagger} \;\rightleftharpoons\; \text{R}\overset{*}{\text{Hg}}\text{X} + \text{HgX}_3^-$$

Figure 7-28 Closed transition state (multicentered) for one-anion-catalyzed exchange

result from reaction between $\text{RHg}\overset{*}{\text{X}}_2^-$ and HgX_2 with one anion from each mercury contributing to the bridging. While applying the microscopic reversibility principle is clearly of mechanistic value, it must be done with caution. Figure 7-29 affords an interesting illustration of two pathways; both individually violate the principle, but in concert they do not. Both the upper and lower paths provide unsymmetrical energy profiles; however the lower route is the mirror image of the upper, and further, since the transition states for both are identical, both processes must occur with the same rate. Under these circumstances the overall sequence is in accord with microscopic reversibility.

The results of the exchange studies of Hughes, Ingold, and coworkers provide evidence for uncatalyzed exchange, one-anion-catalyzed exchange and two-anion-catalyzed exchange. A number of mechanisms are possible for the first two reactions, but only one appears to be reasonable for the two-anion-catalyzed exchange (Figure 7-30). This provides the best substantiated example

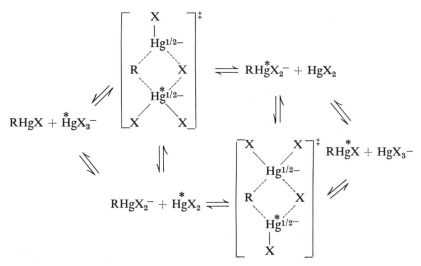

Figure 7-29 Simultaneous unsymmetrical exchange mechanisms

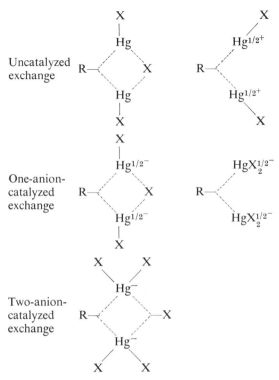

Figure 7-30   Reasonable transition states

of a four-center transition state. The greater the ionic character of the anion the faster the uncatalyzed exchange occurs, while the reverse is true for the catalyzed reactions. It is tempting to choose the open transition state for the uncatalyzed reaction and the bridged structures for the catalyzed reactions, but an unambiguous choice can not be made at this time. For example, it might be argued that in the uncatalyzed reaction the geometry on mercury with sp^2 bonding favors an ionic bridging atom. A properly designed kinetic investigation should allow a decision between the open and closed transition state models for the uncatalyzed reaction. It is expected that the kinetic orders will differ in ion dissociating solvents, and that the reaction with the open transition state will be inhibited by excess common ion. Plausible transition states for these reactions are shown in Figure 7-30.

Bromide ion catalysis has been reported for two first-order reactions in DMSO solution. Hughes, Ingold, and Roberts (reference 7h) found two-anion catalysis for racemization of active ethyl α-bromomercuriphenylacetate and a nonlinear effect has been observed for the exchange of labeled mercuric bromide and p-nitrobenzylmercuric bromide.[16]

[16] V. A. Kalyavin, T. A. Smolina, and O. A. Reutov, *Proc. Acad. Sci. USSR, Chem. Sect.*, **157**:762 (1964).

Table 7-7 Effect of added bromide ion on the rate of racemization of ethyl $(-)$-α-bromomercuriphenylacetate in DMSO solution at 29.8°: concentration of RHgBr, 0.02 M

[Me$_4$ \overset{+}{N}Br$^-$] $\times 10^2$	$k_1(\text{sec}^{-1}) \times 10^4$	$k_3{}^a(\text{liters}^2/\text{mole}^2\text{-sec})$
0	0.52	—
0.75	1.65	1.90
1.00	2.58	2.06
1.25	3.49	1.90
1.50	4.76	1.89
1.60	6.92	2.50
1.80	8.26	2.39
2.00	8.85	2.08
		Av. = 2.10

[a] Third-order rate constants, rate $= k_3[\overset{*}{R}HgBr][Br^-]^2$, for the catalytic part of the reaction.

Ingold et al. reported first-order rate constants for uncatalyzed racemization of the α-bromomercuri-ester and third-order constants with added bromide ion (Table 7-7). These results were rationalized on the basis that RHgBr reacts in preequilibria with bromide ion to form in low concentration RHgBr$_2^-$ and then RHgBr$_3^{-2}$, which dissociates to form R$^-$ and HgBr$_3^-$. The increase in rate with added bromide ion is not enormous and therefore the report that RHgBr and RHgBr$_3^{-2}$ but not RHgBr$_2^-$ (to any appreciable extent) undergo heterolytic scission to form carbanions is surprising.

$$\overset{*}{R}HgBr + Br^- \rightleftharpoons \overset{*}{R}Hg\bar{B}r$$
$$\overset{*}{R}Hg\bar{B}r_2 + Br^- \rightleftharpoons \overset{*}{R}Hg\overset{=}{B}r_3$$
$$\overset{*}{R}Hg\overset{=}{B}r_3 \rightleftharpoons R^- + Hg\bar{B}r_3$$

Figure 7-31 Postulated bromide ion-catalyzed carbanion formation

The effect on rate of other added salts is also surprising. At 59.2° (DMSO), with added salt 10^{-2} M, the following reaction rate sequence ($k_1 \times 10^4$) was reported: no salt, 3.40; KClO$_4$, 2.45; LiClO$_4$, 0.95; and LiNO$_3$, 5.05. These observed salt effects depend markedly on both the cationic and anionic species and suggests that additional work with the system is needed before any mechanistic conclusions regarding anion catalysis are accepted.

Kalyavin, Smolina, and Reutov found that added potassium bromide has a large effect on the exchange reaction of p-nitrobenzylmercuric bromide in DMSO solution (Table 7-8) (reference 16). These results were taken to indicate that, relatively speaking, small catalysis is observed until [Br$^-$] > [$\overset{*}{H}$gBr$_2$],

Table 7-8 Effect of added potassium bromide on the exchange reaction of mercuric[203] bromide with *p*-nitrobenzylmercuric bromide in DMSO solution at 18°C (reference 16)

$[p\text{-}O_2NC_6H_4CH_2HgBr] = 0.03\ M; [Hg^{203}Br_2] = 0.06\ M$								
[KBr]	0	0.01	0.02	0.03	0.04	0.05	0.06	0.07	0.09
$k_1(\text{hrs}^{-1}) \times 10^4$	14.7	23.8	33.0	46.8	70.7	121	2560	69,000	710,000

and when this condition is attained the catalytic effect depends on the concentration of excess bromide ion. In contrast to the conclusions of Ingold and coworkers, these results were interpreted in terms of $RHgBr_2^-$ as the carbanion precursor.

It is remarkable that none of the authors of the work discussed in this chapter made significant comments regarding the rates in air vs. rates in an inert atmosphere. In view of the ease of oxidation of mercurials and the facility with which metal exchange and alkyl exchange occur in the presence of free radicals, the absence of such discussions is disturbing and leaves the reader in a state of uncertainty. The catalytic effects of bromide ion may well be due to the intervention of radical processes.[17] The probable mechanism for the radical catalyzed exchange has been discussed previously (Sec. 4-2). One can in fact write a number of reasonable processes for radical-catalyzed reactions which give mercury exchange with retention of optical activity.

At this stage any discussion of radical-catalyzed exchange with stereochemical detail must be speculative. By invoking reactions such as those shown in Figure 7-32, it is possible to rationalize any combination of exchange and stereochemical observations. Reactions (1), (2), and (4) of Figure 7-32 are free-radical reactions, while formally (3), (5) and (6) represent electrophilic processes even though bonding in the reactive intermediate involves only one electron.

An interesting example of halide complexing of mercurials was suggested by Ledwith and Phillips,[18] who found ethylchloromethylmercury[19] to react faster with sodium iodide in acetone than even the very reactive α-halo-ketones. The rationale for this behavior involved the halogen-bridged transition state shown in Figure 7-33 analogous to that suggested for α-haloketone[20] and halomethylsilane[21] nucleophilic displacements. Although

---

[17] Jensen and Heyman (unpublished results) have found that the rate of the air oxidation of mercurials is increased by the addition of bromide ion to the solution. Presumably this effect is caused by the bromide ion displacing the alkylperoxyl group from mercury and speeding its decomposition to radicals, hence increasing the overall rate of reaction.

[18] A. Ledwith and L. Phillips, *J. Chem. Soc.*, 3796 (1962).

[19] Prepared by the reaction: $Et—Hg—Cl + CH_2N_2 \rightarrow Et—Hg—CH_2Cl + N_2\uparrow$

[20] For a more complete discussion see E. L. Eliel in M. Newman, ed., "Steric Effects in Organic Chemistry," p. 103, John Wiley & Sons, Inc., New York, 1956.

[21] C. Eaborn and J. C. Jeffrey, *J. Chem. Soc.*, 4266 (1954).

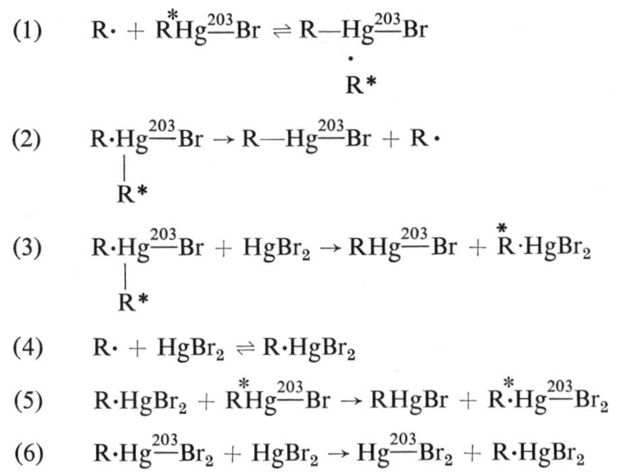

(1) $R \cdot + \overset{*}{R}Hg^{203}Br \rightleftharpoons R—Hg^{203}Br$

$\overset{|}{\underset{}{R*}}$

(2) $R \cdot Hg^{203}Br \rightarrow R—Hg^{203}Br + R \cdot$
$\overset{|}{R*}$

(3) $R \cdot Hg^{203}Br + HgBr_2 \rightarrow RHg^{203}Br + \overset{*}{R} \cdot HgBr_2$
$\overset{|}{R*}$

(4) $R \cdot + HgBr_2 \rightleftharpoons R \cdot HgBr_2$

(5) $R \cdot HgBr_2 + \overset{*}{R}Hg^{203}Br \rightarrow RHgBr + \overset{*}{R} \cdot Hg^{203}Br_2$

(6) $R \cdot Hg^{203}Br_2 + HgBr_2 \rightarrow Hg^{203}Br_2 + R \cdot HgBr_2$

Figure 7-32   Possible free-radical processes
involved in one-alkyl exchange reactions

these transition states have been represented (footnotes 18, 20, 21) in a manner analogous to that shown for the mercurial displacement (Figure 7-33, structure I), applying the principle of microscopic reversibility leads to the expectation, but not an absolute requirement, that structures of form II are more reasonable.

Another example of nucleophilic attack on mercury has been reported by Dessy and Paulik[22] in the anion-catalyzed acid cleavage of methoxycarbonyl-mercurials.

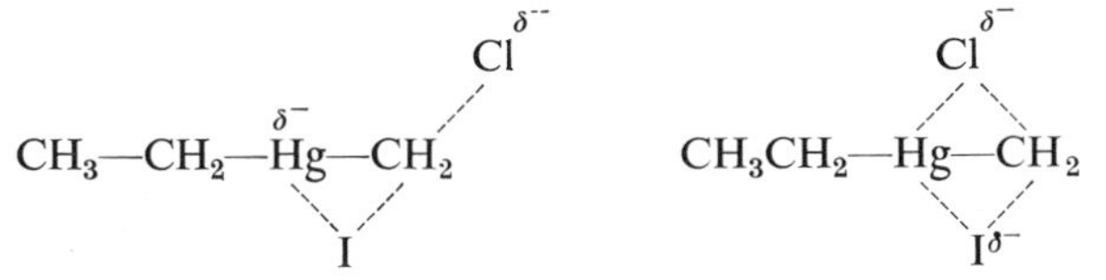

$$CH_3—CH_2—\overset{\delta^-}{Hg}—CH_2 \qquad\qquad CH_3CH_2—Hg—CH_2$$

I   II

Figure 7-33   Transition states for a nucleophilic displacement
reaction involving a halogen mercury complex

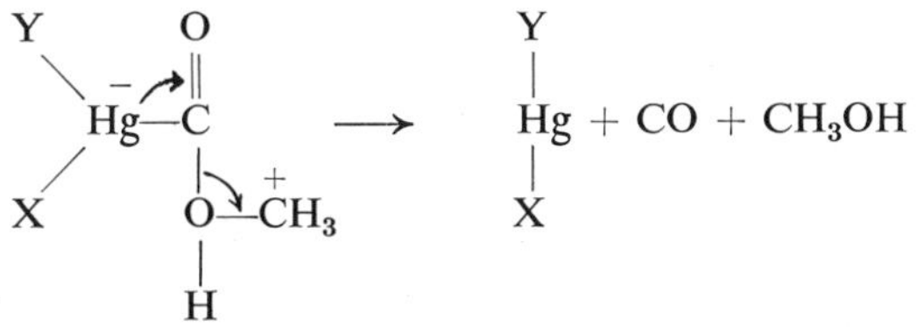

$$\begin{array}{c}Y \qquad O \\ \diagdown \underset{}{\overset{-}{\nearrow}} \| \\ Hg—C \\ \diagup \quad | \overset{+}{\diagdown} \\ X \quad O \diagdown CH_3 \\ | \\ H\end{array} \longrightarrow \begin{array}{c} Y \\ | \\ Hg + CO + CH_3OH \\ | \\ X \end{array}$$

Figure 7-34   Bond scission involving anion attack on mercury

[22] R. E. Dessy and F. E. Paulik, *J. Am. Chem. Soc.*, **85**:1812 (1963).

7-3 Cleavage of Dialkylmercurials by Alkylmercuric Salts

The exchange or cleavage reaction which occurs when a dialkylmercury compound is treated with an alkylmercuric salt was noted and studied by Reutov and coworkers[23] in Russia, and Hughes, Ingold and others[24] in Great Britain. Unlike the halide exchange, this process can be detected either by use of radiomercury or by the use of two different alkyl substituents.

$$RHgR + RH\overset{*}{g}X \rightleftharpoons RH\overset{*}{g}R + RHgX$$
$$RHgR + R'HgX \rightleftharpoons RHgR' + RHgX$$

Figure 7-35 Detection of exchange between a dialkylmercurial and an alkylmercuric salt

Both groups chose to use a doubly labeled pair of reactants to examine the stereochemistry and mechanism of the reaction, as exemplified by the 5-methyl-2-hexylmercury system used by Reutov et al. (reference 23).

The reaction was shown to be reversible and to occur with complete retention of configuration. In the system shown in Figure 7-36 this was

$$\overset{*}{R}Hg\overset{203}{\text{—}}Br + RHgR \rightleftharpoons \overset{*}{R}Hg\underline{^{203}}R + RHgBr$$

$$R*Hg\overset{203}{\text{—}}R \xrightarrow{HgBr_2} \overset{*}{R}HgBr + RHgBr$$

$$R = (CH_3)_2 \, CHCH_2CH_2CH\text{—}$$
$$\overset{|}{C}H_3$$

Figure 7-36 Cleavage of a dialkylmercurial by alkylmercuric halide with retention of configuration (reference 23)

demonstrated by separating the two products, examining the mercuric halide directly, and cleaving the bis-5-methyl-2-hexylmercury with mercuric bromide (a process known to occur with retention, cf. Chap. 5) followed by radiometric and polarimetric examination of this alkylmercuric bromide product. The total rotation of all recovered alkylmercuric halide remained unchanged through the course of the reaction. At the same time it was shown that the rate of radiomercury exchange was equal to the rate of alkyl exchange.

[23] a. O. A. Reutov, T. P. Karpov, E. V. Uglova, and V. A. Malynov, *Bull. Acad. Sci. USSR, Div. Chem. Sci.*, 1223 (1960).

b. *Ibid., Tetrahedron Letters*, No. 19, 6 (1960).

Ibid., Proc. Acad. Sci. USSR, Chem. Sect., **134:**1017 (1960).

d. T. P. Karpov, V. A. Malynov, E. V. Uglova, and O. A. Reutov, *Bull. Acad. Sci. USSR, Div. Chem. Sci.*, 1492 (1964).

[24] H. B. Charman, E. D. Hughes, C. Ingold, and F. G. Thorpe, *J. Chem. Soc.*, 1121 (1961).

The more thorough examination of this reaction by Charman et al. (reference 24) involved the use of the *sec*-butylmercury group. In this study the stereochemistry was determined by showing that the final material, recovered

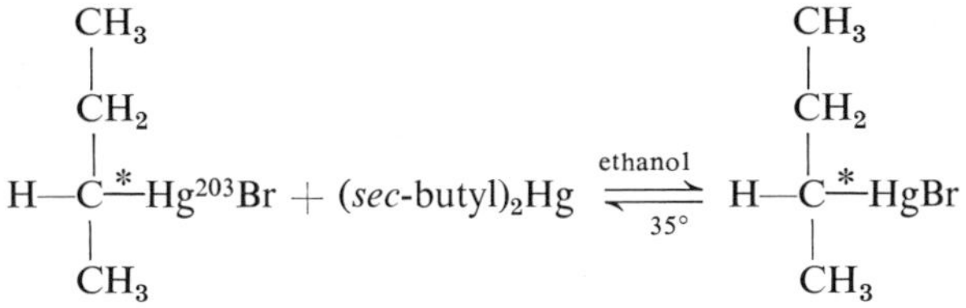

$$
\begin{array}{c}
CH_3 \\
| \\
CH_2 \\
| \\
H—\overset{*}{C}—Hg^{203}Br \\
| \\
CH_3
\end{array}
\;+\;(\textit{sec}\text{-butyl})_2Hg\;
\underset{35°}{\overset{\text{ethanol}}{\rightleftharpoons}}\;
\begin{array}{c}
CH_3 \\
| \\
CH_2 \\
| \\
H—\overset{*}{C}—HgBr \\
| \\
CH_3
\end{array}
$$

$$[\alpha]_D^{20} - 14.5° \qquad \text{after 14 ``half-lives''} \quad [\alpha]_D^{20} - 4.7°$$
$$\text{(1/3 of original)}$$

$$k(\text{Hg exch.}) = 4.6 \mp 0.2 \times 10^{-7} \text{ liter/mole-sec}$$
$$k(\text{alkyl exch.}) = 4.7 \mp 0.1 \times 10^{-7} \text{ liter/mole-sec}$$

Figure 7-37 The "three-alkyl" exchange reaction of Hughes and Ingold (reference 24)

after fourteen "half-lives" of mercury exchange, had exactly its statistically expected rotation. Thus, when starting with equal concentrations of optically active *sec*-butylmercuric bromide and inactive di-*sec*-butylmercury the recovered alkylmercuric halide had one-third its original rotation.

The reaction was shown to be second-order overall, first-order in dialkylmercury, and first-order in alkylmercuric halide. Several plausible reaction pathways may be considered for this exchange; many are obviated by the established kinetic order and stereochemistry. The two principal types differ in the substituent (R or X) that is transferred from the alkylmercuric salt in the exchange (Figure 7-38). The first of these may be disregarded[25] since

(1) $\quad$ R—Hg—R + R*—Hg*—X $\rightleftharpoons$ R—Hg—R* + R—Hg*—X

(2) $\quad$ R—Hg—R + R*—Hg*—X $\rightleftharpoons$ R—Hg*—R* + R—Hg—X

$\qquad$ R*—Hg*—R + R—Hg—X $\rightleftharpoons$ R—Hg—R* + R—Hg*—X

Figure 7-38 Two plausible schemes for cleavage of dialkylmercury by alkyl mercuric halide

inspection shows that while this mechanism can account for alkyl group redistribution, the radiomercury label would remain with the alkylmercuric halide. Both labels are transferred during the reaction (at equal rates).

Two additional lines of evidence were obtained by Hughes and Ingold to argue in favor of an open transition state. The first of these is the effect of variation of the anionic portion of the alkylmercuric salt on the rate of reaction. The rate sequence clearly shows that the more rapid reaction

[25] It cannot be excluded as a very slow concurrent process.

$$RHg^*X + R_2Hg \rightleftharpoons RHgX + R_2Hg^*$$

$$k(NO_3^-) \geq 10^2 \times k(OAc^-) \geq 10 \times k(Br^-)$$

Figure 7-39 Effect of variation of anion on
rate of exchange

occurs with the more highly ionized alkylmercuric salt (in ethanol at various temperatures).

Added salts were shown to have a mildly accelerating effect on rate, with the order established:

$$LiClO_4 > LiBr > LiNO_3 > LiOAc$$

The degree of rate enhancement is not comparable with the halide ion "catalysis" noted in the exchange of alkylmercuric halide by mercuric halide (Sec. 7-2). In the present case the acceleration can be attributed entirely to medium effects, with the more dissociated salts having the larger effect on rate.[26]

These results were interpreted by Hughes, Ingold, and coworkers as precluding all but an open transition state mechanism. Although the details were not given, they inferred the mechanism shown in Figure 7-40. According

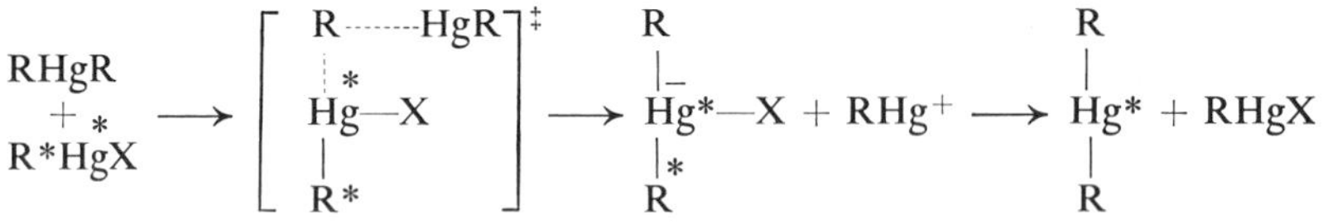

Figure 7-40 S_E2 mechanism forbidden by the principle of microscopic reversibility unless a parallel forward path is proposed which is exactly the reverse of the reaction as shown

to this picture, it is expected that the more ionic the HgX bond, the more electrophilic the mercury and, hence, the faster the rate. This mechanism as pictured is again precluded by the principle of microscopic reversibility (see Sec. 7-2). A related scheme in which ionization of alkylmercuric salt occurs prior to exchange does not present this difficulty, but would not be expected to show the observed kinetic behavior. For reaction with dissociated ions, the dependence would be half-order in alkylmercuric salt with first-order inhibition by added anion; however, for ion pairs first-order kinetics with no inhibition by added anion is anticipated. The reactions were carried out in ethanol and the states of the ionic species are unknown.

[26] The authors pointed out that lithium bromide under these conditions was expected to be very largely dissociated, perhaps even more so than the perchlorate. The salt effects of these two materials were comparable in magnitude.

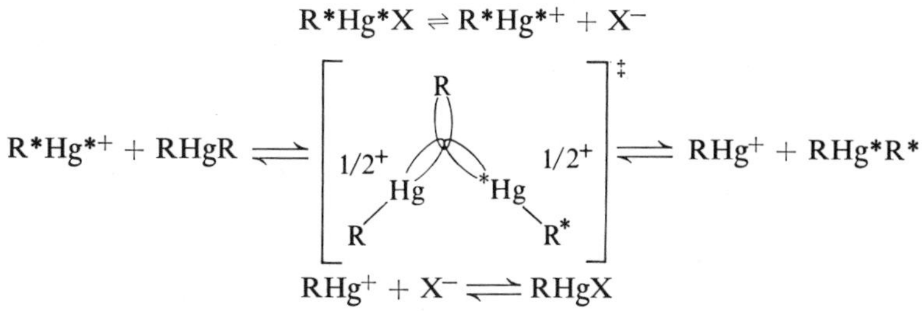

$$R^*Hg^*X \rightleftharpoons R^*Hg^{*+} + X^-$$

$$R^*Hg^{*+} + RHgR \xrightleftharpoons \left[\begin{array}{c} R \\ \underset{1/2^+}{\diagup} \underset{Hg}{\diagup} \overset{\diagdown}{\underset{{}^*Hg}{\diagdown}} \underset{1/2^+}{\diagdown} \\ R \diagup \qquad \diagdown R^* \end{array} \right]^{\ddagger} \rightleftharpoons RHg^+ + RHg^*R^*$$

$$RHg^+ + X^- \rightleftharpoons RHgX$$

Figure 7-41   Electrophilic attack by alkylmercuric cation

As noted above, Hughes, Ingold and coworkers viewed their results as not allowing the intervention of a bridged transition state. However, intuitive arguments no longer carry sufficient force to render mechanistic decisions; factual (rather than circumstantial) evidence is needed before a judgment can be made.[27] Therefore, a bridged transition state with a relatively ionic bridging anion is also possible in cases where the geometry and hybridization favor this electronic distribution. A worthwhile study would

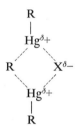

Figure 7-42   Four-center transition
state for the three-alkyl exchange

involve the reinvestigation of the kinetics of this exchange reaction in solvents where the degrees of ionization and dissociation of these compounds are known or may be determined.

7-4   Exchange Reactions of Metallic Mercury

An important and facile reaction of organomercurials, which has been explored by Reutov and his coworkers,[28] is the exchange with metallic mercury. Examination of the reagents and products does not allow a formal definition

[27] However, intuitive arguments do provide an excellent basis for planning future experimental work.

[28] a. O. A. Reutov and U. Yan-Tsei, *Proc. Acad. Sci. USSR, Chem. Sect.*, **117**:110 (1957).

   b. O. A. Reutov, *Angew. Chem.*, **72**:198 (1960); see also references 2 and 12.

of the nature of this reaction. It differs operationally from the cleavage reactions that have been considered previously in that the exchange is apparently more rapid with alkylmercuric salts than with the analogous dialkylmercury compounds.[29] As previously noted, the opposite effect would be expected on the basis of electronic arguments for the attack of an electrophile on the carbon-mercury bond. Because this exchange represents a potential side

$$RHgX + Hg^* \rightleftharpoons RHg^*X + Hg \qquad \text{(faster)}$$
$$RHgR^* + Hg \rightleftharpoons RHgR + Hg^* \qquad \text{(slower)}$$

Figure 7-43   Exchange between metallic mercury and organomercurials

reaction in other electrophilic cleavage studies, the available information is presented.

Although no exact kinetic studies have been carried out with alkylmercuric salts, the order of reactivity shown in Figure 7-44 has been established

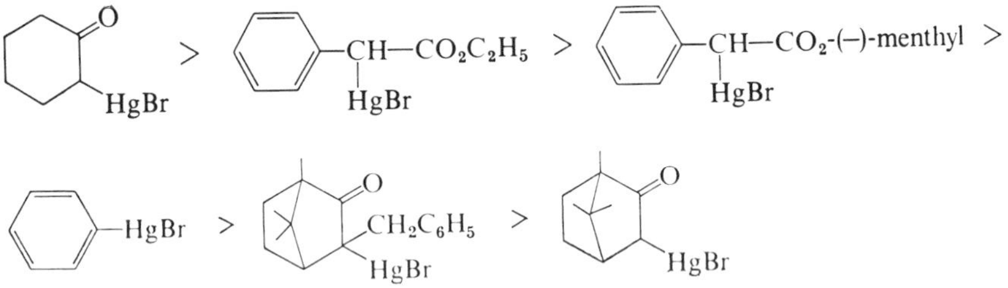

Figure 7-44   Order of reactivity in the mercury exchange reaction

(reference 28b).[30] It is worth noting that under the conditions employed (benzene, acetone, or dioxane solvent at 23°) the only alkylmercurials which undergo reaction are those having an α-carbonyl group.[31] Four other

[29] Very few examples are available for comparison; Reutov (reference 12) has reported that in benzene (23°) the half-life for exchange of (−)-menthyl α-bromomercuriphenyl-acetate is 2 hrs, while under comparable conditions (in chloroform) the symmetrized product exchanges only 10% in 50 hr.

[30] The rates for these heterogeneous reactions were determined using similar conditions and constant stirring rate. It is possible, but not established, that exchange involves dissolved metallic mercury. No information is available regarding the effect of the added mercurials on the solubility of mercury or the rate of dissolution of mercury. It is probably unwise to derive conclusions from the effect of substituents on rate where the rates are comparable until more information regarding the physical mechanism for exchange is known.

[31] The single exception is the 2-methoxycyclohexylmercuric chloride system, where stereochemical results have been reported (reference 28a) but experimental details and reaction conditions are not yet available.

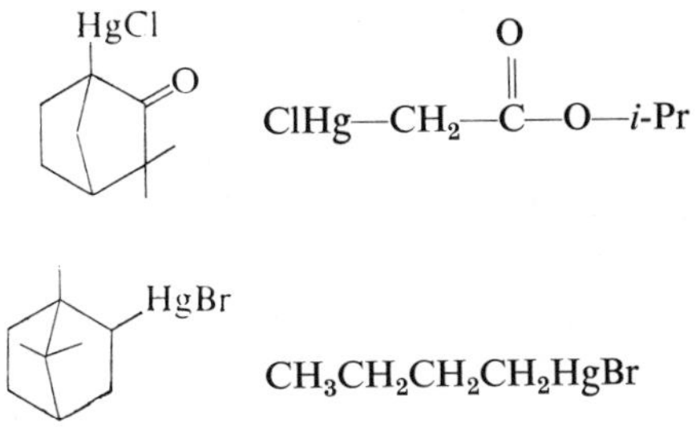
HgCl
O
O
ClHg—CH$_2$—C—O—*i*-Pr
HgBr
CH$_3$CH$_2$CH$_2$CH$_2$HgBr

Figure 7-45 Some organomercurials which failed to undergo mercury exchange

materials failed to give reaction with mercury in benzene solutions (the α-carbonyl compounds at 23° and the simple alkyl materials at 80°). These are shown in Figure 7-45.

With arylmercurials, substituent effects have been determined for both the organomercuric halides and for the symmetrized materials.[32]

Although exact kinetic data were not obtained, it was shown that electron withdrawing substituents tend to decrease the rate in both series, as shown in Figure 7-46. Reaction with the symmetrical materials was slower than with

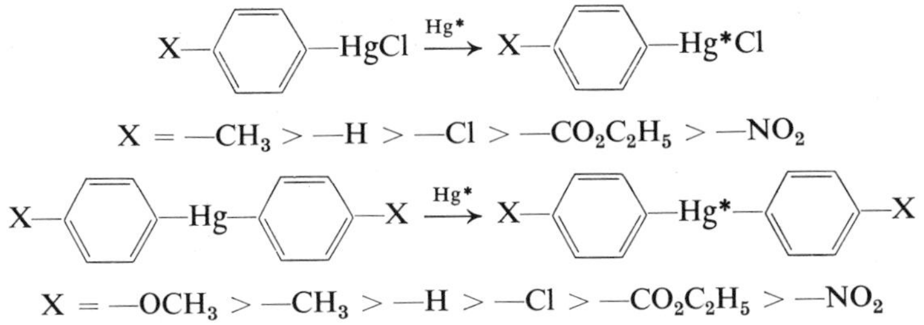
X— —HgCl
Hg*
X— —Hg*Cl
X = —CH$_3$ > —H > —Cl > —CO$_2$C$_2$H$_5$ > —NO$_2$
X— —Hg— —X
Hg*
X— —Hg*— —X
X = —OCH$_3$ > —CH$_3$ > —H > —Cl > —CO$_2$C$_2$H$_5$ > —NO$_2$

Figure 7-46 Substituent effects on relative rates of exchange with metallic mercury

the substituted phenylmercuric chlorides, in agreement with the limited available data on alkylmercurial exchanges. The substituent effects are somewhat surprising in view of the large enhancement furnished by an α-carbonyl group in the alkyl systems. However, the variation in rate for all compounds represented in Figure 7-46 was less than a factor of 12 and the differences noted may be an artifact of the experimental method rather than a true measure of the rates of exchange (reference 30).

[32] a. O. A. Reutov and G. M. Ostapchuk, *Proc. Acad. Sci. USSR, Chem. Sect.*, **117**:1075 (1957).
b. *Ibid.*, *J. Gen. Chem. USSR* (*Eng. Transl.*), **29**:1588 (1959).
c. O. A. Reutov, *Bull. Acad. Sci. USSR, Div. Chem. Sci.*, 663 (1958).

The metallic mercury exchange is classified by Reutov (reference 28) as a homolytic reaction not involving "free"-radical intermediates. Thus, retention of configuration is observed for the diastereomeric (−)-menthyl α-bromomercuriphenylacetates and also for *cis-* and *trans*-2-methoxy-cyclohexylmercuric chloride (references 2, 28a).

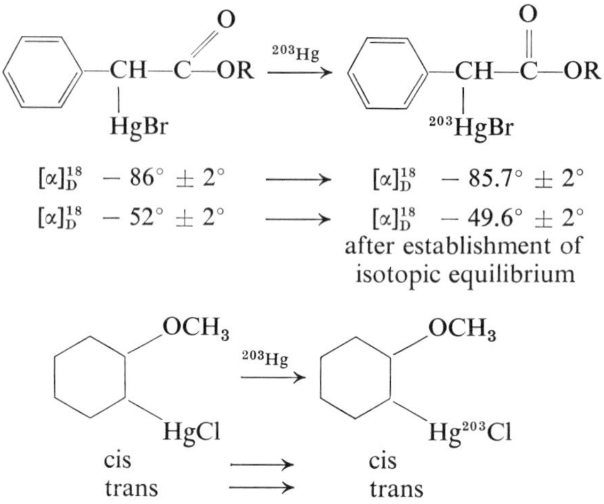

$$[\alpha]_D^{18} \quad -86° \pm 2° \longrightarrow \quad [\alpha]_D^{18} \quad -85.7° \pm 2°$$

$$[\alpha]_D^{18} \quad -52° \pm 2° \longrightarrow \quad [\alpha]_D^{18} \quad -49.6° \pm 2°$$

after establishment of
isotopic equilibrium

Figure 7-47 Retention of configuration in the exchange with metallic mercury (R = (−)-menthyl)

The advent of free-radical intermediates in this reaction was further ruled out by the results obtained when an unsymmetrical diarylmercurial was allowed to undergo exchange. Neither of the two possible symmetrical products was obtained, strongly implying that the two aryl groups do not act independently of each other during the course of the reaction (reference 28a).

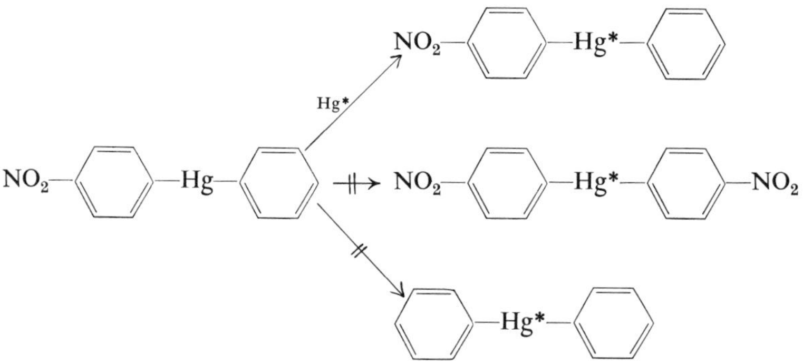

Figure 7-48 Mercury exchange with an unsymmetrical diarylmercurial

$$2RHgX \rightleftharpoons R_2Hg + HgX_2$$

$$HgX_2 + Hg^* \rightleftharpoons Hg^*X_2 + Hg$$

$$R_2Hg + Hg^*X_2 \rightleftharpoons RHgX + RHg^*X$$

or

$$RHgX + Hg^*X_2 \rightleftharpoons RHg^*X + HgX_2$$

Figure 7-49 A potential multistep route for
exchange—disproved

The possibility that exchange is occurring in a multistep process involving prior symmetrization of the alkylmercuric halide, followed by exchange (unspecified mechanism) of the mercuric halide with mercury, and finally cleavage of dialkylmercury by radiomercuric halides appears to be negated by the available data. The reaction with mercury metal is considerably more rapid than the analogous exchange with mercuric halide.[33] Essentially the same compounds were used for both studies by Reutov and coworkers, and it is instructive to compare the two relative rate sequences (Figures 7-19 and 7-44). Although the few examples suggest that two different reactions are under examination, the overall similarity implies roughly comparable electronic demands. Finally, as Reutov has pointed out, if mercuric halide were formed it should react rapidly with mercury to give mercurous halide:

$$HgX_2 + Hg \rightleftharpoons Hg_2X_2$$

Two general types of mechanisms are consistent with the observed stereochemistry, and the available data do not provide sufficient information for a choice to be made.

As mentioned previously, this reaction was described by Reutov as a homolytic but not "free"-radical process. The term "homolytic" was used in the belief that the electron pairs on mercury, halogen, and carbon all undergo unpairing during the course of the reaction. However, there is no reason to believe that electron movements in this reaction are abnormal. Figure 7-50

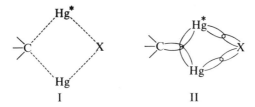

Ⅰ   Ⅱ

Figure 7-50 Representations of four-center
transition states for Hg° exchange

[33] No direct comparison is available because the former reaction is heterogeneous—run with a large excess of metal and high-speed stirring.

shows the four-center transition state depicted by Reutov and coworkers (I), and a possible orbital picture of a conventional four-center transition state. The orbital arrangement on mercury may be of several types, but either *s* or distorted *sp* (structure II) seems most likely.

A mechanism having many attractive features involves organomercurous compounds as intermediates. Substantial evidence is available indicating the existence of such compounds, although in unstable form. The decomposition to the mercuric form may occur by the route proposed previously (Sec. 6-3) for the stereospecific reduction by magnesium of alkylmercuric salts to dialkylmercuric compounds.[34] A reasonable orbital representation of the intermediates is given in Figure 7-51. First, a mercury-mercury bond is

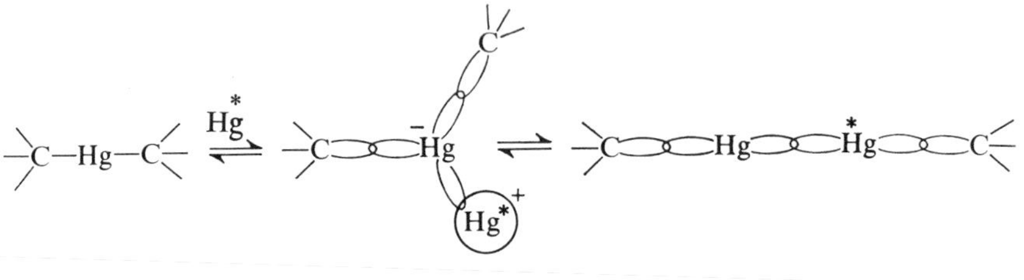

Figure 7-51 Exchange of metallic mercury by an electrophilic process involving an organomercurous intermediate

formed, and then rearrangement occurs with electrophilic reaction on carbon. This mechanism is consistent with the relative rate sequences observed as well as the stereochemistry.

7-5 Exchange between Disubstituted Mercurials

The process which completes the spectrum of exchange of alkyl substituents between organomercurials is that involving two molecules of dialkyl- or diarylmercurials (or combinations thereof). The only data bearing directly on this reaction are those of Reutov and coworkers (reference 12).[35] At 60° in pyridine, diphenylmercury labeled with radiomercury underwent exchange with di-*p*-chlorophenylmercury without formation of unsymmetrical products. It is this feature which distinguishes this reaction from the other exchanges and cleavages of organomercurials which have been examined. That is, cleavage involving a four-center transition state would be expected to give rise to some of the unsymmetrical product (Figure 7-53). While it is possible that the two symmetrical mercurials could be highly favored thermodynamically,

[34] F. R. Jensen and J. A. Landgrebe, *J. Am. Chem. Soc.*, **82**:1004 (1960).
[35] O. A. Reutov, H. Hun-veng, and T. A. Smolina, *Izv. Akad. Nauk SSSR, Otd. Khim. Nauk*, 559 (1959).

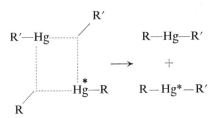

Figure 7-52   Exchange between diarylmercurials

this prospect seems unlikely in view of the many reports of isolation of similarly constituted unsymmetrical diarylmercurials (see Secs. 3-3 and 5-2).

Other systems which were examined are shown in Figure 7-54. The limited data available again indicate a rate enhancement associated with the α-carbonyl substituent, demonstrated by the facile exchange in the cold of diacetaldehydomercury with the two diarylmercurials. The apparent rate depression caused by the *p*-chloro- substituent would seem to put this reaction in the same category as many other exchange reactions which have been discussed previously, i.e., the carbon seat of reaction (in the aromatic series) is relatively more positive in the transition state than in the initial state. The extreme difference in relative rates is, however, surprising.

This same relative rate sequence is noted in the exchange with metallic mercury, and leads to the suspicion that this may be the active "carrier" of radioactivity. Thus a small amount of mercury, either as a heterogeneous

$$R—Hg*—R + Hg \rightarrow R—Hg—R + Hg*$$
$$R'—Hg—R' + Hg* \rightarrow R'Hg*—R' + Hg$$

catalyst or in solution,[36] may explain this exchange; it certainly offers a

$$
\begin{array}{ccc}
& R' & \\
R'—Hg\text{------} \diagup & & R—Hg—R' \\
\vdots & \vdots & \\
& & \longrightarrow \quad + \\
\vdots & \overset{*}{\underset{}{}} & \\
\text{------}Hg—R & & R—Hg*—R' \\
\diagup & & \\
R & &
\end{array}
$$

Figure 7-53   Formation of unsymmetrical dialkylmercurial by a four-center mechanism—not observed

[36] Although Reutov and his coworkers used a large excess of free mercury in their studies of metallic mercury-organomercurial exchange, the necessity for this procedure was never stated. As is well known by researchers in this area, it is difficult to work with mercurials without at least some decomposition occurring. If the reaction proceeds between organomercurial and mercury in solution, this may offer an explanation in the reaction presently under discussion; if a surface phenomenon is involved, this suggestion becomes much less probable.

$$\left(\underset{\overset{|}{CH_3}}{\overset{CH_3}{\diagdown}}N-\!\!\!\left\langle\!\!\!\bigcirc\!\!\!\right\rangle\!\!\!-\right)_2 Hg + \left(\left\langle\!\!\!\bigcirc\!\!\!\right\rangle\!\!\!-\right)_2 Hg^* \longrightarrow$$ facile exchange in dark at 23°, toluene solvent

$$\left(CH_3O-\!\!\!\left\langle\!\!\!\bigcirc\!\!\!\right\rangle\!\!\!-\right)_2 Hg + \left(\underset{H}{\overset{O}{\diagdown}}C-CH_2-\right)_2 Hg^* \longrightarrow$$ immediate exchange; acetone, 20°

$$\left(\left\langle\!\!\!\bigcirc\!\!\!\right\rangle\!\!\!-\right)_2 Hg + \left(\underset{H}{\overset{O}{\diagdown}}C-CH_2-\right)_2 Hg^* \longrightarrow$$ immediate exchange; acetone, 20°

$$\left(Cl-\!\!\!\left\langle\!\!\!\bigcirc\!\!\!\right\rangle\!\!\!-\right)_2 Hg + \left(\underset{H}{\overset{O}{\diagdown}}C-CH_2-\right)_2 Hg^* \longrightarrow$$ no reaction at 20°

Figure 7-54   Other examples of exchange between disubstituted mercurials without formation of unsymmetrical product

rationale for the lack of scrambling of alkyl and aryl substituents. Much more information, both kinetic and stereochemical, is needed to ascertain the exact nature of this reaction. In the event that no alternate explanation is found, a novel transition state appears to be involved. One possibility is pictured in Figure 7-55; the bond angles and hybridization required for mercury as illustrated would appear to be more reasonable in a complexing solvent, where nonlinear bonding has been well established. The transition state shown might require the use of d orbitals in a state of hybridization which is open to speculation but leading to the nonequivalence of R and R'.

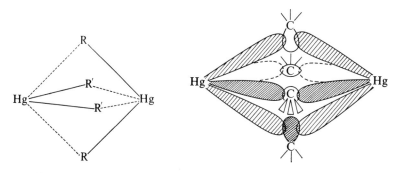

Figure 7-55   Possible transition state for dialkylmercury exchange

As depicted in Figure 7-55, this nonequivalence can be simply a matter of geometry, i.e., the two groups R are situated para rather than ortho to each other.

Once again both mechanisms which have been examined would imply retention of stereochemical configuration at the substrate carbon. Although the actual data are not available, Reutov has stated this to be the case.[37]

Comparable exchange reactions involving fully alkylated organometallics and with two different metals have been examined by McCoy and Allred.[38] Using nuclear magnetic resonance spectroscopy, it was possible to establish either minimum or maximum pre-exchange average lifetimes for the alkyl groups on different metals.[39] Pertinent to the present exchange reaction is the observation that methyl group-nmr peak coalescence did not occur with mixtures of dimethylzinc-dimethylmercury or with dimethylcadmium-dimethylmercury. With metals other than mercury, very rapid exchange resulted. Similar data have been obtained by Dessy, Kaplan, Coe, and

$$(CH_3)_2M + (CH_3)_2M' \rightleftharpoons (CH_3)_2M' + (CH_3)_2M$$

Figure 7-56   Exchange reaction of like alkyl groups on unlike metals— observable by nmr

Salinger.[40] These authors also used perdeuteriodimethylmercury with various other dimethylmetallics; only with dimethylmagnesium was exchange sufficiently rapid to be observed at room temperature. Of particular importance is the observation that the unsymmetrical product was formed in this reaction. It was further shown that the unsymmetrical product is formed

$$CD_3HgCD_3 + CH_3MgCH_3 \rightleftharpoons$$
$$CD_3MgCH_3 + CD_3MgCD_3 + CH_3\!-\!Hg\!-\!CD_3 + CH_3HgCH_3$$

Figure 7-57   Exchange between dimethylmercury-d_6 and dimethylmagnesium— with formation of unsymmetrical product

more rapidly than the symmetrical product, illustrating that the exchange observed is not due to some minor side reaction. Further, a mixture of dimethylmercury and dimethylmercury-d_6 heated at 65° for 78 hours gave

[37] O. A. Reutov, 17th Congress for Pure and Applied Chemistry, Munich (1959), Plenary Lecture, as quoted by J. H. DeBoer, "Proceedings of the Symposium on the Mechanism of Heterogeneous Catalysis, Nov., 1959," p. 11, Elsevier Publishing Co., Amsterdam, 1960.

[38] a. C. R. McCoy and A. L. Allred, *J. Am. Chem. Soc.*, 84:912 (1962).

   b. A. L Allred and C. R. McCoy, *Tetrahedron Letters*, No. 27, 25 (1960).

[39] For a discussion of the general technique see J. D. Roberts, "Nuclear Magnetic Resonance," p. 63, McGraw-Hill Book Company, New York, 1959.

[40] R. E. Dessy, F. Kaplan, G. R. Coe, and R. M. Salinger, *J. Am. Chem. Soc.*, 85:1191 (1963).

evidence of exchange with formation of dimethylmercury-d_3. While it is of questionable validity to extrapolate the mercury-magnesium results to the reactions examined by Reutov et al., the results of Dessy et al, shown in Figure

$$(CD_3)_2Hg + (CH_3)_2Hg \rightleftharpoons CH_3HgCD_3$$

Figure 7-58 Exchange between mercurials

7-58 are more directly comparable. Although Reutov's studies involved only α-carbonylalkyl or arylmercurials the formation of mixed product with dimethylmercury strongly suggests the need for further work in this area.

7-6 Anion Exchange Reactions of Mercurials

Generally the anion or potential anion of an alkylmercuric salt may be viewed as fairly mobile and subject to exchange in solution. Three modes of exchange are available; one involving ionization, another the intervention of a complex anion, and a third direct displacement.

(1) $R—Hg—X \rightleftharpoons RHg^+ + X^-$

(2) $R—Hg—X + Y^- \rightleftharpoons R—\overset{\displaystyle X}{\underset{\displaystyle Y}{\overset{\diagup}{\underset{\diagdown}{\bar{Hg}}}}} \rightleftharpoons RHgY + X^-$

(3) $RHgX + Y^- \rightleftharpoons RHgY + X^-$

Figure 7-59 Plausible mechanisms for anion exchange

Such exchange is often of secondary interest when anions like halide, nitrate, acetate and other inorganic species are involved; however, when one of the exchanging groups is a carbanion, the process becomes of considerable importance in the study of electrophilic substitution. In fact, one of the least explored areas of organomercurial chemistry involves their use as substrates for S_E1 reactions. The data collected in this and earlier sections will help to illustrate the specific features needed by the carbon substituent in order to insure reaction by this mechanism. Suggestions for the groups *abc* in Figure 7-60 would include halides,[41] sulfoxide, sulfone, and other electron-withdrawing substituents.

Reutov and Lovstova[42] found that treatment of variously substituted mercuric chlorides with chloroform and potassium *t*-butoxide in benzene

---

[41] Substantial substitution of this sort can lead to the mercurial existing in the ionic form, i.e., with the equilibrium depicted in Figure 7-60 lying far to the right. See, for example, the description of perfluoroalkylmercurials, H. B. Powell, M. T. Maung, and J. J. Lagowski, *J. Chem. Soc.*, 2484 (1963).

[42] O. A. Reutov and A. N. Lovstova, *Bull. Acad. Sci. USSR, Div. Chem. Sci.*, 1599(1960).

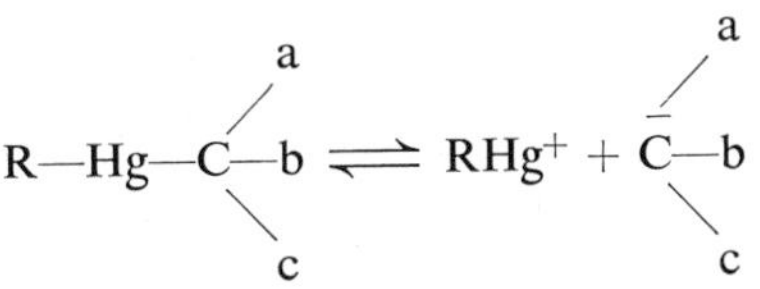

$$R—Hg—\overset{\displaystyle a}{\underset{\displaystyle c}{C}}—b \rightleftharpoons RHg^+ + \overset{\displaystyle a}{\underset{\displaystyle c}{C}}—b$$

Figure 7-60   Mercurial ionization—S_E1 reaction

solution leads to the formation of trichloromethylmercurials. Thus, mercuric chloride itself gives trichloromethylmercuric chloride while phenylmercuric chloride yields phenyltrichloromethylmercury. The formation of these

$$R—Hg—Cl \xrightarrow[\text{t-BuOK}]{\text{CHCl}_3} R—Hg—CCl_3$$

Figure 7-61   Formation of trichloromethyl
mercurials

materials was attributed to the insertion of dichlorocarbene into the mercury-chlorine bond.[43] This suggestion has subsequently been refuted by Seyferth and Burlitch.[44] The correct scheme and evidence presented by these workers is shown in Figure 7-62. Using phenylmercuric bromide, it was shown that

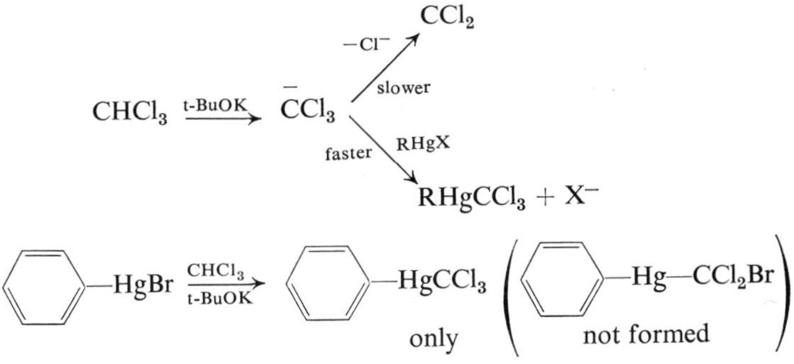

Figure 7-62   Example of anion exchange involving a carbanion

only replacement product (trichloro) and no insertion product (dichloro-bromo) was formed. Suitable controls were carried out to show that the product did not arise by chloride-bromide exchange either prior to or after reaction. These results suggest that the exchange is occurring by complex ion formation (Figure 7-63), or alternately, direct displacement. Additional

[43] Compare the reaction of substituted mercuric chlorides with diazomethane to give insertion products, footnotes 18 and 19.

[44] D. Seyferth and J. M. Burlitch, *J. Am. Chem. Soc.*, **84:**1757 (1962).

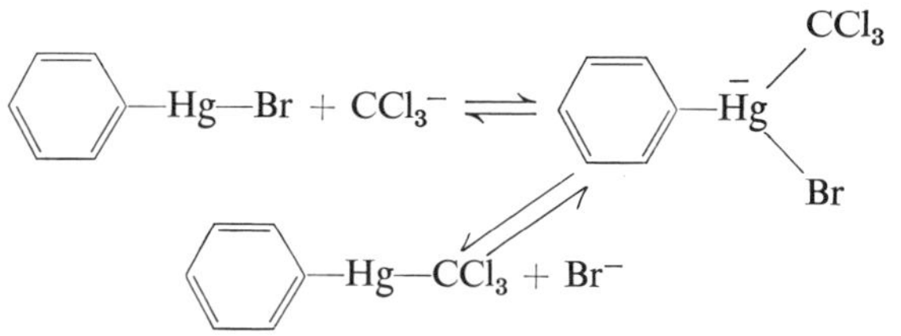

Figure 7-63   Anion exchange via complex formation

information regarding this reaction is found in the work of Logan,[45] who demonstrated that trichloromethyl anion exhibits substantial selectivity in its reaction with mercuric chloride.

$$\underset{\text{(1 mole)}}{HgCl_2 + CCl_3CO_2Na} \xrightarrow{\Delta} CCl_3Hg{-}Cl$$

$$\underset{\text{(2 moles)}}{HgCl_2 + CCl_3CO_2Na} \xrightarrow{\Delta} \underset{71\%}{CCl_3{-}Hg{-}CCl_3}$$

Figure 7-64   Selectivity of trichloromethyl anion in the anion exchange reaction

This behavior is in keeping with the predicted degree of complex anion formation: $HgX_2 > RHgX > R_2Hg$ (cf. Chap. 2). It could also arise from steric hindrance towards displacement on mercury, or possibly by mercuric chloride cleavage of bis-trichloromethylmercury.

[45] T. J. Logan, *J. Org. Chem.*, **28**:1129 (1963).

AUTHOR INDEX

SUBJECT INDEX